Rehabilitating Apartments

Editorial Consultants
Louis A. Danzico, CPM®
James S. Peacock, CPM®
Lyn E. Weiland, CPM®

Joseph T. Lannon
Publishing and Curriculum Development Manager

Caroline Scoulas
Senior Editor

Rehabilitating Apartments
A Recycling Process

Robert A. Cagann, CPM®

Institute of Real Estate Management
of the **NATIONAL ASSOCIATION OF REALTORS®**
430 NORTH MICHIGAN AVENUE · CHICAGO, ILLINOIS 60611

333.338
C

This publication is designed to provide accurate and authoritative information in regard to the subject matter covered. Forms or other documents included in this book are intended as samples only. Because of changing and varying state and local laws, competent professional advice should be sought prior to the use of any document, form, exhibit, or the like.

This publication is sold with the understanding that the publisher is not engaged in rendering legal, accounting, or any other service. If legal advice or other expert assistance is required, the services of a competent professional should be sought.

The opinions expressed in this book are those of the author and do not necessarily reflect the policies and positions of the Institute of Real Estate Management.

Library of Congress Cataloging-in-Publication Data

Cagann, Robert A., 1939–
  Rehabilitating apartments : a recycling process / Robert A.
Cagann.
    p.   cm.
  Includes index.
  ISBN 0-944298-90-7
  1. Apartment houses.   2. Housing rehabilitation.   3. Real estate
investment.   4. Real estate management.   I. Title.
HD1394.C34   1994
333.33'8--dc20   93–27771
                                                        CIP

Printed in the United States of America

1 2 3 4 5 6 7 8 9 10 Printing/Year 02 01 00 99 98 97 96 95 94 93

To my Sandy
whose love and encouragement
kept me focused on the task at hand.

Preface

The term rehabilitation has been used rather loosely by real estate professionals to illustrate creativity. There is no question that rehabilitation requires creativity, but the cynicism within the real estate industry implies that all one must do is "doll it up and change the name" for creativity to be present—rehabilitation seems to have become the buzz word for the 1990s, just as conversion was the buzz word for the 1970s. It is important to understand, however, that the change resulting from rehabilitation is more than cosmetic, and it is the extent of this change that this book addresses.

Rehabilitating Apartments: A Recycling Process takes a realistic approach to apartment rehabilitation to give real estate professionals and private individuals the information they need to transform nonperforming or low-performing apartment properties into viable, performing assets. As an apartment recycler, your objective is to create perceptions of the property in the marketplace that will arouse in prospective renters a desire to live there. The rewards of recycling are great; in terms of dollars, the profits can be outstanding. For the rehabber, however, there is also a profound sense of accomplishment for having transformed a former blight on a neighborhood into a desirable place to live.

About this Book

Rehabilitating Apartments: A Recycling Process is not a theoretical text; rather, it is a reflection of what I have learned in some twenty-plus years of buying and rehabilitating apartment properties. As such, it is intended to be a practical "handbook" to assist you in making salient, economic decisions about your apartment investments.

Chapter 1, Apartment Recycling, outlines the role of real estate in the U.S. economy, how it compares with alternative investments, and what makes recycling desirable. It also introduces the major challenge of the recycling process, which is changing the image projected by the property—i.e., how it is perceived.

Chapter 2, Finding the Right Property, explains the array of data to be collected and analyzed in making this type of investment decision. This is the first step in the recycling process. The next step is to develop a comprehensive plan of action. Chapter 3, Planning the Rehabilitation discusses feasibility, organization of the work, preparation of specifications, and budget considerations. What the rehabber must scrutinize are the intended changes, the costs of making them, and the time required to achieve them.

Chapter 4, Financing the Recycling Process, discusses the market for financing and specific considerations in applying for construction loans and permanent financing. In chapter 5, Analyzing the Investment, considerations of risk, return, and the value of the property are addressed.

Throughout the recycling process, the property and its operations must be managed. The rehabilitation activity itself must be monitored. These issues are covered in chapter 6, Managing during Rehabilitation. After the rehabilitation is completed, it is time to reassess the marketplace, the property's operations, and the goals of ownership—all with an eye toward refinancing the investment for the longer term. These considerations are the substance of chapter 7, Evaluating the Results. Chapter 8, The Recycling Process, revisits the various steps discussed in the preceding chapters and provides an overview summary of the rehabilitation process.

The tone of the book is conversational—as in a dialog, the reader is addressed as "you." Throughout the book, my experiences and personal opinions have been distinguished from general information and management practice. Since I often collaborate with business partners and my property management business has a construction management affiliate, the words "I" and "we" are both used, sometimes interchangeably.

Care has been taken to define terms where they are introduced, precluding the need for a separate glossary. However, details about information sources would have interrupted the flow of the text, so a compilation of resources has been included as an appendix.

Other Considerations in Apartment Recycling

In writing this book, I have recalled my own particular experiences and approach to the recycling process. Where my methods may be at variance with local requirements others might encounter, I have made a point of indicating this. Issues of law vary with jurisdictions; financing requirements vary according to dollar amounts and lenders' protocols, and analytical calculations may vary depending on the calculator or spreadsheet program used. Because of all these potential differences, I strongly recommend consultation with expert professionals both to protect your investment decisions and to assure accuracy in the data and the analytical results used to make those decisions.

The Americans with Disabilities Act is mainly concerned with public accommodations in commercial properties and therefore is not addressed in this book. Another topic I have not covered is conversion to metric measurements. Real estate professionals doing business with the U.S. government after October 1, 1993, must use metric measurements in proposals submitted to the General Services Administration. This will impact proposals for space leasing or acquisition of existing buildings. In terms of construction, metric units will have to be used for dimensions in drawings and specifications for components. While most construction products (piping, lumber, switch plates, etc.) will not be changed in size, they will be labeled in metric units. On the other hand, modular products such as doors and plywood sheeting will be produced in standardized metric sizes, and this change will likely impact the way you specify materials for a recycling project. Another consideration is that availability of metric-measure construction materials may vary, potentially affecting materials costs and work scheduling. To learn more about the impact of metrication on construction, write to the Construction Metrication Council of the National Institute of Building Sciences, 1201 L Street, N.W., Suite 400, Washington, D.C. 20005.

ACKNOWLEDGMENTS

A text of this nature is not a work that is assembled based on research. It is the culmination of many experiences accumulated over my thirty-year career in the real estate business. A great many people have been involved directly and indirectly in the experiences from which I gained the knowledge to successfully recycle apartment properties.

In 1966, I convinced Keith G. Wurtz, M.D., to purchase an apartment property in Arlington Heights, Illinois. Aside from my education, I am sure it was my youthful exuberance that convinced Dr. Wurtz to buy the property and allow me to manage it and rehabilitate it. This was my beginning. I am proud that Dr. Wurtz remains an investor with me today.

A major thrust in rehabilitating apartments through the recycling process requires an understanding of market perceptions—what they are and how to change them. Charles L. Hulin, Ph.D., Professor of Psychology at the University of Illinois at Urbana-Champaign, was very instrumental in quantifying the process of perception change. My relationship with Dr. Hulin began with a seminar we prepared together on "How to Manage People" and offered throughout the United States and Canada in the early 1980s. It is Dr. Hulin who taught me the requirements for changing people's perceptions.

Robert T. Lincoln, Senior Vice President of NBD Bank, took a chance on me when I needed help and gave me the encouragement and impetus to alter my career path to focus almost exclusively on the apartment recycling process. Another lender, Stephan J. Chevalier, Treasurer of Towne Realty in Milwaukee, Wisconsin, provided help and forbearance while I learned a costly lesson about the time required to change the perceptions of the market.

David M. Knight, CPM®, who was assigned the awesome task of turning around and liquidating $400,000,000 worth of nonperforming assets, hired me as an outside consultant and virtually gave me a free hand to work my plan on many projects. The successes achieved in this arena paved the way for my personal acquisitions.

Any perceived change must be initiated by a physical change in a property. I am very fortunate to have the services of Mark A. Sanders, a fine artist and a noted American Impressionist who has used his skills with color, texture, and design to provide physical changes to properties where many felt there was no hope. The cover of this book is yet one more manifestation of Mark's ability.

Lelia and Mark Jabin, real estate and legal professionals in their own right, have assisted me with their financial strength and their rock-solid support in the acquisition and rehabilitation of several properties. In this same vein, I offer a sincere acknowledgment to all of the limited partners who have given me unwavering support and allowed me to apply the recycling process to our mutual investments.

Within my own organization, the entire staff has been supportive of this endeavor, and without them, this book would never have become a reality. Specifically, Nancé J. Prahl, my assistant for eight years, typed the manuscript. Her knowledge of the real estate management business in general and our own operation in particular allowed her to provide constructive criticism so that the main thrust of the manuscript stayed on track. My son, Roger M. Cagann, a CPM® Candidate and Project Director for Eagle Properties, critiqued the manuscript from the standpoint of the pragmatic aspects of our business and provided a plethora of insights, especially regarding the analysis of the investment.

Martin J. Freed, Esq., a noted real estate and environmental attorney and my personal attorney for more than ten years, assisted with the legal aspects of this book and specifically applied his expertise to the section on environmental considerations.

The Institute of Real Estate Management, the publisher of this book, has given me untold support and encouragement, specifically: Joyce Travis Copess, Staff Vice President, Communications and Education, who took my idea about this book and helped me make it a reality; Joseph T. Lannon, Publishing and Curriculum Development Manager, who allowed me the freedom to attack the subject of the recycling of apartments in my own way; Caroline Scoulas, Senior Editor, who illustrated her tremendous talent in making all sections of this book readable and understandable; and my IREM teaching colleagues—I have been a CPM® member of the Institute since 1967—who helped me through the years to understand new concepts and to manifest them in my work.

Specifically relating to this text, I wish to thank the following individuals who reviewed the manuscript and offered their valuable insights to improve the contents of this book: Louis A. Danzico, CPM®, President of Management Enterprises, Inc., in Scranton, Pennsylvania, who has extensive experience in rehabilitation and management of office and apartment buildings; James S. Peacock, CPM®, Senior Vice President of Peacock Construction, Inc., in Lafayette, California, who has extensive experience in the rehabilitation, construction, and management of commercial and residential properties; and Lyn E. Weiland, CPM®, of Blackhawk, Colorado, one of the authors of *The Successful On-Site Manager* published by IREM, whose experience includes rehabilitation and management of commercial and residential properties.

Although this book bears my name as its author, those mentioned above are only a few who have helped shape my career and provided me the practical everyday experiences necessary to write a book of this nature. It has truly been a humbling experience.

Robert A. Cagann, CPM®

Contents

Apartment Recycling

"Recycling" is a concept not commonly associated with apartment properties. The public focus in recent years has been on the recycling of glass, metals (especially aluminum cans), paper, and plastics. In the past, glass bottles from soft drinks and other beverages were returned to the bottler, cleaned, inspected, and refilled; new bottle caps were added, and they were packed into new cartons. (Remember the two-cent—later a nickel—deposit on Coke and Pepsi bottles?) By contrast, used newsprint is ground up, de-inked, repulped, and formed into new paper stock. The one process constitutes cleaning up and repackaging; the other requires disintegration and re-creation—both are examples of recycling.

The fairly commonplace rehabilitation of buildings to reclaim them for adaptive or continuing use is also a form of recycling. Finding an apartment property that is not performing, buying it, and investing in improving its physical components, its rental performance, and its reputation in the community are the components of apartment recycling. The key is knowing the potential pitfalls in apartment rehabilitation as well as what makes such projects successful. This chapter provides an introductory overview of apartment recycling. In discussing fundamentals and benefits of this process, reference will be made to planning, financing, and management considerations. Because these are important issues, they will be addressed in detail in separate chapters.

Fundamental Concepts

The idea that apartment rehabilitation consists of simply painting, doing some needed repairs, and changing the name of a property is no longer acceptable. Once something is perceived as "bad," making it "good" again requires more than mere physical change. While the investment community views a physical change from "bad" to "good" as positive, it is the perception of this change by renters in the marketplace that dictates how long it will take the investment to move from a low level of performance to a higher one. Obviously there is a certain amount of risk inherent in any kind of change, but the psychological aspect of such change—the need to alter the perception of a property in its market—is a critical part of the apartment recycling process. That is why the psychology of change and its attendant risks will be explored throughout this book in conjunction with the manifested physical changes. Understanding this important psychological component can mean the difference between success and failure when you truly "recycle" an apartment property.

The Scope of Recycling. Rehabilitation is often used interchangeably with such words as restoration, renovation, reconditioning, remodeling, refurbishing, modernization, and recycling. Yet each of these terms differs from the other in subtle ways. *Rehabilitation* of a property is restoration to a state of functional efficiency and good management while *restoration* itself relates to physical repair and is concerned with correction of deferred maintenance. *Renovation* and *reconditioning* are extremely close to restoration and similarly relate to returning a property to good physical condition. *Remodeling,* on the other hand, relates mostly to physical change of the property short of changing its use (i.e., reconstruction), and *refurbishing* refers more to superficial change (i.e., the minimum that one might do to a property)—to clean is to refurbish. *Modernization* is adaptation to modern (current) needs, taste, or usage and is clearly related to market perception of what is currently acceptable. *Recycling* is processing for reuse, a concept that has broader implications and encompasses the whole of the process needed to turn around a poorly performing, physically rundown, and functionally deficient apartment property.

Recycling truly represents the extensive change imposed on a property from the outside (not by the residents themselves), and it is the magnitude of this process that has the greatest impact on a property. More than a general sprucing up, recycling means replacing such things as appliances, cabinets, and light fixtures; installing new carpeting, and making other changes to update apartment features and fixtures. In an overbuilt market, it is often difficult to obtain financing for new construction. In such a market situation, recycling of existing apartments can be a more realistic approach to enhancing the local housing supply.

Because the recycling process represents change, it is appropriate to characterize this term as well. To *change* something means to alter or modify it, making it different in some particular way but not actually converting it into something else. However, change also means to transform something or convert it into a radically different form. Thus another distinction emerges: An *alteration* is a partial or superficial change that preserves original integrity, while *transformation* represents more substantive change that leads to a distinctly different result. This latter is the scope of the change involved in apartment recycling.

Although the physical transformation of a property takes place quite rapidly, the loss of value that preceded it has occurred over an extended period; and the causes and consequences of this depreciation are far-reaching, encompassing the property itself, the people who live there, and the surrounding neighborhood. That is why physical transformation is not necessarily enough. The truth is that physical change is relatively straightforward—it proceeds in accordance with market dictates—while social change and market reacceptance are much slower and more difficult to achieve.

How Properties Depreciate.   One of the primary goals of real estate managers is to enhance or create value. Value is created by maximizing net operating income (NOI) over the life of the investment. When making a purchasing decision, a prospective investor examines the quantity, quality, and durability of the income stream an investment will generate. In apartment recycling, the investor will be dealing with property that has been depreciated (i.e., lost value). One of the keys to successful recycling is the ability to (1) identify different types of depreciation as they affect a property under consideration and (2) quantify the loss as it relates to the market (perceived deficiencies, consumer desires and preferences).

There are three types of depreciation: physical deterioration, functional obsolescence, and economic obsolescence. Only the first two can be controlled; they are inherent within a property. Physical deterioration can and must be addressed in any recycling process, and functional obsolescence is something that recycling can overcome.

Physical deterioration is a loss of value due to physical wear and tear. This is the easiest form of depreciation to identify and quantify. To a great degree, physical deterioration will be visible. A property in need of paint (evidenced by peeling, fading, or exposure of the original surface) is just one example. Unkempt landscaping, potholes and cracks in the pavement in parking areas, and missing roofing material are others. These all typify *deferred maintenance.*

Other types of physical deterioration, which may not be as readily apparent, can be an even greater hindrance to the marketing effort. While the mechanical equipment in a building is not shown to prospective residents, if it is not functioning properly, the impact on residents—and therefore on resident retention—can only be negative. A heating system that functions poorly or not at all during cold weather will be well-remembered at lease renewal time. Improper drainage that causes sewers to back up periodically will lower resident morale. Outdated electrical wiring is a safety hazard, and residents are inconvenienced when blown fuses have to be replaced regularly. Yet these types of mechanical problems are commonplace in properties that are candidates for recycling.

In my experience, there is a direct relationship between the amounts of observable and unobservable physical deterioration. In such situations, it is reasonable to assume that if money is not being spent to maintain the physical condition and appearance of the property, preventive maintenance of mechanical systems is not being done either. The greater the observable physical deterioration, the more intensively one must scrutinize the unseen areas of a property.

In most instances, physical deterioration is measurable in terms of move-outs and lost rental income. A roof that leaks at several points and affects apartments, a totally inoperative heating system, and no hot water are problems that must be totally corrected for apartments to be livable and therefore leasable. In the absence of such corrections, there will be no rent.

Functional obsolescence is somewhat more esoteric because it is a loss of value due to out-moded style and design—i.e., it is no longer fashionable. What makes this element of depreciation so ethereal is that what is fashionable will differ from market to market and among segments of the population. The apartment recycler must identify the segment of the market to be attracted and determine what this group of people considers desirable. This is not always an easy task.

Some obvious examples of functional obsolescence are present in properties built between 1968 and 1972. This so-called Mediterranean era featured heavy dark furniture and included very dark kitchen cabinets. In an effort to brighten the kitchen, Chinese red countertops were often installed. Wrought iron was used extensively in apartment fixtures as well as in the common areas. Hallways in these buildings looked like they had been transplanted from the medieval castles of Europe. There was also the long shag carpeting. The "beauty" of the long shag was enhanced by the two most popular color combinations: red with black and green with yellow. Vacuuming it was a two-step process—first you vacuumed, then you raked the shag. Quite frankly, almost any changes to these items would have a positive impact on a property. However, it is the more subtle areas of functionality that must be addressed.

A phrase commonly used in real estate is, "the most bang for the buck." While correction of functional obsolescence should have an immediate positive impact on the property, it must have a lasting impact as well. It does not pay to be trendy or to follow fads. Children's toys provide good examples why not. Massive promotional efforts created great demand for Cabbage Patch dolls and Hoola-Hoops when they first entered the market, and advertising had an immediate positive impact on their sales. However, within one or two years, these toys became obsolete (each was probably replaced by another trendy toy). At any rate, when there was no longer a market for Cabbage Patch dolls or Hoola-Hoops, no amount of money spent to promote them would increase their sales. Fad items are short-lived, and that is why I caution about trendiness in apartment recycling. It is important that a property not become dated; ideally, it should appear stylish long after the recycling process has been completed.

The third type of depreciation is not inherent in the property and therefore cannot be controlled. *Economic obsolescence* is a loss of value due to negative external forces. These external forces can take many forms.

- Adjacent land uses.
- Population movements that change the character of the neighborhood (social and economic changes).
- In-migration or out-migration of workers due to shifts in local industry.

All of these can have a drastic effect on the demand for your apartment product. I recall a particularly striking example of economic obsolescence from more than 20 years ago. In this instance, location was the true key to value.

I was appraising a detached single-family home in a subdivision which was typical of the period in that there were some five basic models repeated throughout the tract. In working out the appraisal, adjustments were made for condition, time of sale, and other slight differences among examples of the same model. When checking sale prices, however, I noted that a particular model in one half of the subdivision was selling for several thousand dollars more than the identical model located in the other half of the subdivision. At first this was baffling to me because there were no immediately discernible differences attributable to house location. However, I eventually found out that the difference in home values was directly related to school district boundaries—one district was known to be excellent; the other did not have such a favorable reputation.

That was the first time I realized how intelligent the market and market forces are. Obviously a new coat of paint for a house located in the poor school district would not affect the value of the real estate much because the market was penalizing the property for its location. Physical and functional changes to that property would only improve its position within the same school district-defined area of the subdivision. No physical or functional change could overcome the price differential in comparing it with homes located in the better school district. This clearly illustrates why only those items that are inherent within the property can be controlled. Physical and functional enhancements cannot and will not overcome external forces that have a deleterious effect on the property.

Many dollars have been spent to "improve" properties only to find that a return on the incremental increase in investment was not achievable because external forces working against the property precluded its financial success. A property tends to be what it is. It can be changed and improved as long as the changes or improvements are consistent and compatible with the influences of the market. If additional improvements or changes will yield no measurable increase in a property's economic value, it is expedient to make only such improvements as are needed to keep it competitive in the market where it is located.

Physical Change versus Perceived Change.   In this book, "market perception" refers to the mental image or impression of an apartment property held by actual and prospective residents. Properties that are candidates for recycling usually have a negative perception; the goal of rehabilitation is to reverse that perception. The physical change and perceived change must be synchronized for a rehabilitation to be successful. The goal is to change the perception in a way that will stimulate the senses of prospective renters, creating in them a desire to call your apartment community home.

Perception is awareness developed through the senses; it is synonymous with recognition and discernment and implies knowing and understanding. In a more utilitarian sense, specific perceptions are reinforced by additional stimuli such as stated opinions. For example, what makes a restaurant an "in" place to go could be anything from the people who go there to the exquisite food, the wonderful service, or the fact that being seen there enhances one's image. While food, service, and atmosphere are all part of its acceptability, what really creates an aura of "in-ness" for that restaurant is what others have said or written. You may be impressed by a glowing review that notes the restaurant's positive features and comments on the beautiful people who have been seen there. In addition, a friend or acquaintance might have mentioned how exciting and wonderful it was to go there. Thus, your desire to go to a particular restaurant will be stimulated by others' characterizations of it.

What does all this really mean? It means that something is only good to the extent that it is perceived as good. The reverse is also true. If someone tells you that a particular movie is bad, you might think twice about going to see it. If someone else independently comments about the movie being bad, the two negatives combined will probably be enough to keep you from seeing it.

The problem with perceptions is that they are often more emotional than intellectual. This makes them particularly difficult to overcome. The market perception of a property undergoing rehabilitation is a case in point. With the proper organization, funding, contractors, and suppliers, the physical transformation of the property itself can be accomplished over a period of months, in most cases less than one year. The physical image of the property is changed just as soon as the work is completed. However, the change in the perceived image is more ethereal. The foregoing examples of the restaurant and the movie demonstrate that desirability or undesirability is largely a matter of opinion. In the same manner, the community has an opinion about a property. Individual opinions can range from very positive to very negative, but the largest segment of the community holding a particular opinion—positive or negative—will have the greatest overall impact.

Market acceptance of a property as a desirable place to live is the key to financial success in the recycling process. Suppose you were new to a community, and you were thinking about renting at Wishful Vista Apartments. You might try to learn more about the area by striking up a conversation with someone who had lived there for some time and asking about the Wishful Vista Apartments. What if that person said, "I know someone from the police department who told me they have had many police calls at Wishful Vista Apartments because there are lots of drug dealers living there." Would you even bother to go to the property and see it for yourself? It is perceptions like this that control the success or failure of a rehabilitation. How rapidly the market perception of the property changes from negative to positive will dictate how long it will take to achieve investment success.

When you meet someone for the first time, you have an impression of that other person instantly. You probably do not know why you like or dislike someone at your very first encounter—your reaction is a feeling, a perception. If it is positive, the relationship can endure for a long time, even if the other person tends to do things you do not like. Conversely, if your first impression is negative, no matter what that person may do that is positive, it will likely take a very long time to win you over, if he or she ever can. Negative impressions are often far more lasting than positive ones.

A perception can be a one-time thing, but in the business of apartment recycling, it is important to accentuate the positive, always. The first positive results when someone familiar with the property's past perceives that real change has taken place and is willing to make a commitment to live there. The second and ultimately the most important positive occurs when that person, after living in the property awhile, realizes that his or her perception of the change was correct and begins to tell others. This third-party referral or testimonial will be the greatest impetus to success for an apartment property that is being recycled.

One of the most successful rehabilitations I was involved with maintains occupancy at greater than 98 percent, with virtually all of its new residents coming as referrals from those who live at the property. However, for almost five years following the rehabilitation, this particular property received phone calls from prospective residents who would say, "Oh! Are those the little houses on Craig Avenue?" and then they would either say, "No thank you," or just hang up. Although this type of reaction diminished with time—the numbers were greatly reduced each succeeding year—it is obvious that old perceptions die hard.

It takes time to change negative perceptions in the market. Classical appraisal theory defines the market as buyers and sellers who are ready, willing, and able to consummate a transaction. It is my firm belief that, in the context of apartment recycling, this definition of the market must be expanded to include other people, whether knowledgeable or not, who have an opinion about the subject property. Their expressed opinions, which come from impressions they have received, do have an influence on the renting market.

One of the sources of particular inferences about a property is its current residents. Consideration for the needs of residents once they have moved to the property is paramount. Although residents want a nice place to live, they also want to be treated as valued customers. This includes prompt action when service is required. On the other hand, the landlord needs residents who pay their rent promptly and care for the property. This includes respect for the other residents. The old adage, "birds of a feather flock together," is certainly true in the apartment business. The negative aspects of this premise become increasingly apparent when a property begins to decline.

There are two main reasons for the failure of an apartment property. One is money—or the lack of it. The other is the lack of sound professional management. The latter is most important because even if money is tight, good management can sustain a property longer than inexperienced or unknowledgeable and unsupervised people can. When a property begins to decline, the attitude of the site personnel seems to be the first thing to change, and as a result, residents become increasingly dissatisfied. As vacancies increase, the marketing effort must be increased to replace the lost residents.

Concurrently, there tends to be a lack of timeliness in handling residents' requests for service, and the work that is done declines in quality. This, in turn, increases resident dissatisfaction further, and the property begins to show signs of deferred maintenance. Thus begins the decline of the physical appearance of the property. Furthermore, these events do not take place over only one or two months; rather, they occur over a period of one or two years or longer.

As the need to market becomes greater, there is a tendency to lower resident qualification standards. This only compounds the problem because it will be readily apparent to established residents that the newcomers do not match the intended resident profile, and this may lead to some friction. When such interpersonal tensions develop, there is even more reason for resident dissatisfaction and, consequently, greater turnover. If money was not a particular problem before, it certainly is now. Occupancy is down, the quality of the residents has been lowered—along with their ability to pay rent—and this results in less rent being collected. The lack of money is now an even greater factor, and deferred maintenance begins to be even more obvious than before.

The process of decline begins very slowly; it is almost evolutionary. However, as each ingredient is magnified the process gains momentum. If allowed to go unchecked, the residents will ultimately gain control of the property, and any rules and regulations or community policies that existed will no longer be followed. The decline and fall can take several years, and all the while, the neighborhood surrounding this property is seeing the telltale signs. Rumors begin, and as they are substantiated, the negative perceptions of the property are amplified.

Once the recycling process is begun, new policies and procedures will be established. The physical changes to the property will not only correct deficiencies that exist but, more importantly, they will address the need for modernization and correction of functional obsolescence. Still, the market will not perceive the change immediately—the change may be completed, and the market may know that something has happened, but the negative perception prevails. Remember, it took considerable time, perhaps years, for the market perception of the property to become negative. Consequently, it will take considerable time to overcome that negative perception.

My own approach to apartment recycling is one of overt action to start the process moving in the desired direction. As soon as financing has been obtained and the acquisition is finalized, I start to work. Exterior improvements and more attractive landscaping are done to clearly signal a transformation. These very visible signs communicate to the marketplace—the neighborhood as well as the current residents—that real change is taking place, thus providing a foundation for the perception to change as well.

Risk as a Function of Degree of Change. An apartment property can be likened to a great mass that is in motion. If it is moving in a positive direction, it will gain positive momentum and project a positive image from the existing residents to the outside market. If it is moving in a negative direction, the opposite will be true—its negative momentum will increase, and the perception by residents and the market will be increasingly negative. This was demonstrated in the preceding discussion. A key fact to remember is that before the direction of a property can be changed, the negative momentum must be stopped. An impression of tranquility at a property is the first step toward overcoming the negative perception fostered by previous turmoil.

Risk accompanies change. The greater the change required, the greater the attendant risk. In apartment recycling, risk has two major components—market forces and time. The market and all attendant influences must be thoroughly examined, and the physical changes and policy changes must conform to the desires and preferences of the market. Time must be a factor in budgeting, particularly with regard to financing the rehabilitation. Provision must be made to cover the carrying costs (real estate taxes and mortgage interest) during and after the rehabilitation when the property's rental income is likely to be reduced.

The *degree of change* is also an important consideration. The more a property has depreciated, the lower its acquisition price, and the greater its potential return. It must be understood that the time required to change the negative perception in the market will be commensurate with the magnitude of the negative image. The most striking example in my experience was a property in Alexandria, Virginia.

> The property had lost all of its occupancy permits and had stood vacant (boarded up) for several years. Many factors had contributed to its demise. It started with very poor management that included little or no screening of prospective residents. As the resident profile changed for the worse, delinquencies increased. This reduced collected income and simultaneously increased the need for maintenance. However, due to insufficient income, the maintenance performed was inadequate, and the effects snowballed from there.
>
> On the upside were three positives, all of which existed prior to the acquisition and ultimate rehabilitation in 1981. The first was size—the property comprised more than 2,000 units. It was a neighborhood unto itself and amounted to almost 28 percent of all multi-family units in the city. The second was the fact that the surrounding neighborhoods were well-accepted by the market. Third and most important was time. At least three years had gone by since there had been any drug dealing or gang activity at the property. It is often said that time has a way of healing all wounds. This is certainly true about a property that has had serious problems. In this case, because there were no residents, there was no longer a negative image being projected.
>
> Finally, actual construction on this rehab was far more than cosmetic. Buildings were gutted, new roofs were installed, and new roof lines were created. The buildings were given new facades, and apartment configurations were changed, improved, and modernized. It was more than a year before the newly recycled property was ready to go to market. At that point, even more time had passed, and the community had been watching to see what was going to happen. The bottom line is that we were able to rent up the entire property of more than 2,000 units inside of 14 months—in one month alone, we rented 276 apartments. Yes, there was excitement. The point remains, however, that it took several years for this property to reach bottom, and then even more time to turn it around completely. Old perceptions die hard, but *they will die* over a period of time if the proper steps are taken to cure the ills of the property.

It should be obvious from this example that the most serious risk factor in apartment rehabilitation is the time it will take to change the market perception of the property from what it was at acquisition or at the beginning of the recycling process to what you want it to be. Compounding this risk is the desire to begin remarketing the newly rehabilitated property. If you market too soon, you will surely continue to attract the same type of resident as had been living there previously. It certainly can be argued that one can wait too long to market, and during the delay, the carrying costs will consume whatever resources are available (reserve funds or rental income), but it is advisable to seek a middle ground. It is necessary to wait long enough and have enough of the rehabilitation work completed for the image of the property to have changed as well. Thus time and the market are interrelated. When apartment rehabilitations fail, they often do so because an aggressive marketing campaign was launched *immediately* after the physical defects had been corrected. In many instances, the change in the market perception did not keep pace with the physical transformation, and that difference was being ignored.

Too much physical change presents another market-related risk. There is no question that the greater the amount of physical change required, the longer it will take to change the market perception. The operative word is "required." Some rehabbers would argue that the more done to enhance a property physically, the better its chances for success. Yet, if market analysis reveals a certain level of quality or a particular array of amenities to be the accepted or expected standard, any improvements beyond this standard will not generate any more income and, in fact, will only increase risk. There will be no return on the excessive capital expended.

Misinterpretation of the resident profile is yet another risk factor. A property will be, not what the owner wants it to be, but what the market says it will be. The demographics of the market must be scrutinized to determine the characteristics of the prospective residents for a rehabilitated property. Then the changes to the property must be matched to this market indication. (Risk analysis is addressed in chapter 5.)

Benefits of Recycling

Apartment recycling is a complex process. Those who pursue this venture need to have some understanding of the role of real estate in the U.S. economy, how it compares with alternative investments, and how recycled apartments meet an existing market need.

Real Estate and Economics.   The Tax Reform Act of 1986 has caused real estate to lose much of its appeal because it must stand on its own economic merits as an investment—no longer can real estate be used simply to provide a tax shelter. These rules did not become fully effective until 1991. Most economists agree that one of the reasons the recession that began in 1989 lasted so long was a massive oversupply of developed real estate. The primary reason for that glut was Congress' vote to change the rules on depreciation of real estate (the Economic Recovery Tax Act of 1981), allowing investors to take huge financial losses (on paper) and use these losses to offset tax obligations from other profitable pursuits. Deals that produced these valuable "losses" were packaged into tax shelter investments, and such programs flourished in the early 1980s. Investors seeking to shelter income from taxes did not really care whether a real estate development had "economic" value. Subsequently, the Tax Reform Act of 1986 devalued real estate, causing many of the more highly leveraged properties to fail.

Real estate values continue to fluctuate. Many owners have had to default on loans because the income generated by their properties was not sufficient to cover operating expenses and debt service. There has also been a great deal of restructuring of loans—in many cases, lenders have written down loans on nonperforming real estate in an effort to make such properties economically viable.

As the glut of overbuilt real estate has been absorbed by the market, developers, investors, purchasers and lenders have readopted an age-old standard in viewing real estate investments. The question now asked is, "Does the real estate investment make solid economic sense?" This means, will the income generated by the real estate investment be adequate to support operating expenses, provide necessary reserve funds, and service the debt while still providing an adequate return? (Investment analysis as such is discussed in chapter 5.)

Investment Alternatives. As the prime lending rate fell in the early 1990s, interest paid on savings accounts also languished (at very low single-digit rates). The lowered rate forced investors who previously relied solely on passbook and money market accounts to consider alternative investment opportunities. Thus, the aspect of risk inherent in investments is being evaluated by a broader spectrum of the investing public. This has been good for the real estate industry for two reasons: First, investors are making conscious investment decisions based on what they must give up or risk in order to receive a higher yield on their invested dollars. Second, and most important to the real estate industry, is the lowering of demanded yield rates because so-called safe investments such as passbook savings accounts now yield much less than they did in the past.

Real estate has always been viewed as "risk capital." That has not changed. However, the amount of demanded yield has been reduced in relation to other investments—today when an investor measures loss of liquidity and ultimate risk compared to other investments, real estate looks good. When passive losses can be used to offset some or all of the passive income generated, real estate looks even better. A key factor will be the competence and integrity of the manager of the real estate.

The Institute of Real Estate Management Foundation commissioned a nationwide survey of property owners (real estate investors) by the national accounting firm of Arthur Andersen and Company. The results of this survey, which was published in 1991, identified the following as the top nine characteristics that property owners seek in property managers and management firms.

1. Integrity
2. Reliability
3. Quality of individuals assigned (to their properties)
4. Financial responsibility
5. Professional competence
6. Tenant relations
7. Reputation
8. Timeliness of reports
9. Local market information

These all precede the array of specific property management skills such as maintenance, budgeting, reporting and record keeping, marketing and leasing.

Investors are now analyzing real estate managers the same way they have analyzed managers of corporations before they would invest in the stock of that corporation. The climate is such that real estate compares very favorably with other investment opportunities because the same criteria are being used to measure all investments. This has come to pass because real estate is now being measured solely on its ability to produce an economic return on invested capital.

Multifamily Real Estate as an Investment.   Many trends have evolved in the real estate industry out of economic necessity. One example is the way large, sprawling offices have given way to smaller, more utilitarian spaces as companies have downsized their personnel and space requirements in efforts to maintain a more competitive market position. Another is an increase in self-employment, with more people working out of their homes. In the retail segment of the real estate market, merchants have been able to take advantage of technological innovations to reduce requirements to maintain a large inventory and the space to store it. Similar downsizing has been taking place in industrial real estate. This downsizing by space users is one of the reasons why the office, retail, and industrial sectors of the real estate market have been so slow to recover from the overbuilding.

Apartment investments have suffered similar problems due to overbuilding. Although the management of apartments is more labor-intensive (in comparison to other types of properties), there is a stability in this sector that is not enjoyed by the others—even in bad times, people need somewhere to live. As the real estate market moves toward equilibrium, the multifamily segment of the market will continue to provide solid investment opportunities.

Older Properties.   Most of the properties that are good candidates for rehabilitation were built between 18 and 25 years ago (many of them have been
neglected severely for a variety of reasons). These older properties provide
many opportunities for profitable recycling. Due to community growth, these
properties tend to be quite well located, and a good location can overcome
many functional deficiencies that a property may have. Those suffering from
depreciation in its various forms can be purchased at a lower per-unit price
and returned to a competitive position in the market for far less invested
capital than new construction. This works well because many people who are
interested in enjoying maximum benefits of living in a quality environment
prefer to do so at a reduced cost. Recycling is a means of restoring a property
to a competitive position in the market while yielding an adequate return on
the invested capital.

Changing Consumer Attitudes.   There are generally two types of apartment renters: *Renters by necessity* comprise those who cannot afford to buy
a home; this group includes those who are trying to save enough money for
a downpayment on the "American dream" of homeownership. *Renters by
choice,* on the other hand, are committed to renting, usually high-end luxury
apartments, even though they can afford to buy a house. Although there used
to be a large gap between these two groups, people's attitudes toward rental
apartments have changed over the last several years, and so have apartments.

Developers began to offer midline or semiluxury apartments because
several factors in the single-family home-buying equation had been altered.
In particular, the price of the average detached single-family home increased
dramatically. This meant it would take longer to accumulate the funds for a
downpayment. It also meant that first-time homebuyers would be older than
those in the past. While interest rates have been moving downward in recent
years, lending institutions have been tightening their mortgage qualification
standards. All of these changes tend to favor renting over buying.

Two other considerations are encouraging for the apartment recycler.
One is that today's first-time homebuyers have been raised with much higher
expectations. Often called "conspicuous consumers," they are not willing to
make the sacrifice of living in marginal housing while they amass the necessary capital for a downpayment, and consequently they have little or no savings. The other consideration is that today's renters who expect to buy a home
eventually are accustomed to more-spacious and better-equipped housing.
They are basically unwilling to compromise their "me generation" lifestyle,
even for the short term. They are, however, better educated and more aware
of the amenities offered in a particular market. These renters are perfect
prospects for the recycled property where apartments have been rehabbed
to offer the lifestyle equivalent of high-end units without the accompanying
high monthly rents.

Here is a key thought when you consider recycling a property that is
18–25 years old: The high-end amenity-loaded properties that were built dur-

ing the late 1980s—replete with health clubs, socializing facilities, and every appliance imaginable—are losing significant market share to well-managed and well-rehabilitated properties. Also, many renters are less confident about their employment future and income-generating potential. They cannot afford to live in the high-end properties, or they choose not to spend a large proportion of their income on housing. Renters in this market segment are prime candidates to rent in a good rehab that is able to charge less rent.

This situation will prevail wherever apartment rentals remain soft because overbuilding has created excess supply at rents beyond the means of those seeking "affordable" housing. In other words, demand for rehabbed apartments renting at modest rates will likely be sustained into the future. In particular, a well-conceived rehabilitation combined with professional property management will flourish. Remember, while today's consumers are more knowledgeable, they are also more frugal—they continue to demand a certain ostentation that is found in new properties, but they do not want to pay a high rent. Recycling an apartment property offers a way to meet both of these requirements.

2

Finding the Right Property

The search for a property to recycle must be conducted with extreme care. Investment in a multifamily building requires a large amount of capital, most of which will likely be borrowed. Both you and your lender will want to be assured of a reasonable, acceptable return on the investment. Such assurance will result from specific analyses of a property's physical and fiscal condition, the marketplace in which it competes, and its specific competition.

Properties that are candidates for recycling can be characterized in one of two ways. *Nonperforming assets* are properties whose "as is" value is below that which would be acceptable to a lending institution's board or whose upside potential is marginal or achievable only in the distant future. The goal of recycling such properties is to restore the value that has been eroded. *Performing assets* are currently profitable properties that could do better; recycling affords an opportunity to enhance their performance.

There are several potential sources of apartment properties to which the recycling process can be applied. You may be aware of a particular property in the community where you work or live or in an area with which you are generally familiar. Once you have made known your interest in recycling apartment properties within a geographic area, available candidates will likely be brought to your attention. Local real estate professionals who learn of your search may even direct you to properties in their sales portfolios (networking).

Federal agencies such as the Veterans Affairs Department (formerly Veterans Administration), the Department of Housing and Urban Development

(HUD), and the Resolution Trust Corporation (RTC) are also owners of distressed properties. These include multifamily apartment buildings acquired through defaults on federally guaranteed mortgages, many of which may be suitable candidates for rehabilitation, although single-family homes predominate among VA and HUD properties. Properties available from HUD are often prominently advertised, and dealings must be through a HUD-approved broker using special bid forms. There are no guarantees on HUD properties so careful inspection before purchase is mandatory. RTC properties are often sold through auctions, and there are some special programs for financing bulk real estate purchases from them.

Lenders are a very good source, perhaps the best one. Many major banks have REO (real estate owned) departments whose holdings comprise primarily properties acquired through foreclosure. Occasionally REO properties are sold through brokers, but the banks themselves are the most direct source. Price-wise, the bank will try to minimize its loss. The outstanding mortgage (usually quite large) as well as the bank's take-over costs will probably determine the starting point for negotiations; the asking price may be close to market value. However, REO properties have the advantage of being free of encumbrances, and title can be transferred easily.

There are other possibilities although these may be less readily accessible. Institutional owners of real estate include insurance companies and others who manage assets for pension fund investment. Their real estate portfolios comprise mostly commercial properties (office buildings and shopping centers), but they often include apartment buildings as well. When their real estate investments are not performing to their expectations or requirements, divestiture may be considered. Networking with real estate asset managers may provide an opportunity to acquire an apartment property and recycle it.

Investment Preliminaries

The decision to invest in a particular property proceeds in two stages. The first is a preliminary, somewhat superficial evaluation which is the basis for offering a purchase contract to the seller. The second stage is a more comprehensive analysis of specifics—the *due diligence* that examines the feasibility of recycling that particular property. This, in turn, is used to develop a formal plan for the rehabilitation, which will be submitted to a lender to secure financing.

Most people equate analysis with "number crunching," and rightly so. Analysis of the investment is precisely that type of activity (see chapter 5). Frankly, crunching numbers is the easy part. The hard part is determining what numbers to use in the first place. You have to decide what risks you are willing to take before you decide what you are willing to do. From personal experience, I can assure you that there is no substitute for the laborious and often cumbersome task of gathering information. On the other hand, before I even look at a property, I apply some quick arithmetic and ask some basic questions. I want to know four things—

1. The asking price
2. The number of units
3. What the neighborhood is like
4. The property's current state

At this very early stage, I want to know what it will cost, per unit, to buy the property (price divided by the number of units equals cost per unit); whether it can be fixed, and whether it can be marketed. Past experience suggests what it is reasonable to spend, per unit, so that I can raise rents and get a return on the investment.

If I decide I am interested, I will do a preliminary evaluation. This comprises an initial inspection to get an overview of what must be done to the property and prepare some cost estimates. This particular exercise requires knowledge of price ranges for materials and labor at the local level. (Access to professionals with construction sources and expertise is very helpful.) Simultaneously, I conduct a basic market analysis. At this point, I am interested in potential market rents and the market perception of the property and its neighborhood. These preliminary data provide a basis for drafting a specific purchase offer and negotiating a deal. Among other specifics, the negotiated contract includes the dollar price, required financing, and sufficient time to conduct an appropriate *due diligence* evaluation. (I specifically negotiate a deal in which the due diligence period constitutes a "free look"—nothing, including the earnest money, is at risk. If, as a result of the due diligence, I decide *not* to go through with the purchase, the contract allows for a clean break—no penalties.) Actual terms of purchase depend on factors peculiar to the particular deal.

The due diligence effort includes the specific analyses discussed in the remainder of this chapter. This is the data-collection process that provides the information used in developing a rehabilitation plan, obtaining financing, and analyzing the investment, which are the subjects of separate chapters. Although the analyses and other activities are discussed separately, they will often overlap each other. For example, inspection may suggest installation of new bathroom fixtures in the apartment units, and when this is evaluated as part of the rehabilitation plan, it may become desirable or necessary to replace plumbing pipes as well. In a similar vein, rather than replace metal kitchen cabinets with wood ones or vice versa, it may be equally appropriate and more cost-effective to replace cabinet doors and drawer fronts or just repaint them. While comparative costs are a major consideration, what can actually be accomplished may depend on the level of financing that can be obtained. Due diligence comprises a determination of what must be done to the property physically and what additional enhancements can be made to maximize the return on your investment. It is an examination of the feasibility of recycling the particular property.

Analysis of Existing Properties

When presented with a property that appears to be a candidate for recycling, you must ask yourself the question, "What can I do differently (than existing management and ownership) to make this property successful as an investment?" This is the starting point in the data-gathering process. What must be determined is how the property came to its present state of decline and whether it is a likely candidate for rehabilitation. Five factors are critical to this evaluation, and these must be examined carefully. The first is its current management—management is the catalyst for success of any real estate venture. The second is the property's current fiscal position—its ability to generate sufficient income to meet its financial obligations. The third is its current physical condition—the extent of depreciation. (This can be studied concurrent with the examination of its management.) The fourth is the existing financing—if a property is severely over-leveraged, debt service may be given priority over operating expenses such that maintenance standards cannot be met. The fifth is the marketplace—something may have changed the market within the past several years to reduce demand for apartments. Each of these five factors will be addressed in its turn.

Current Management. Many of the deals made before the Tax Reform Act of 1986 was enacted had little solid economic basis. The Tax Reform Act changed all that, and the 1990s bring a totally new perspective to multifamily investment. Today, success is founded on professional property management. All the work involved in the recycling process is likely to be of no avail unless competent professional management is in place.

The first thing to look for is the *attitude* of the site staff. Attitude will be reflected in their dress and appearance and in the neatness and organization of the paperwork in the office. Real estate management is an extremely detail-oriented business. The only way that it can be done successfully is through organization such that many of the details can be handled on a routine basis. A few minutes spent in friendly conversation with the site staff can save endless hours later. The problem could be as simple as the competence of the resident manager. (The checklist in exhibit 2.1, page 22, provides a guide for the assessment of current management.)

Another area to analyze are service requests or maintenance work orders. You also want to know whether there is a maintenance log and how many maintenance people are employed at the site. (Exhibit 2.2 lists specific items to look for when examining a maintenance log.) In the absence of such

Components of Due Diligence Analysis

Comprehensive physical inspection should be performed to determine current condition, what absolutely has to be done, and what enhancements would maximize the return on the investment. It may be necessary or appropriate to call upon other professionals, especially if the rehabber suspects problems. A *structural engineer* may be needed to evaluate the roof, supports, and the physical structure in general. A *civil engineer* may have to be called in because of drainage problems or obvious signs of potential for flooding.

Current zoning should be reviewed to determine whether zoning matches current use and whether there are any violations. It may be necessary to request a zoning change or variance—e.g., if the number of units will be increased or decreased as a result of the rehab. If the original building was constructed under a zoning variance, that fact may preclude the purchaser's ability to alter (rehabilitate) the property. Also check that the property is not located in a special local or historical district.

Liens against the property (e.g., for nonpayment of taxes or other debts) can impede financing. Title to the property when it becomes collateral for construction or other financing (first lien) must be free of all other liens and encumbrances. A check of title records is mandatory.

Local codes should be checked very carefully to determine current requirements and the property's compliance status. It should be possible to ascertain the existence and extent of any recorded violations of building codes, fire or life safety requirements, etc. There may be local requirements regarding access for handicapped individuals as well. It is important to know not only what problems exist but also whether they can be remedied. Operating and occupancy permits (when required) typically are contingent on periodic inspections; their status and renewal dates should be ascertained. It may be prudent to meet with the individual in charge of the local building or planning department as well as obtain copies of signed inspection reports, notices of violations, etc.

Real estate taxes are assessed by local authorities. Current assessed value, its basis, the amount of the tax, and the reassessment schedule—and whether a notice of reassessment has been sent to the seller—are key things to check. Taxes should be current—not delinquent. (A tax protest may be in order.)

Leases should be audited to assure that they are matched to current occupants and to verify rent amounts and lease expiration dates.

records—or in addition to reviewing them—it may be prudent to talk to some residents about the quality of the services being provided currently.

In addition, existing policies and procedures should be evaluated carefully. Not only should they be scrutinized for clarity and reasonableness, but you need to ascertain whether they are being followed.

Many lenders, real estate venture companies, and private investors make the mistake of having the initial site inspection made by someone who lacks property management experience and looks at a property far too analytically. There is never a better opportunity to acquire information about a property than that presented on the very first visit to the site. I would argue that while

---

Components of Due Diligence Analysis (*cont.*)

Resident files should be reviewed to determine who the occupants are, where they work, their employment status, etc., as a starting point in constructing a *resident profile*.

Collections information is critical—delinquent rents reduce income; nonpayment of rent is cause for eviction. Rent roll and delinquency reports (minimally current month and year-to-date) should be reviewed. More specific data may be found in resident ledgers, if such are being kept.

Current financial status should be evaluated. Minimally you need to know current occupancy (vacancy) levels, current income and expenses, and its potential to generate additional rental income.

Current policies and procedures—and their enforcement—should be reviewed as part of the evaluation of current management.

Market analysis should identify what is most deleterious to the perception of the property in the market—also what is its most favorable feature. Meeting and talking with the residents and visiting local stores are critical components of this exercise. What has to be determined is the position the property can ultimately attain in the market. Evaluation of the competition is part of this analysis.

Environmental compliance status should be reviewed. Regardless of lender requirements for the purchase, a Phase I assessment is the minimum that should be done. (It will be absolutely necessary for any refinancing or for resale.) Such an assessment should be conducted by a qualified environmental professional. Apart from inspecting the property, it is important to check the "chain of title" to be assured that prior uses of the land did not create any "hidden" environmental problems.

Rehabilitation costs and time should be estimated. A rehabilitation plan (including a budget) will be needed to obtain financing.

NOTE: Those conducting due diligence analyses need to be aware of costs that may be incurred. To this end, professional consultants (e.g., engineers) should be asked to provide a statement or estimate of their fees in advance. There may also be charges for access to or copies of liens, title records, code violation reports, tax records, etc., all of which are important components of due diligence. The information compiled in this analysis will be used in the analysis of the investment as well as in creating the budget and other components of a comprehensive rehabilitation plan (as outlined in the next chapter), and some specifics may have to be submitted to the lender as part of the loan application.

---

many property analyses consist of site inspections that place initial emphasis on physical condition and occupancy levels, evaluation of the staff will be a far more productive initial activity.

Management Personnel.   Even if your plans call for dismissal of the entire staff, it is a major error to overlook any factor in the analysis of a piece of real estate. Time spent gathering information from the staff on your first visit to the site will save time in the long run. Most properties that are for sale have been examined by numerous potential buyers. Site personnel are likely to be physically tired and emotionally drained because they are very uncertain

E X H I B I T   2.1

Example Current Management Checklist

Property: _____

Date: _____ Compiled by: _____

Staff Position (Name)	Appearance	Professionalism	Attitude	Salary
Manager				
Assistant Manager				
Leasing Agents				
Other Office Staff				
Maintenance Supervisor				
Maintenance Personnel				
Janitorial Staff				
Other Site Staff				
Comments:				

This type of form may be used in compiling evaluations of the site staff as a group. A format with larger cells would permit more extensive notes regarding the characteristics of individuals.

about their future. That being the case, they are likely to show you exactly what you ask to see and answer specific questions, but they will rarely volunteer additional information. While this makes it easy to look at the physical property, it minimizes contact with the staff. Therefore, evaluating the staff will require your best people skills. This means prudent inquiry, withholding

E X H I B I T   2.2

Example Maintenance Log Checklist

Property: _____

Date: _____ Compiled by: _____

	Notes
Overall Setup	
Who Uses It	
How Often Updated	
Most Frequent Calls	
1	
2	
3	
4	
5	
Call Backs (same problem)	
Call Backs (new/different problem)	
Response Time	
Items Repaired?/Replaced?	
Preventive Maintenance Schedule	
Located	
Last Update	
Equipment Inventory	
Comments:	

This or a similar form should be used to compile information regarding an existing maintenance log and program for purposes of evaluation and planning.

---

of judgment, and suitable conversation—nothing more than you would have if you were getting to know any new person.

Spend time visiting with the site manager. Ask questions: "Where are you from?" "How long have you been in real estate management?" "How long at this property?" "What do you like to do for recreation?" Whether someone is married or has children is more personal but also likely to come out in conversation. However, if the manager thinks he or she is being grilled, the lines of communication will break down immediately. (Direct questions about personal characteristics are best avoided because they can be considered discriminatory.)

One of the best ways to acquire information from or about a site manager is to build a relationship during the tour of the property. While the good things about the property are likely to be happily pointed out, negative aspects can also be discussed without putting the manager on the defensive. His or her responses regarding the negatives will be helpful in measuring the level of competence of the manager and identifying the policies that have been established by the manager or others in the management company.

Resident Profile.   Another excellent way to begin an analysis of the property and further evaluate its management is to glean as much information as possible about the current resident profile. (Exhibit 2.3 is a general checklist for gathering resident profile information.) The current resident profile is a reflection of the competency of the current management, and both of these factors are important in determining the current status of the property. The resident profile becomes the basis for all decisions that are made with regard to enhancement of the physical asset. The higher the social and economic caliber of existing residents, the less change will be required to attain the desired profile and the lower the risk.

It is important to understand the relationship between change and risk. The potential for enhancement of the value of the real estate is a prime consideration. That is why you must establish the "as is" status of the real estate as rapidly as possible. During your initial visit, review the lease files and examine the relevant rental applications, which should be included in each resident's permanent file. Ask the manager about move-outs as well. He or she should be able to tell you about the length of residency, reasons for leaving, results of exit interviews, and any changes in resident quality during his or her tenure. These are very tough issues, and if the manager is even slightly defensive, the information may not be accurate.

It is wise to ask the manager what he or she believes the resident profile to be. Are most of the residents singles in their twenties, families with small children, or senior citizens? You want to know what age groups, income levels, and space needs are represented, as well as how a "typical" resident would be characterized. (In other words, does the manager really know and understand the resident profile?) Also important is whether residents pay their rent (in full, on time) and generally get along with their neighbors.

As you tour the building, you will certainly examine some or all of the vacant units. You should try to enter some occupied units as well. (During the due diligence process, you will have to inspect *every* apartment.) Engage the residents in conversation—ask what they do for a living and how they like living at the property. Ask them questions about the property; this will elicit some very interesting responses. The extra time spent talking with res-

E X H I B I T　2.3

Resident Profile Data Checklist

Property: _____

Date: _____ Compiled by: _____

Information Source:	
	Notes
Who Lives Here:	
Household/Family Size:	
Pets:	
Turnover:	
What do you like best about the property?	
Would you recommend the property?	
(Resident) Are you renewing?	
Comments:	

This form is used to characterize the resident profile for the property as a whole. Sources might be the resident manager, another staff person, and selected residents. A separate form should be completed for each source surveyed. Several people's insights should be sought and compared.

idents while inspecting their apartments will expand your knowledge of how the property is perceived in the market.

Remember, those who work and live at the property (staff and residents) have valuable information you need. All you have to do is extract that information from them. Good use of people skills can save considerable investigative time.

Current Fiscal Condition. There are many "rules of thumb" in real estate, and one must be careful not to let these rules control the decision-making process. Nevertheless, examination of a property's operating statement for the past twelve months can be quite revealing. The first thing to do is compute the expense-to-income ratio (operating expenses divided by receipts). If the ratio is 50 percent or less, the expenses would be considered typical. More often than not, the expenses exceed 50 percent. This is due to two main problems, usually in combination. The first relates to income, and the key considerations are the number of vacancies and the level of collections (amounts due and owing versus actual receipts). The second relates to expenses. In particular, the payroll figure tends to be quite revealing. Typically the property is over-staffed, and the employees are being paid higher than average wages. Under maintenance expenses, the costs of parts and supplies tend to be inordinately high, even in the presence of extensive deferred maintenance.

An example from my own experience is a property in a lender's REO portfolio. Even though there was 30 percent vacancy, not one apartment was ready to show. There were eight maintenance men for approximately 250 units. Some units had new carpeting, others had been freshly painted, and still others had new appliances. Yet no one of these apartments had all of these items completed.

Reviewing the operating statement before the property is inspected may point out potential problems which can be verified during the physical inspection. Again, there is no substitute for experience. Line items in an operating statement can be revealing in other ways. For example, advertising costs usually are high even when a property is not ready to be marketed.

One final thought about fiscal condition. If at all possible, try to review operating statements for the past two or three years as well. Look for trends in both income and expenses. Often this information will not be available on your preliminary inspection, but you should see as many years' prior data as possible before committing to a rehab. Even if no startling revelations are forthcoming, you will be better informed about the property in general.

Current Physical Status.   Most people examine a property from a very personal perspective—their prejudices about renting and apartments contribute to their point of view. This happens because most preliminary inspections are made prior to a thorough market analysis. However, market wants and desires must be considered in your evaluation of a property's physical condition. The greater the experience of the person making the inspection, the easier it will be to distinguish between personal prejudices and the true market position regarding desirability.

Also to be considered are items that detract physically from a property's marketability, diminishing its capacity to both attract prospective new residents and retain existing ones. I would argue that, regardless of the kind of depreciation prevalent within the property, correcting it will have the direct effect of increasing the property's marketability.

Before you even enter the property, your first impression of it will be meaningful. Think a moment about your own experience at a particular property. What is the first thing you see on arrival? Better yet, what is the first thing a prospect sees? The landscaping? The monument sign? A fence? A wall? Any one of these—or a combination of them—is going to create an impression.

Your very first impression results in a feeling—a prejudice—that will color your initial evaluation of the property. Before you do anything else, you should drive around the entire property. This is no time to be taking notes. What you want to do is see if your first impression is altered at all. Your "gut" feeling is a valid one. If there are other people with you, now is the time to talk about their first impressions as well. Is there consensus? No matter how hard you try not to be prejudiced, it is impossible to completely suppress your feelings and impressions. However, a word of caution is in order. First impressions should not be allowed to become entrenched; you should not discount or ignore new information, especially if it contradicts your initial reaction or response. Remember, you cannot conduct a proper analysis until all the data have been gathered.

To be productive, even a first inspection of the property should utilize a checklist. (Exhibit 2.4 provides a generic example that should be workable for most preliminary inspections.) However, bear in mind that every property is different. When a more detailed inspection is to be done, as in the context of due diligence, you should use an inspection form that is specific for the property. Such a checklist will include details regarding fixtures and features that are common to most or all of the apartments. If your initial inspection reveals one or more recurring problems, a checklist tailored to the property will provide ample space for making notes about each type of problem and its extent.

Not long ago, I was doing an initial inspection and noted that each bathroom included a medicine cabinet. In addition, there were two recurring problems with these medicine cabinets—spots of rust on one side and discoloration of the plastic covers for the built-in lights (due to age). This raised the question of how much it would cost to solve the rust problem and replace the light covers. I had to know how many medicine cabinets had to have remedial work done. Note that the example checklist in exhibit 2.4, under bathroom condition, includes space to note the overall condition. However, this generic list makes no provision for indicating the presence of a medicine cabinet, let alone its condition. I needed a checklist tailored to the property that had more space to make notes about the bathroom in general and its component fixtures in particular. The more personalized the checklist, the more accurate and complete the information gathered will be.

There is no rule of thumb about how much time the initial inspection of a property should take. Obviously it depends on the size of the property, and it should not be hurried. The due diligence inspection requires an even more careful look at all physical aspects of the property as well as accurate note taking. (Single copies of apartment building exterior and unit interior inspection forms can be purchased from the Institute of Real Estate Management.

E X H I B I T   2.4

Example Property Inspection Checklist

Property: _____

Date: _____ Compiled by: _____

First Impression		Waste Removal	
Exteriors		Fire Prevention	
Structure		Floor Plans	
Decor		Square Footage	
Number of Buildings		Number of Rooms	
Number of Units		Number of Baths	
Roofs		Last Renovation	
Age of Improvements		Kitchen Styles	
Landscaping		Appliance Package	
Parking Lot		Floor Coverings	
Parking Availability		Window Treatments	
Lighting		Hallways	
Signage		Mailboxes	
Leasing Office		Light Fixtures	
Management Office		Decoration	
Models		Heating System	
Percent Occupied		A/C System	
Rental Rates		Laundry Facilities	
Neighborhood		Amenities	
Boundary North		Bathroom Condition	
South			
East			
West			
Street Access			
Security			
Comments:			

This type of form is intended for a preliminary inspection to gather certain types of information about the property as a whole. The list of characteristics to be examined should be tailored to the property. A more comprehensive form should be used for a detailed inspection, and it should include provision for recording information about condition, specific work needed, and estimated costs as appropriate.

These forms provide an even more comprehensive starting point for developing a property-specific inspection checklist.)

Existing Financing.   Analysis of the existing financing can help to establish whether the acquisition of a property is feasible. If the total amount of indebtedness on the property exceeds its current value—as may be the case for an REO property in a lender's portfolio—it is impossible to make the property successful unless the amount of debt can be reduced. This also has an impact on operations—the larger the amount of debt, the larger the debt service payment, and the less income available for operating the property. If the current lender is unwilling to write down a portion of a loan that exceeds the property's value, not even the shrewdest professional can overcome the problem. Apart from its impact on the asking price—which may itself preclude further consideration of the property—outstanding debt creates a lien against the property and inhibits the transfer of title. (Financing is discussed in chapter 4.)

The Marketplace.   Of all the data you will need, information about the market will be the most difficult to obtain. The information exists, and it is available. Unfortunately, you cannot just go to a store and purchase it off a shelf. Analysis of the market requires tireless searching, and some of the data you gather will have no effect on the property or on your decision. (Specific analytic techniques are beyond the scope of this book, but some information sources are provided in the appendix.)

There are three questions an examination of the market is intended to answer:

1. Is there a demand for this apartment property?
2. At what rent level?
3. Is the economic climate in this market such that the property will yield an income stream of sufficient quantity, quality, and durability to warrant my undertaking the risk?

The answers to these questions will establish how much the property must be changed in order to create and maintain its niche in the market. Remember, the goal of property management is to maximize NOI. The same objective applies ultimately to a property that is being recycled.

A proper economic analysis must take into account current events in the United States and the world. Due to worldwide advancements in communications and technology and increased speed of travel, the global economy is becoming more important each day. As foreign investment in and outright ownership of U.S. industries increases, political and economic activities in other parts of the world will have greater impact on regional and local economies in the United States, and this in turn will have an effect on individual apartment properties.

The Region.   The region is a fairly large geographic area, one for which specific demographic data can be obtained. Population shifts and other demographic changes are tracked by the U.S. Department of Labor, Bureau of the Census. (For purposes of regional economic analysis, a *region* can be defined as the Metropolitan Statistical Area (MSA) in which a property is located.) The objective is to establish demand for your rehabilitated apartments—not just for today, but for the long term—a durable demand that gains strength from the market. In order for there to be demand, there must be people who are ready, willing, and able to rent your apartments. A particularly important consideration is whether there have been any major movements of industry into the region or out of it.

The two aspects of the region that must be examined before any others are its industry (economic base) and its particular characteristics (infrastructure, recreational amenities). From these, one should be able to develop a solid opinion regarding the strength of the region. Note that analyzing current industry is not enough. You want to know what new industries have purchased land, obtained permits to build, and are firmly committed to the region. Real estate brokers and economic development councils can be valuable resources for this type of information.

It is not enough to know that a company employs 400 people. You need to know how long it has been in the region, what product or service it provides, and its place in the larger industry of which it is a part and in the national economy overall. You also want to know about the soundness of its financial footing and its potential for growth and expansion of employment opportunities. The types of companies and the jobs they make available will impact living costs in the region, including rental rates. An area dominated by manufacturing businesses will have a work force comprised mostly of skilled and unskilled workers, and union contracts may determine wage rates and employee benefits. As the U.S. economy shifts away from manufacturing to service-oriented industries, job opportunities shift as well. In an area where research, high technology, and service businesses are prominent, there will be jobs for both laborers and highly trained professionals. (Exhibit 2.5 lists the kinds of information you should try to obtain about local businesses.)

The mix of businesses and their potential for change should be considered. The company or plant that employs most of the people in a town is extremely rare these days, although there are metropolitan areas where a single industry is dominant—the automotive industry in Detroit comes to mind as an example. Information on the future potential of any industry or business within the region will be scant, and your projections based on it can only be tentative. Because you do not sit in a company's board room, you can only correlate specific facts you gather locally with whatever you can learn about the industry as a whole. You can only hope to find out what an industry contributes to the local economy in terms of number and types of jobs, prevailing wage rates, and potential for economic growth. You also want to know

E X H I B I T 2.5

Information for Evaluating Local Businesses

1. Name of company
2. Type of product or service it provides
3. Number of employees
4. Length of time at present location
5. Ten-year recap of annual employment figures
6. History of labor conflicts such as strikes or other work stoppages
7. Financial footing
   —If publicly held, a synopsis of stock prices for the past five years
   —Stock broker's opinion of company
8. Plans for expansion or increased growth or retrenchment
9. Random opinions of the business within the neighborhood

In the context of "location," it is also important to ascertain the suitability of the premises for their business activities, especially their ability to respond to technological advances if the company or industry is going in that direction. The likelihood of a business remaining in a particular location—and therefore being a source of employment—should be explored. Technology has changed attitudes toward location because physical proximity to sources and markets is less important today.

---

that it will continue to employ a comparable number of people at comparable and better wages into the future—i.e., that it is stable.

What attracts industry to a region is a population base and its characteristics and an established infrastructure—police and fire departments, schools, public transportation, etc. The quality of the infrastructure is what attracts people (the work force) to live there and will be a consideration in bringing industry to a region and encouraging it to remain. When infrastructure components are high quality, real estate taxes will be high. The question is whether industrial and commercial uses and their tax contributions will be sufficient to relieve the tax burden on homeowners. (Real estate taxes have a direct effect on an individual's ability to purchase a home.) The tax base will be a strong attraction for both industry and individual homeowners. Homeownership stabilizes a region, and this has a positive influence on rental apartments.

It is also important to catalog the recreational amenities within the region. Different recreational activities attract different kinds of people. Natural resources such as forests, lakes, and mountains are attractive to people who like outdoor activities (camping, hunting, fishing, skiing, etc.). Cultural amenities such as museums, performing arts (theater, symphony, opera), and institutions of higher learning tend to skew the social and economic levels of the population upward.

While the region's industrial base determines its economic strength, population size and characteristics establish the hard numbers that comprise demand. Raw population data are relatively easy to acquire. Elements of the decennial census are updated annually. Sources for this information include the U.S. government (Department of Labor, Bureau of the Census) and private marketing research companies that provide more focused tabulations. State and municipal governments, regional and local planning commissions, utility companies, business bureaus, and chambers of commerce are possible resources for more location-specific figures. Census data are rapidly dated; this makes it essential to determine trends.

The current population count should be compared with annual figures for the past decade. The only thing the raw population numbers provide is the total population for the region, and a comparison of these totals from one period to another indicates trends—whether the size of the population is increasing, decreasing, or essentially stable. The size of the population does not determine the demand for housing; that is determined from the number of households. For example, if the total population of a region is 275,000, and the average household comprises 2.75 people, then the number of households in the region is 100,000.

The analysis continues with an examination of its *demographic characteristics.* One of the first things to look for is population shifts within age groups. If you know the population has increased, you want to know whether this was because the number of births exceeded the number of deaths or if there was a major influx of people into the region. If the population increase is due to births exceeding deaths (a marked increase in the percentage of the population below age 10), the average household size will have increased slightly, but the impact on demand for housing will be negligible if the population has not been particularly mobile. A sharp increase or decrease among adult groups (ages 20–29, 30–39, or 40–49) would suggest movement of people into or out of the region. Age is an important characteristic; a static population tends to be an aging population whose housing needs are probably already met.

Income is another important demographic characteristic. In the preceding example, the number of households was calculated to be 100,000. This does not mean that all 100,000 households would be prospects for a rental property—the total number of households does not represent total demand. This must be adjusted for homeownership. The "American dream" of homeownership is still very strong, and many people will choose to buy a home if they can afford to do so. It is important to determine the "breakpoint" at which people will choose to rent rather than buy. The breakpoint is important because if the monthly rents at your property are comparable to the mortgage payments on an average home, you will be competing head-to-head against homeownership.

Household income is a key factor in the decision to rent or buy. Also to be considered is the fact that people tend to spend the maximum they can afford for shelter. There are exceptions to this, but they tend to be at the upper end of the income range. For the most part, apartment properties that are being recycled are in the middle income range of affordability. Typically, qualification for a home mortgage or for a rental apartment will be based on approximately one-third of an individual's or household's income being spent for shelter. Relative affordability will be related to the average home price within the region. In general, the higher the average house price in the region, the greater the demand for rental housing.

Assume the average home in the region sells for $90,000. If loans are available at 90 percent of value, the average loan would be for $81,000. Assume further that such loans are for a term of 30 years at 9 percent interest. The annual amount for principal and interest would be $7,820.93. To this mortgage amount must be added real estate taxes and insurance, which are commonly accumulated in an escrow account by the lender. Assuming taxes and insurance total $1,800 per year yields a total annual obligation of $9,620.93 or $801.74 per month. In this example, the monthly mortgage payment of $801.74 means that $800 per month would be the breakpoint for rents.

If we further assume that lenders are qualifying purchasers based on 30 percent of their income, an annual income of at least $32,000 would be required to purchase an average home in the region. This does not necessarily mean that every household with an income of $32,000 will be a homebuyer. Two other factors must be considered—what homeownership means and what it actually costs. Some people are more transient by nature—the permanence of homeownership is not for them; they choose to rent rather than buy. Others are renters by necessity—saving for a downpayment is something they are unable (or unwilling) to do. To accumulate the downpayment, the prospective homebuyer must be able to set aside money that is not needed for day-to-day living expenses. Low interest rates on bank savings accounts and increasing prices for food, clothing, and other necessities make saving increasingly difficult. As to specific costs, purchase of a $90,000 home with a 10-percent downpayment ($9,000) would require paying an average of two points ($1,620—one *point* equals one percent of the loan amount) to secure the loan, plus title charges and application and legal fees (around $850), or roughly $11,500 up front.

This type of analysis should be done for the prospective rehab property, both as it exists today and after the recycling process. This will help to determine the number of households capable of paying rent at its current rent level and at the projected rental rate. Demographic data will allow you to determine whether the population of the region includes adequate numbers of households with the income levels and social characteristics needed to qualify as renters at your property, currently and after the rehabilitation is completed. If not, the rest of the analysis is moot.

The Neighborhood.   Regional analysis gives you the big picture. It provides the basis for determining the economic soundness of the entire area. Neighborhood analysis, on the other hand, is more specific. The neighborhood has a direct and immediate impact on a property. For example, in an area of predominantly detached single-family homes, the quality of the school district will influence the demand for real estate in the neighborhood as well as its value. In a suburban environment, transportation will be a key factor in a neighborhood's desirability. Sociologists have found that people of similar backgrounds—income, educational level, social status, etc.—tend to gravitate toward each other. There is a sympathetic attraction among those who share common interests. This is part of what characterizes a neighborhood. A region is comprised of a series of neighborhoods.

It is essential to determine the boundaries of the specific neighborhood in which the subject property is located. In a small town or a suburb, the entire community may be one neighborhood; in a big city, a neighborhood may consist of a single block or both sides of a stretch of a single street. Major thoroughfares, nearby commercial activities, and school districts often establish neighborhood boundaries. The number and types of businesses located near a property or on streets adjacent to it will define the products and services immediately available to local residents and attract nonresidents into the neighborhood. These components of the area surrounding the property should be evaluated carefully. For example, are the businesses beneficial or detrimental to the neighborhood? Are their clienteles desirable or undesirable as prospective residents?

Boundaries are important because influences, trends, or perceptions within one neighborhood may be totally different from those in another. It would be most unfortunate to identify a particular neighborhood as having positive trends and perceptions when, in fact, those trends and perceptions apply to a different neighborhood, and the neighborhood in which you are interested actually has negative trends and perceptions.

This is the part of the analysis that requires legwork. As you attempt to ascertain the boundaries of the neighborhood, you will find out about neighborhood trends and learn how the neighborhood is perceived in the market. Real estate brokers who handle properties there and in adjacent neighborhoods can be invaluable. However, it is essential that you talk to several brokers in different offices locally so you can begin to indicate neighborhood boundaries on a map. Everyone you talk to may have a different idea of the boundaries of the neighborhood. While real estate brokers should be the most knowledgeable, you should also interview municipal planners, local merchants, service station attendants, and others.

Your own senses can tell you a great deal. The types of cars parked in driveways and parking lots can be considered a reflection of income level;

their condition indicates the amount of care they receive. A preponderance of current model cars in prime condition tells a different story than large numbers of older cars that need repairs. The types of commercial uses add to the picture. Fine jewelry stores and similar upscale retail establishments have a different clientele than do pawn shops and tattoo parlors. One thing that makes a neighborhood strong is people's pride in where they live. The Christmas holidays are an outstanding time to drive through neighborhoods. Neighborhood pride will be manifested in outside decorations, regardless of the economic level. I have acquired properties in which only a few Christmas trees and virtually no window decorations had been displayed prior to rehabilitation. After the property was recycled, it was amazing to see the extent of the holiday decorations that symbolized the pride of the new residents in their rehabbed homes.

The ultimate purpose of the neighborhood analysis is to determine its current status and project its future trends. Neighborhoods tend to evolve through three stages which can be plotted on a bell curve. The first is a period of growth in which construction turns raw land into improved property. As vacant land diminishes, this development phase peaks, and the neighborhood reaches a plateau. This maturity or stabilization phase may be very brief or endure for decades. Ultimately, however, the neighborhood begins to decline. First there is a change in the physical condition of properties within the neighborhood. Deferred maintenance and physical deterioration become apparent. This begins quite slowly but soon accelerates down the backside of the bell curve. Unless this trend is stopped, the neighborhood will continue to decline until it is virtually blighted.

Obviously, the best opportunity to recycle real estate is when the neighborhood is strong, either still in the development phase or with most of the property in the neighborhood in the stabilization phase. Once there is general decline in a neighborhood, and it develops a reputation based on that decline, the economic obsolescence of the neighborhood will have a negative impact on individual properties. You will have a far better chance for success in recycling an apartment property if the rest of the neighborhood is still perceived as a nice place to live. Your personal observations of the neighborhood and your conversations with different people should give you a clear sense of how the neighborhood and your candidate for rehabilitation are perceived.

Analysis of the Rental Market

Market analysis is a more focused evaluation of a property and its place within the local rental market. It deals with specifics and should provide answers to the following questions:

1. How many units are vacant at the property (total and by unit type and rental rate)?

2. Can the vacancies be characterized as to the dominance of a single unit type or rent level?
3. How does the vacancy rate at the property compare with those at competing apartment properties (the neighborhood)?
4. How does it compare with the vacancy rate for the larger market (the region)?
5. What changes need to be made to the property so that it can compete effectively in the market?
6. Can the property achieve higher rents and greater occupancy if those changes are made?

Answers to the first four questions are related to housing supply and demand. Answers to the last two are found by comparing the property, feature for feature, with comparable properties nearby.

Supply and Demand.   As you conduct the market analysis, one thing you want to find out is the market supply of units. While the number will not be difficult to ascertain, it will never be totally accurate either. The supply of rental housing includes both occupied and vacant units; the latter is especially difficult to pinpoint. Although issues of supply and demand are usually examined in the context of regional analysis, they are an important component of the neighborhood analysis for a proposed rehabilitation.

The apartment communities located within the market will account for a large percentage of available housing units. It should be possible to find out the number of units in each property—total and by unit type (one-bedroom, two-bedroom, etc.). The smaller scale properties in the market are sometimes more difficult to quantify as to total units and unit types, and the number of detached single-family homes in the area that are rented (rather than owner-occupied) is also difficult to ascertain. Real estate brokers sometimes handle rentals of single-family homes and small residential properties, and locally active brokers may be able to assist your research. Local newspapers can also be a useful resource in characterizing the housing market. Want ads (apartments for rent) usually include a description of the property and its location as well as the unit being offered and its rental rate. The real estate section will cover planned new developments, property openings, and related "news" about apartment housing. Announcements or articles may include descriptions of properties, the features and amenities they offer, and the rents they charge. The general "condition" of the local real estate market will be a recurring topic. Vacancy rates and the use of concessions, especially in larger urban markets, are always newsworthy items.

One of the most closely guarded secrets in the apartment rental business is the vacancy factor on a property. Rarely will the figures stated by real estate managers or in publications be accurate. Often you will have to research vacancy data on your own. Drive-by observation of apartment properties during both daylight and evening hours used to be a good way to approximate vacancies based on a count of apartments with no curtains at their windows. Today, however, many apartments have mini-blinds or curtains provided by the owner. This assures uniformity of window treatments; it also disguises any existing vacancies.

One of the best ways to find out the vacancy rate at a particular property is to simply walk into the entrance area and count the units for which there are no names in the directory or on the mail boxes. This exercise, together with your personal impressions of different properties and the number and types of ads being run in the local newspapers, will give you an indication of the condition of the market. If there are few ads and those are for widely dispersed locations, vacancies are probably at low levels. The absence of in-centives offered to rental prospects suggests that the market is rather solid.

Some vacancy figures may be available from local associations of real estate professionals (this is more likely in large metropolitan areas than in small towns or suburbs). You must understand, however, that such data may be optimistic because the information is compiled from numbers provided by owners or managers of apartment complexes rather than an independent source and may not be representative of the market as a whole.

The most difficult information to obtain is the vacancy rate by unit type. Apartment managers and leasing agents can be asked which types of apart-ments are most in demand and which have the highest vacancy rates, but, here again, the information they provide is likely to be suspect. Careful analy-sis of newspaper ads may shed some light on the types of units that are most difficult to rent, and repeated phone calls to the same property—each time requesting a different size apartment—can be helpful.

Another important consideration is the *absorption rate*—how many units are rented compared to how many units (total) are available for rent. Absorption is typically measured within a defined geographic area for a spe-cific period of time (usually one year). It accounts for construction of new rental housing as well as demolition or removal from the market of existing housing. In the context of regional analysis, demand for rental housing was said to be based on households, income level, and the average price of homes being sold in the market area. Absorption rate can be computed in the following manner.

	Units vacant at the beginning of the period
Plus	Units constructed new during the period
Minus	Units demolished during the period
Minus	Units vacant at the end of the period
Equals	Units absorbed during the period

In computing the absorption rate for the period, a closer look at new con-struction and demolition is needed. The formula does not account specifically for rehabilitation that creates additional rental units; nor does it address conversion to condominiums, which removes rental units from the housing supply. Absorption is *favorable* when demand exceeds supply—i.e., vacancy declines. Absorption is *unfavorable* when supply exceeds demand. A negative absorption rate indicates a softening of the rental housing market and a general inability to raise rents.

The housing supply can change substantially in the time required for the recycling of a property. Both new construction and demolition require permits. Close reading of the minutes of local governing agencies and examination of permits issued by the municipalities in the market area will provide accurate information on numbers of units and dates of completion or removal.

Comparison Grid Analysis. A critical step in the analytical process is establishing market rents for your apartment recycling candidate—the subject property—as it exists today. What you want to define at this point is the extent of the market in which your property must compete for prospective renters. The only way to do this is to examine comparable rental properties in the neighborhood. It would be pointless to examine properties that are not affected by the same factors that influence the subject property. This is why it is so important to establish the neighborhood boundaries. It is these same boundaries that define your market. This is not to say that some renters will not come to your property from other neighborhoods or that some of your current residents will not move to another neighborhood, only that it is not possible to factor these particular elements into the market analysis.

Market analysis is a tedious task. Regardless of your level of experience, there is only one way to obtain the information you need, and that is to physically inspect each of the properties in the subject property's market. This can be done in one of two ways. You can act as a "shopper" and present yourself as a prospective resident for the competing properties. This approach takes shrewdness and acting skill. If you are believable, you will be able to ascertain the effective rent for the properties. However, you will only see the model they are showing and the areas used for marketing. You will not be able to obtain a complete picture of its operations.

The second way is to introduce yourself to the manager and explain that you are conducting a market analysis. This approach requires good people skills because you will be asking for information that could, in fact, be used against these properties. However, you are likely to have an opportunity to see more of the property and, perhaps, get a better sense of the market. On the downside, you may get no cooperation and virtually no information.

I recommend using both methods—and different people, of course. Additional information can be found by contacting Certified Property Manager® (CPM®) members of the Institute of Real Estate management (IREM) and other real estate professionals who work in that market. Experience exchange publications such as *Income/Expense Analysis: Conventional Apartments* (published annually by IREM) can provide additional comparison data. The market analysis exercise compares other properties in the market with the subject property—in this case, a candidate for recycling. Your purpose, initially, is to establish whether the subject property is achieving true market rent in its present condition. It is possible that a property could be performing poorly solely because of poor property management. If this is so, it stands to reason that improved management and a better marketing program could raise rent levels at a property. In most cases, however, poor management is not its only problem.

Exhibit 2.6 shows an example of the type of form used for comparison grid analysis. Here again, it is important to tailor the form to the characteristics of the properties being analyzed—the features of the subject property should prevail. If the property is a garden apartment, there need not be a line item for elevators. However, if the properties being compared have swimming pools, then "swimming pool" should be an item for evaluation. Most comparison grid forms do not provide much space for the analyst's notes. Therefore, additional notes should be made (on a separate sheet, as needed) to remind you about particulars. For example, notes about the swimming pools might relate to their size, condition, and overall appeal.

Inspection of the recycling candidate (subject property) will provide the primary list of features for comparison. The number of units, their size and arrangement, and components of their common areas are some of the considerations in identifying comparable properties. To be truly comparable, properties should have very similar characteristics (building size, number of units of a given type, amenities, etc.). Comparability is what gives weight to the calculation of market rents. As the sample form indicates, features and amenities are listed at the left and columns are provided for making the comparisons. The subject property is evaluated in the column adjacent to the features list; the comparables are evaluated individually in successive columns to the right. Building amenities such as laundry facilities, a party room, or any other special component of the common areas should be listed for comparison. Lease concessions affect the amount of rent paid, so they should be recorded as well (or the rent amount on the form should be adjusted appropriately), and the property's signage and curb appeal may be rated.

Typically, dollar amounts are used to indicate adjustments to the monthly rent of the comparables for the presence (or absence) of comparison features as indications of their relative desirability. If rent at the subject property includes a parking space for the resident's car at no additional charge, and residents at a comparable property pay $25 per month extra for parking, $25 would be the adjustment amount. If a feature at a comparable property is superior to that at the subject property, the value entered should be negative; conversely, if the comparable feature is inferior to the subject property, its value should be positive. Adding the positive and negative adjustment

E X H I B I T   2.6

Example Form for Comparison Grid Analysis

Property: _____   Unit Type: _____
Date: _____   Compiled by: _____

Item	Subject	Comparable #1		Comparable #2		Comparable #3	
		Description	+(-) Adj.	Description	+(-) Adj.	Description	+(-) Adj.
Property							
Area of Unit							
Current Rent							
Location							
Age and Condition							
Appearance							
Parking							
Amenities							
Carpeting							
Appliances							
Drapes or Blinds							
Storage or Deck							
Utilities							
Net Adj. (Total)							
Adjusted Rent							
Rent per Sq Ft							

This type of form is used to compare the subject to competing properties for purposes of determining what to "match" in a rehabilitation as well as in setting rents. In use, it should be tailored to the fixtures and amenities of the properties being compared. If concessions are prevalent in the market, a separate line entry should be provided for this adjustment.

Adapted with permission from Kelley, E. N.: *Practical Apartment Management, Third Edition* (Chicago: Institute of Real Estate Management, 1990).

amounts yields a net total adjustment to the rent of the comparable. (Dollar amounts should reasonably anticipate what a typical renter is likely to pay as a part of his or her rent to have the feature.)

The best grid analyses compare a subject with at least three comparable properties. Analysis of the three rent values should indicate an appropriate market rent for the size of apartment being compared. Separate grids should be prepared for each different size of apartment. If the majority of apartments in the market are one-bedroom units, a comparison based on one-bedroom apartments may suffice. If the properties include a mix of apartment sizes and arrangements (e.g., studio, one-bedroom, two bedroom, one-bedroom plus den), it is best to compile comparison data for each unit type.

In this context, it is also important to view market potentials. You should be trying to determine what improvements should be made to the subject property so it can achieve the optimum rent that the market can generate. The features and amenities of comparable properties and the rents those properties achieve indicate what the renters in this particular market are paying for and getting. Comparison grid analysis will tell you how well the subject property "fits" into its market and what the recycled property must "match" in order to compete effectively with the comparable properties. The market study is one of the most critical analyses that you will conduct during the due diligence period.

Also important to be included in the market analysis is an examination of the management of each of the competitive properties. In my personal experience, the situation has often been that the subject property suffered from extremely poor management compared to its competition. However, once recycling had been completed and better management established, the situation was effectively reversed.

Remember, market analysis is inexact at best. There are many minor considerations that have a major bearing on the financial performance of a property. Once all of the data have been gathered and the analysis has been completed, the time for calculations and adjustments is over. Now it is time to review the results of the analysis and ask these questions:

Does this property currently meet market standards or is it substantially below them?

If changes are made to the property to enhance its position in the market, will the property be stronger in terms of the quality, quantity, and durability of the income it will generate?

The answers to these questions must be a solid "yes" if you intend to proceed with the recycling of a particular property. (The importance of ongoing market analysis is reiterated in chapter 7 in the context of evaluating the results of recycling.)

Other Considerations

The due diligence evaluation should take into account other factors that can affect the decision to proceed. It is important to determine whether the property is being put to the highest and best use. A growing body of environmental regulations promulgated at the federal, state, and local levels requires examination of the environmental compliance status of the property. Determination of the property's value "as is" and how it arrived at its depreciated state is an important predecessor to deciding what the recycling process is to accomplish. Finally, the approach to recycling is different for a poorly performing property with little upside potential and one that is performing adequately at present but could do better if the right changes are made. These additional considerations are addressed in the following sections.

Highest and Best Use.   In appraisal terminology, *highest and best use* is defined as the reasonably probable and legal use of vacant land or an improved property that is physically possible, appropriately supported, financially feasible, and results in the highest value. Highest and best use is determined from careful evaluation of prevailing market conditions, trends affecting market participation and change, and the existing use of the property under consideration. The test of highest and best use must be applied to all property, regardless of whether capital improvements and changes are contemplated. The highest and best use of a specific property may not conform to its present use.

There are two key issues to consider. One is the existing zoning for the particular property and whether it is reasonable to secure a zoning change (if desired). The other is the value of comparable vacant land in the market area that is available for other uses. The easiest way to establish highest and best use of a particular property is to compare the value of the land as though unimproved with the value of the existing property with the improvements in place. The issue of highest and best use becomes most important when the physical property requires substantial rehabilitation to bring it up to an existing market standard. In most cases, continuation of the existing use is the highest and best use because improvements are already wedded to the land. (This subject is developed further in the context of investment analysis in chapter 5.)

Environmental Considerations.   Over the past several years, lenders have had to comply with ever more demanding and complex environmental regulatory requirements. A lender usually will not make a loan of any kind on a real estate purchase unless there has been at least a Phase I environmental assessment of the property. The importance of environmental considerations was brought home to me a few years ago when seven of the twelve pages of the mortgage commitment from a lender (to refinance a property for the purpose of rehabilitation) were related to environmental concerns. (Exhibit 2.7 is a list of some common sources of environmental problems.)

For properties constructed more than ten years ago, environmental status is the largest negative in obtaining financing for rehabilitation. Newer construction should be in compliance with then-current environmental regulations, but historical review is needed to ascertain previous uses of the land and rule out the possibility of soil contamination from hazardous waste. It is doubtful that one would be able to determine, on initial inspection of a property, whether there was ever a hazardous substance in or on the ground. Residential properties are not likely to exhibit staining of the building or damaged vegetation consistent with such contamination. However, it is possible that a residential use may have been developed on previously contaminated vacant land. The chain of title is one way to document land use over time.

Probably the biggest single concern in older buildings is asbestos because abatement can be extremely expensive. Asbestos was once commonly used because of its fire-retardant properties and may be present in structural elements (insulation in walls and roofs; piping), in finishing materials (floor and ceiling tiles; siding), and as a component of cement. Because of its multitude of uses, lenders are concerned about asbestos in any form. Some lenders exclude properties with certain environmental problems (asbestos, contaminated groundwater, elevated levels of lead and/or other heavy metals in tap water, radon, "poor" indoor air quality) from their loan portfolios because of the risks involved as well as the expense of remediation. Alternatively, a lender may impose restrictions on the loan (a lower loan-to-value ratio, a higher debt coverage ratio). In addition to (or instead of) restrictions, a lender may require environmental testing and—depending on the results—long-term monitoring of a discovered problem. The lender may insist that a problem be corrected prior to funding a loan. If, in your judgment, there is some likelihood of a costly abatement being required, you may wish to abandon further consideration of a property. However, it would be most unfortunate to have expended considerable time, energy, and money in analyzing a property and its market only to be thwarted by a cost that could destroy the financial viability of the rehabilitation project. An alternative approach is to negotiate for a reduction of the purchase price based on the cost of abatement.

On the other hand, you may be trying to purchase a property which is being transferred from a lender's REO portfolio. Although this may be done without an environmental survey being required for the purchase, at some point in time you may want to refinance the property or sell it, and an environmental assessment will surely be required at that time. It is best to deal with environmental problems at the outset. If they can be solved without

E X H I B I T   2.7

Some Common Sources of Environmental Problems

Hazardous Materials
- *Asbestos* in construction materials (insulation), finishing materials (floor and ceiling tiles, adhesive compounds, other components), and fireproofing and specific fire-resistant materials/installations (blown-in insulation, fire doors)
- *PCBs (polychlorinated biphenyls)* in electrical transformers (may be utility's responsibility)
- *CFCs (chlorinated fluorocarbons)* and related compounds used as refrigerants and coolants in large-scale air-conditioning systems
- *Radon gas* (enters buildings and air circulation systems through basements)
- *Lead* in paints on floors and walls and in solder or joint seals in plumbing connections as well as the pipes themselves*

Problems Affecting Water Supply
- Soil and/or groundwater contamination
- Storm water and wastewater discharges
- Plumbing and piping systems (lead solder)

Problems Affecting Air Quality
- Inadequate ventilation, poor air circulation, and other HVAC problems that adversely affect *indoor air quality*†
- Hazardous (or noxious) fumes generated within HVAC system (circulated within the building and/or discharged to the atmosphere)
- Enclosed parking areas (vehicle exhaust fumes—carbon monoxide)

Other Considerations
- Garbage and waste disposal (state and/or locally mandated requirements for recycling of specific materials)
- Storage, use, and disposal of hazardous materials such as cleaning chemicals (especially organic solvents), insect control and lawn care chemicals (pesticides), paints, etc.
- Use and condition of adjacent land (potential to contaminate the site being purchased)

*A new federal law (Residential Lead-Based Paint Hazard Reduction Act of 1992) is one that will have particular impact on properties that are candidates for recycling. While the federal government banned lead-based paint in 1978, when the new law (known as *Title X*) becomes effective in October 1995, all owners of properties built *before* 1978 will be required to notify new renters about the presence of lead-based paint. The same information will have to be provided to prospective buyers if the building is sold. Minimally, buyers should inquire about the presence of "known" lead-based paint hazards when they are seeking apartment properties to rehabilitate. (Some state and local governments banned such paints even earlier, so the cutoff date in a particular locale should be researched.)

†There is no specific environmental law regulating indoor air quality (IAQ), but poor IAQ is a problem, particularly in buildings where windows do not open, and legislation is likely to be promulgated in the future.

NOTE: The list presented here is not intended to be all-inclusive. The array of potential environmental problems expands as more becomes known about hazardous substances and as air emissions, water pollution, waste disposal, wetlands preservation, and endangered species are more extensively regulated over time. It is particularly important to understand that environmental regulations exist at all levels—federal, state, and local—and that compliance requirements are derived from the law that is most stringent. Review of the regulatory situation as it applies locally in general and to a specific property in particular is the investors' best means of identifying prevailing standards.

damaging the economic viability of your rehabilitation plan, you can be reasonably assured that refinancing or sale of the property at a future date will not be impeded.

You should be aware, too, that any environmental problem, even if it is not a consideration today, could very well be important in the future. If you have any knowledge about the problem, you could be legally responsible. It is wise to consult a qualified environmental attorney regarding the purchase, the rehabilitation, and potential future liability. "Due diligence" in environmental parlance takes on an even larger dimension with regard to careful examination of a property.

"As Is" Value of the Property.   In order to know what to change in a property, it is essential to know where the property is in relation to the current market. (Valuation techniques, as such, are discussed in chapter 5.) There are two reasons why an "as is" value is so critical in the analysis. First and foremost, a value must be established for the purpose of acquisition. Regardless of statements from brokers or sellers, the value of a property is what it is. A property is generating a certain amount of income today, and a certain amount of money is being spent to operate it today. Thus, it can be argued that if the property could generate more income, based on the ability of its current management and the policies and procedures that are in place now, it would. Similarly, if expenses could be reduced, they would. It is indeed possible that better property management—i.e., tighter controls on spending and more efficient operations—could lead to an increase in NOI. However, determining hypothetical "what ifs" is not the purpose of your analysis. The value of the property *as it is today* is the basis for making the purchase.

If a property is suffering from depreciation, its current value (based on its current NOI) will not be the same in the future if the existing deficiencies are not corrected—the value will be reduced, Likewise, any plans the seller has to correct these items do not add to the property's value today. When making a purchase with the intent of enhancing value in the future, it is imprudent to pay a premium price if you will have to undertake the risk and utilize your expertise to achieve the hoped-for greater value. In the preceding chapter, the market perception of the neighborhood in general and the property in particular were discussed. The capitalization rate—the rate of return on the investment—must take into account any negative perceptions. The more negative the perception of the neighborhood, the longer it will take to bring the property up to its ultimate potential. The property cannot achieve its maximum value until the perception of the neighborhood in the market has been improved. This is the most difficult part of the analysis because you are required to make a value judgment about the neighborhood based solely on the data you have been able to gather.

On the other hand, if the perception of the property is the only thing that is negative, then the time required to achieve full value enhancement will be shorter. A word of caution is needed in regard to how long it will take to alter the negative perception of a property. The negative perception developed over a long period of time, and it will take more than a rehabilitation project to correct these negative perceptions. Time will be the ultimate corrective measure. When calculating an internal rate of return or conducting any other type of investment analysis, it must be assumed that it will take longer to manifest the upside potential of the income stream than the time needed to complete any physical rehabilitation.

Identifying the Cause for Loss of Value.   The next step is the precise identification of specific problems. This begins the real decision-making process as you sort through the information you have gathered. This is a difficult task because many problems are interconnected, and correction of one problem might eliminate two or three other problems which would never be addressed at all if the first problem was not remedied. A particular example is property management. In my experience, most of the problems at a property are the result of poor property management. The management philosophy being applied at the property should be examined. The goals of management should be to provide a physical environment and a level of service that will attract residents to the property who will pay maximum rent and want to live at the property indefinitely. Hand in hand with these goals should be the desire to maintain efficiency and control costs. It is the way the goals are carried out that makes the difference between good management and mediocre or poor management.

As indicated earlier in this chapter, quality of management is reflected in the attitude of the staff, the size of the payroll, and the ratio of expenses to income. Management aside, debt service is sometimes so high that there is not enough money available to maintain the property adequately or to correct deferred maintenance. Another item to examine is the size of the debt on the property and the amount of the debt-service payment.

Once you have determined that improving management could improve the property and that debt service is not a hindrance to operations, you can turn your attention to the physical and functional problems of the real estate. Physical deterioration—the need for painting and fixing up in general—is easy to identify and estimate the costs of correcting. A property's functional obsolescence can only be determined from an examination of its competition. Economic obsolescence, on the other hand, has to do with the neighborhood and its perception in the market. If the neighborhood is perceived as declining, it is declining. Neither correction of all the physical and functional problems at a property, nor a change in management, nor even a whole new image will change a negative perception of the neighborhood. Conversely, if the neighborhood is perceived to be fine, but the property has a negative perception, this loss of value can be corrected. However, sufficient time must be allowed to achieve a new perception of the property in the market.

Changes Needed to Maximize Value. A fundamental goal of the recycling process is to maximize NOI—in quantity, quality, and durability. In terms of physical change, it is just as bad to overdo a rehabilitation as to not do enough. It may be possible to upgrade an existing property substantially, but it will never be absolutely equivalent to the top grade or class of property in the market. Real estate professionals sometimes classify buildings as A, B, C, or D based on their condition, location, and the services they offer. Although this is more common for office buildings, similar criteria can be applied to apartment properties. In essence, class A refers to buildings that command the highest rents because of their location and amenities. Usually these are the newest properties with the most complete arrays of features and amenities. A class B property would command lower rents due to a less desirable location, fewer amenities, or apartment configurations that are less in demand in the market, but otherwise such buildings are generally well-maintained and comparable to class A. Sometimes a class B building is next door to one that is class A—the structure that is newer being considered the better of the two. As buildings age, it is more difficult to maintain them at the highest levels. Class C buildings may be older and reasonably well maintained, but they can no longer command class A or B rent levels because they are not as well located. Their rents are more "affordable." A building that is class D commands very low rents and probably has extensive deferred maintenance. Such classification descriptions are not precise, but they allow me to provide a specific example.

> A rehabber I know purchased a property in class D condition. I was familiar with the market area, and it was obvious to me that the best this property could hope to be was class B. However, the rehabber decided that each room should have a ceiling fan and that each kitchen should have not only a dishwasher, but also a trash compactor. As a result, far too much money was spent on the physical changes to this property. Achievable rent levels would never provide an adequate return on the additional capital expenditures. In fact, the property was ultimately foreclosed by the lender.

The market will dictate how much or how little improvement can and should be made to a property. If most of its competitors have newer carpeting, the rehabilitation should probably include new carpeting so the property will be more desirable than its competition. If the competition provides dishwashers, then dishwashers may have to be part of the basic appliance package in a rehab. Competition is a key element in this decision. It is rare that a property being recycled is ever going to be able to compete favorably with brand-new class A properties. If class A rents cannot be achieved, installation of class A amenities is not warranted. It has long been my personal goal to exceed in kind the types of improvements offered by my direct competitors in a particular market. I would argue, however, that a well-done rehabilitation that meets or only slightly exceeds the competition will achieve its maximum potential value.

Properties with Little "Upside" Potential.   As noted in chapter 1, prior to the Tax Reform Act of 1986, there were many real estate syndications that were essentially tax-driven. These over-leveraged deals were counting on inflation to achieve their success, and many of them failed. As a consequence, lenders have taken back properties whose value is far less than the outstanding debt.

There are two reasons why these properties have little upside potential. First, many of them are so debt-ridden that while previous ownership was attempting to service the debt, they had to, by necessity, forego much of the maintenance. This resulted in not only a physical deterioration of the property, but also a decline in the quality of its residents, both socially and economically. Second is their locations. In many instances, the market analysis performed at the time of the original purchase was inadequate or inappropriate. In one of his lectures at the University of Illinois, the late Robert O. Harvey, Professor of Real Estate, stated that most properties that failed would never have been built if proper feasibility studies had been performed initially. He made that statement well over thirty years ago, and it never ceases to amaze me how true it is. A corollary to this statement comes from Martin J. Freed, a respected real estate and environmental attorney, who said that often the deal itself has its own life, and the relevant economics take a back seat.

Regardless of the cause, the effect is the same. A property has lost tremendous value due to neglect, poor management, and in some cases failure to recognize changes that have been taking place within the neighborhood. A property that goes into default is already suffering from these negative factors. The time that it takes to complete foreclosure only serves to further accentuate the problems that originally forced the property into default. In this situation, a lender has only two choices. First, and probably the easiest—but also the most costly—option, is to immediately write down the asset to a point where it can be purchased by someone who will assume all of the risks of restoring the property to viability. The entrepreneur will measure the risk against the potential reward. The entrepreneur benefits from the write down because it lowers the purchase price and, thus, the investment basis to a level that economic viability (return on the investment) can be attained sooner.

The lender's other option is to hold the property in its portfolio and essentially try to restore it to viability so that a higher sale price will permit the lender to recoup most or all of its investment in the property. This obviously is a slower process because the desired value is considerably higher than the value at foreclosure. The key to achieving success by this route is patience on the part of the lender coupled with a management team that does not interpret that patience to mean the lender will hold the property in perpetuity.

A higher level of rent must be achieved, and in many cases, this can be accomplished by working closely with housing agencies in the local area. There is always a need for decent, affordable housing. However, appointment of strong, competent management is a must; this assumes that economic obsolescence is not a problem. Ridding the property of problem residents and performing a systematic rehabilitation can go a long way toward turning a property around so that the lender can sell the asset at a profit.

The point is, the purchase price will determine when and how much profit will be generated. It is much easier to return a property to economic viability in the market if the original cost is $10,000 per unit as opposed to $20,000 per unit. If virtually identical steps are taken to rehabilitate a property, it is reasonable to assume it will take longer to achieve rent levels that will restore it to economic viability if you paid $20,000 per unit initially.

Currently Performing Assets.   Even though an asset is performing, it may not be generating maximum NOI. This might be due to a management deficiency or because it is beginning to deteriorate. Sometimes, in these cases, the subtlest changes can yield surprisingly positive results.

Let us make an initial assumption that a property has maintained a high level of curb appeal, which is obviously what attracts prospects to it. Many things can be done to enhance such a property that will not disturb current residents or disrupt existing income. Many of these enhancements can be paid out of reserve funds and thus have no impact on NOI. It must be understood, however, that noncapital expenditures such as painting and landscaping will affect NOI because they will be paid as operating expenses. Since there is no great need for major change, even these operating expense items can be budgeted so they will have a lesser impact.

A key point to remember is that any maintenance-related changes should improve operating efficiency. Energy conservation and reduction of the repetitiveness of maintenance are worthwhile goals. For example, systematic window replacement using windows with a superior R rating will conserve energy winter and summer. If heat is included in the rent, obviously the property owner will save money. If heat is at the residents' expense, their heating costs will be similarly reduced, and such savings can make possible a rental increase.

An excellent area to begin subtle changes is the landscaping. Altering the flowerbed configuration at the entrance to the property will give it a slightly new look. Changes in the kind of plant material, even something as subtle as different colors of flowers, will likely please existing residents.

The leasing office may be beginning to show its age. New carpeting and redecorating (e.g., new wallhangings) can make it more appealing to your customers (residents and prospects). For many of them, the office is their first impression of the property.

A review of upcoming lease expirations will indicate where the greatest number of turnovers are likely to occur. Replacing the carpeting in common areas or redecorating the entrances and hallways *before* renewal letters are sent out is a good idea. These changes will make positive impressions on new prospects who will be looking at the vacated units and may encourage renewals.

Changes made to landscaping, the leasing office, and the common areas will give an impression of the property that is certainly superior to what it had been. However, it is within the units themselves that the most dramatic changes can take place. This is where new kitchen cabinets and new appliances can make a great difference in the appeal of a particular apartment and in the rent that it can achieve. Before you make any changes, complete a thorough market analysis. You should be doing this every three to four months regardless. The best of your competitors in the market should be your guide; your apartment should become equal to or slightly better than that competitor's unit. This is not an obvious recycling of the property as a whole. This type of rehabilitation is evolutionary rather than revolutionary; instead of the whole world being able to see that the property is undergoing a drastic change, the changes within units will be done only after occupants move out. No changes will be made in units where residents renew their leases, nor will their rents be raised as much.

Organization is a must. Otherwise the loss of rent for a protracted period will offset any rental increase that can be achieved. Speed is not the only answer. There is no question that there is an economy of scale when purchasing appliances, kitchen cabinets, or other capital improvement items in large numbers. As stated at the beginning of this section, there is already a positive flow of income, and there is no reason that it has to be eroded during this evolutionary type of rehabilitation. With the market as a guide, your efforts should be directed to providing changes that will enhance the value of the real estate by keeping residents' satisfaction high. Frankly, this is just good management.

3

Planning the Rehabilitation

It often seems quite easy to identify cosmetic changes that should be made to a property and, in doing so, to see few pitfalls. However, while new construction is rarely accomplished without problems, rehabilitation of an existing property that is suffering from physical neglect adds a new dimension to construction problems. The rehabilitation process is replete with pitfalls. By way of example, I recall a Chicago property we rehabbed in the mid-1970s. The building was approximately seventy years old and required a change of plumbing fixtures in both the kitchen and the bathroom. The problem was that nearly half of the plumbing connections broke inside the walls. Replacing the connections required additional time and effort and added substantially to the cost of completing the job. This experience taught me a valuable lesson: In planning for rehabilitation, *expect the unexpected.*

Just as the key to time management is planning—for the day, for the month, etc.—in a rehabilitation, one must plan for the job. A properly developed rehabilitation plan will provide as complete a picture of the process and its outcome as possible. Careful attention must be given to management of the property as well as feasibility, costs, scheduling, and other considerations related specifically to the rehabilitation. (A written plan or at least a pro forma budget for the rehabilitation will be required by the lender.) Analysis of the economics of alternatives may suggest the need for a better, more cost-effective (or more profitable) approach to the project. Multiple revisions to fine-tune the budget component and the plan as a whole are to be expected. This chapter addresses the spectrum of issues that must be considered in developing a rehabilitation plan.

Issues of Feasibility

Planning for the rehabilitation of a particular property is both a component and an outgrowth of the due diligence process. Feasibility of the project will depend on the goals of ownership, the physical changes required, and the costs that are likely to be incurred.

Ownership Goals.   The goals of ownership must be the starting point for any rehabilitation plan. It is interesting to note that the Institute of Real Estate Management begins each of its qualification courses for the Certified Property Manager® (CPM®) designation with a discussion of owners' goals and objectives. You may develop an outstanding plan of action, one that is both economically and financially correct in adapting to market conditions, but the owner may choose not to accept it. On the surface, the choice should be straightforward: Either the owner will conform to your wants or you will conform to the owner's wants—or the two of you cannot work together.

Often one's ideas evolve out of personal perceptions of what should be done. A good example could be the holding period for the property once the rehabilitation is complete. The rehab planner may believe that the potential for the property can be maximized by holding onto it for eight to ten years, and the planner's market analysis may support this belief. The owner, on the other hand, may have certain financial obligations that preclude following the planner's recommendation for a longer holding period. This would more than likely make a difference in the approach to the rehabilitation—e.g., material purchases might be somewhat different. If something that will correct an existing deficiency but has a useful life of only five years (instead of ten years) can be purchased at a lower cost, it may be prudent to purchase the less-expensive item if the owner's goal is to sell the property on completion of the rehabilitation. Remember, the goal is always to maximize the return on the owner's investment.

Money is the driving force of any rehabilitation. The bottom line is always how to maximize the return on the investment. If you are actually the owner of the real estate, you will be wearing two hats—owner and rehabber. Before any decisions are made, it is essential to examine the property, the market forces acting on it, and the estimated cost of the proposed changes. This should be done carefully and with every attempt at setting aside your personal prejudices. It is quite possible that your goals and objectives may have to be changed once you analyze the results of a truly accurate assessment of current conditions and future potential.

Some of the items that should be considered in relation to the holding period are the roof, driveway, and parking areas; the landscaping; and cabinets, doors, and other millwork. This is by no means a complete list, but it touches on items of highest visibility. The property will look its best at the completion of the rehabilitation. The key is to maintain the property as close

---

Types of Physical Changes
• Structural
• Environmental
• Cosmetic

---

as possible to that optimum appearance throughout the holding period. Long-term appearance should be a criterion in the selection of materials.

An important additional consideration is the availability of funds. Rarely will there be unlimited funds to create the perfect rehabilitation for a property. The rehabilitation plan will therefore be based on a series of compromises and the hope that the owner's goals and objectives can be tempered to meet the indicated market demands, a situation which will maximize the return on the available dollars.

Physical Changes Required. Identifying physical problems is sometimes quite easy. Shutters that need painting, windows that are broken, roofs that leak, carpeting that is threadbare or badly stained, and landscaping that is poorly maintained are only a few of the very obvious physical problems that a property can have. It is far better, however, to identify the physical problems by category.

There are three types of physical problems—structural, environmental, and cosmetic. The first two categories are the most distasteful to both the owner and the rehabber. Often the correction of structural and environmental problems will have no measurable impact on the amount of rent that can be charged. If rents cannot be raised, there will be no measurable increase in the value of the real estate. However, it must be understood that if structural deficiencies are not corrected, a property could lose its occupancy permits (if such are required). Violations of building codes and compliance with habitability requirements of landlord-tenant laws are specific concerns. If environmental problems are not solved, it may be impossible to obtain permanent financing.

Structural Problems. Determination of specific structural deficiencies may require examination by a structural engineer. (Note that in some jurisdictions, examination by a structural engineer may be prescribed by law.) The vast majority of properties that are likely to be considered for rehabilitation are more than fifteen years old and, in many cases, well over twenty years old. Often the initial construction was marginal (at best). When a property has been neglected over a long period, many shortcuts taken during construction will have become apparent, mostly as structural breakdowns and failures. Sometimes even a cursory initial examination of a property will reveal structural problems. An especially obvious example is cracks in the foundation. These cracks must be inspected closely to determine whether there is any evidence of water seepage into the building. Often such cracks traverse upward and horizontally throughout the various courses or levels of bricks, leaving cracks and gaps along the face of the building. This type of structural problem has cosmetic implications as well—it detracts from the property's curb appeal.

Another problem is a sag or dip along the ridge line of the roof. There may have been a visible shifting of rafters—due either to settling of the building or, in some cases, to improper construction. The results of excessive settling will also be apparent from an examination of the doors and doorjambs. Often a door will have been planed on one end (to hang level), leaving a rather large gap at the other end.

An excellent way to determine structural deficiencies is to check the municipal records and examine all citations that have been issued to the property for violations of building codes and other legal requirements. (Note that there may be a fee for this.) The decision to correct any structural deficiency will depend on (1) whether failure to do so poses a hazard to the life or safety of the building's occupants now and (2) whether the deficiency is a violation of an existing requirement of the municipality. Even if neither of these is an issue, it is reasonable to question whether failure to correct the deficiency now might result in a hazard to life or safety later on or have the potential to become a violation of some municipal code in the future. Obviously, if there is any potential danger to life or safety, the deficiency must be corrected now. Apart from the humanitarian aspect, the negative publicity resulting from any kind of catastrophe that occurs during your holding period could be permanently damaging to the property. As for code violations, there may be no prior ones, but review of the municipal requirements may indicate potential for problems—either from citations arising out of an official inspection of the property or from anticipated changes in the existing code.

Sometimes there may be structural deficiencies that, in the opinion of a structural engineer, would result in no further damage. However, if such a deficiency is deleterious to the appearance of the property (i.e., has a negative impact on its curb appeal), the question has to be asked whether the expenditure to correct this type of deficiency would result in a more attractive property that would ultimately yield higher rents. If the answer is yes, it should be corrected. If the answer is no, it is better to spend that money elsewhere; even if the answer is inconclusive, I am convinced that there will be better places to spend the money and achieve a measurable result.

Environmental Problems. As indicated in the preceding chapter, environmental considerations are critical, both for financing the investment and for selling the property later. It is to be hoped that any environmental problems will have been identified at the time of acquisition. In which case, funds should have been set aside at the closing to correct the problems, or the previous owner should have been required to correct them (and done it) prior to closing. A lender will always require an environmental assessment. However, properties may sometimes be acquired by assuming an existing loan or with seller financing, and an environmental assessment may not be required. If that is the situation in your case, it is essential that you have an environmental study done—at your own expense. Money spent now for an environmental assessment can save you thousands of dollars later.

Cosmetic Problems.   Cosmetic changes are what make "a silk purse out of a sow's ear." This is truly the exciting part of recycling apartments—where color and texture combine to change the physical image of a property. How much cosmetic change is enough? Your creative people will tend to want to do too much. However, cosmetic change is the one area for which a return on invested capital can be measured. The measurement will come directly from the work that you have done in the market. As discussed previously, cosmetic changes will no doubt include correction of functional obsolescence. When considering functionality, it is important to upgrade the property to a currently acceptable standard. However, I offer this word of caution: Sometimes what is "current" is also very "trendy," and such fad items will soon be out of date. The goal should be to overcome functional obsolescence with items whose style and design will be acceptable in the market over the long term.

The owner's goals and objectives will be a major consideration in the amount of cosmetic change to the property. Availability of capital is always a major constraint. Another consideration is how much "improvement" to the property will actually yield higher rents. At some point, additional monies spent for more cosmetic changes will no longer result in any increase in rent. It is important to be aware of this point of diminishing returns, especially as you evaluate cost estimates.

A final consideration regarding physical changes is the time of year when the work will be done. Weather conditions can be a major obstacle to exterior work in some locales. Extreme weather conditions can also have a dramatic effect on costs. Interior work may have to precede exterior changes. The inconvenience to residents must be considered, too. If there are current residents whom you want to retain, inconvenience to them during construction should be minimized.

Cost Considerations.   Once potential physical changes have been clearly identified, it is important to determine just how these changes will be accomplished, because that will ultimately determine the cost. In many situations, there may be two or more possible approaches to effecting the desired change. For example, you may identify kitchen cabinets as an item to be upgraded. The question is whether to install new cabinets or merely replace the doors and drawer fronts of the existing cabinets. Your decision will be based on (1) the comparative cost of installing all new versus replacing selected parts and (2) which of the two approaches will most effectively accomplish the goal of the rehabilitation. Obviously, changing the fronts of the cabinets will cost less than complete replacement. However, the basic cabinets and drawers which remain in place will be older, and this will be apparent no matter how satisfactory the new fronts appear. How bad the insides of the cabinets look in contrast afterward will depend on their condition beforehand. Ultimately, the decision to replace or refinish will be based on the market analysis and the market niche in which this property is expected to compete. Even if the change in door and drawer fronts makes a dramatic difference in the overall appearance of the kitchen, it may not be acceptable to the market. The more discerning your potential residents, the more likely they will be to examine the kitchen (and other rooms) in detail.

Specifying What Is to Be Done.   Before rehab costs can be estimated, there must be specifications for what is to be done. Staying with the example of kitchen cabinets, the more drawers you specify, the higher the price. The market analysis will facilitate preparation of the specifications. (Market analysis must be completed before any specifications or cost estimates can be anticipated.) If the market has indicated that the property should provide only fundamentals, meeting minimum housing standards in terms of amenities, extra drawers in kitchen cabinets will not even be a consideration. However, as the socioeconomic level of the target market (resident profile) moves upward, prospects will be more critical in their evaluation of your apartments. This is where comparison grid analysis data are most helpful. Look at what your competitors are offering. You will probably find that the vast majority of kitchens in class A apartments have base cabinets with only one drawer. This is important because of the difference in cost—a base cabinet that has three or four drawers will cost approximately $35 more than one that has one door and one drawer. I would argue further that spending $35 more on a base cabinet will not result in a single dollar of increased rent. Spread over a 200-unit rehab, this is an excess expenditure of $7,000, and this figure is for only one base cabinet—not the two or three usually found in each unit. (In some areas, cabinet costs can average $25–$50 *per additional drawer,* which would have an even greater impact on the total expenditure.)

As you specify different items for your rehabilitation project, you must consider the economic viability of each item—i.e., whether it will result in any more rent. On the other hand, some things must be done regardless of the return. Obviously, if the roof has to be replaced, that expense cannot be expected to generate any additional rent. The difference is, if the roof is not replaced, you will get no rent at all. The same applies for furnaces, water heaters, broken windows, and the like. (Preparation of specifications is discussed in more detail later in this chapter.)

Provision of Materials.   Materials for the job may be supplied by the owner-rehabber or by the contractor. In our rehabilitation projects, we supplied all material that was not incidental to the job. Being in the business of apartment management, we already had an established relationship with various suppliers, and this usually meant we had greater purchasing power than most of the contractors who would be engaged to do the work. As it is, we have national contracts with some appliance manufacturers, and this allows us to choose grades of appliances that best suit the profiles of the residents we hope to attract. For rehabilitation projects, we contract with a particular supplier for all the appliances needed. We have similar arrangements for cabinetry and countertops. (Note that while this approach works well for us, it may not be possible or practical for some rehabilitation projects or in some areas of the United States.)

Purchase of materials by the rehabber can be disadvantageous as well as advantageous. On the one hand, the rehabber gets a better price; the unit cost is only inflated by the amount of the construction management fee. On the other hand, all the material belongs to the property owner from the time it is delivered, instead of when it is installed by the contractor. This poses a security problem which can be very serious. If any cabinets, appliances, or other items "disappear" from the property, the savings on the purchases will be quickly eroded.

Buying in Bulk.   Usually there are economies in volume buying, which means that, in estimating costs, the amount of material to be ordered at one time is another consideration. For example, if the decision is to install new kitchen cabinets, purchasing a truckload of cabinets (enough for 30 or 40 kitchens at a time) will greatly reduce the cost. This method of purchase, however, is not without pitfalls. Unless all these items can be utilized as they are delivered, a storage area will have to be provided. Then, unless extremely tight security is maintained, there will more than likely be some shrinkage—a euphemism for pilferage—which would require the purchase of one or two of some items to complete some kitchens. These additional purchases can substantially reduce the cost savings effected by the bulk purchase.

No matter how tight the security, there is always a way for someone to steal. An example from my own experience tells quite a tale.

> We had purchased new windows for one building at a property and stored them in a vacant apartment that had been re-keyed and triple locked. Only the manager, the maintenance supervisor, and the project director had keys to the storage unit. As installation was started, it was discovered that three windows were missing. They had been properly inventoried on delivery, so the loss had to have occurred since then.

The pieces began to fall into place when someone recalled that we had stored unit air conditioners in this apartment in addition to the windows. Over a period of time, the maintenance men had been using the maintenance supervisor's key to access the storage unit. They were supposed to remove one or more air conditioners (as needed) for installation in apartments that had been rehabbed. It was apparent that more than the air conditioners had been removed.

Only by chance was the true situation discovered when the project director drove by the home of a maintenance man who had quit about a month earlier. There were the three missing windows, neatly installed in his home. In this case, luckily, there was full restitution. It has not been that way in every instance.

Rehabilitation of individual apartment units rarely progresses in any orderly fashion—i.e., from one unit to another in the same building until that building is completed. Inevitably there is greater confusion and additional opportunities for deception and theft.

The decision to buy in bulk or one at a time ultimately depends on the ability to store the material as well as the divergent cost factor. However, both ways should be examined initially. Remember that if you do decide to buy one at a time, continued availability of a particular product must be considered along with possible unit cost increases. Shipping costs, whether something is delivered by the vendor or picked up by one of your maintenance staff, must also be considered. We try to avoid having site staff deal with any pick-up or delivery of construction materials unless absolutely necessary. Not only is there the cost of the person's time, but this worker is taken away from a previously assigned maintenance task, consequently adding to both maintenance and rehabilitation costs.

Contracted Services.   Contractors will be a major cost factor and a major consideration from the standpoint of their ability to perform the work—and the rehabber's ability to complete the rehabilitation as planned. While a comparison of costs for contracted services is beyond the scope of this book, there are a number of factors that will impact the rehabilitation costs at a particular property. First there is regional location. The state of the local economy will affect availability and costs of materials. Climatic conditions (seasonal variations, protracted periods of inclement weather) will impact scheduling of different types of work. There is also the question of contractor availability and how that will be affected by current demand for construction work at the time the specifications are put out for bid. Another concern is the type of financing the rehabber is trying to obtain and any governmental restrictions that may apply at the time—use of "minority" contractors or other types of equal employment opportunity requirements may have to be met to obtain government-backed financing. In some cases prevailing wages (i.e., local market rates for the construction trades) may have to be paid—it might even be necessary to deal with union labor.

We have had mixed success with contractors whose services at one location commended using them again in a different location. Some small contractors have been very willing to work in a totally new market area even though it has required them to move to the new location temporarily. In large part, a willingness to "relocate" will depend on the availability of work. In my own experience, when contractors we have worked with previously solicited additional business from us in another locale, and we agreed to a finite time frame for the work up front, both the quality of the contractors' performance and the price have been relatively good. However, the best success in terms of both price and quality of work resulted when local contractors were used. There is a direct correlation between the distance from the contractor's home base to the property and the amount of time it takes to complete the job—and the difficulty in getting the contractor back to correct any defects.

Something else that has worked well is finding contractors who will provide turnkey services for the individual apartment. This is not always possible, but it is highly desirable. Carpentry, tile-setting, electricity, plumbing, and painting are the typical "trades" for apartment interior work. If one contractor can supply all of the required trades, the work will be much easier to coordinate.

Permit Requirements.   The cost of a rehabilitation will include fees for construction permits. Fees for such permits are often based on the type of work to be done and an estimate of its cost. (Note that for some types of work proposed as part of a rehabilitation, there may be no requirement for a permit.) Ability to obtain appropriate permits may be contingent on bringing the property up to current standards (eliminating existing building code violations), and this may necessitate changes to preliminary estimates of material costs, time requirements, and actual work to be done. The best way to determine the specific requirements is to investigate this issue with municipal officials (e.g., the building commissioner)—in some areas, use of an architect is required, and some of these issues become the architect's responsibility. This assumes the due diligence investigation has established that the zoning of the property is correct (i.e., no variance is required).

It is vital to establish and maintain a working relationship with the officials in the municipality so as to foster cooperation. This becomes apparent when you search their records of code violations at the property and try to obtain the necessary construction permits for the rehabilitation. Check the codes and "violations" carefully. As new materials become available and technological advancements require different approaches to construction, governing bodies change and upgrade or tighten the standards in building codes to match those capabilities. It is also common practice to "grandfather" older existing structures under the codes and not require strict compliance with the newer standards. However, when a building is to be rehabilitated, the door is opened for requiring compliance of the planned rehab construction with the newer, stricter codes. This can affect both the work to be done and the materials to be used, both of which affect the cost of the project. It is important that such contingencies are not overlooked in the development of the rehabilitation plan.

Whenever a permit is required, the appropriate permit must be obtained. However, the rehabilitation process often has gray areas with respect to the necessity for a permit. These arise because there may be specific permit requirements for construction, as such, but no need for permits to do what generally is thought of as "maintenance." Much of the work done in a cosmetic rehab can be construed as maintenance—e.g., removal of an electrical fixture or outlet to install a new one or replacement of plumbing fixtures. These types of work are often considered maintenance by building department officials in the municipality and, for that reason, no permits may be required. On the other hand, while the rehabber might also consider replacement of drywall (sheetrock) that has holes and water damage to be a maintenance item, municipal officials may insist on a permit for this type of work. (We have never had problems with these kinds of distinctions because we have always advised the municipality of our plans beforehand and obtained permits when there was a definitive requirement.)

The recycling process will take many months, during which you will be subject to permit requirements and building inspections. A good rapport established at the outset can make the difference in your ability to control "extra" costs such as fees for permits and downtime while you await inspections. Being up front with municipal officials about rehabilitation plans may mean not only a saving on the cost of some permits, but also that much of the work done on the property may be overlooked by the assessor when it is time to reevaluate the assessment basis for real estate taxes. Usually the rehabber is in a very good position if the property is blighted because municipal officials are very desirous of having a nice-looking property within their boundaries. However, they also have requirements that must be met. What I am suggesting here is not an impropriety but rather that a good rapport can minimize "official" impediments to the recycling process. Most of the time you will be told, "We will work with you if you play by our rules." If you tell them what you intend to do and then do it—meanwhile openly communicating what you are doing—the cooperation will be there. Often these people truly want to cooperate. All the rehabber has to do is give them an opportunity to do so. The rule to follow is: If there is any question about the need for a permit, talk to the building commissioner.

For the most part, my experience has been that municipal officials are pleased that someone is taking a property that has not been a very good neighbor in the past and making it better. The benefits of establishing a good line of communication with the building commissioner or building inspectors are indicated in the following example.

We purchased and planned to rehabilitate a property that was under the threat of a court order to replace the entire parking lot. Quite frankly, installing a new parking lot at the beginning of the rehab was not the way we wanted to proceed. The parking lot would have to be used for dumpsters (for debris removal) and for unloading appliances and other items for installation in the individual apartments. These activities can and do damage the paved surface. It was obvious, however, that the parking lot was a major concern, so it was resurfaced immediately. Having seen that we "performed" in this respect, the municipal officials happily permitted installation of a site monument as a median in the center of the city street. This incident was the beginning of a wonderful relationship with officials in that municipality.

Aside from the types of responses already indicated here, there is another intrinsic benefit of having a good relationship with officials. As the property is turned around and the recycling process is completed, referrals of prospective residents will come. This obviously cannot be forced. The point is, when those in power are happy with what you have done, the benefits are great.

Organization of the Work

Before the perception of the property can be changed and it can be rerented, the planned physical changes must be made. This requires careful organization of the work that is to be done. At first, rehabilitation may seem to be a much simpler process than new construction because the building or buildings already exist. In fact, it is the opposite. What makes rehabilitation more difficult is that it requires removal of existing fixtures and components before any actual construction can begin. This is further complicated by the presence of existing residents who must be accommodated or worked around during construction.

No other type of construction tests the organization of the job and its timetable for completion as much as apartment rehabilitation does. Even new construction contracts include a caveat that deadlines can be voided in the event of "war, civil commotion, strikes, material shortages, etc." This is usually encompassed in a *force majeure* clause in contracts. The fact that there is uncertainty as to exactly what contractors will find when they begin to tear out walls and remove plumbing parts and electrical fixtures adds to the challenge of construction in the context of rehabilitation. To this must be added the inconvenience caused by the presence of existing residents. Still another consideration is the fact that the individual apartment units will require different amounts of work because their condition at the time the rehabilitation begins will vary. This last point deserves some discussion.

Tile-related work and drywall repair and replacement tasks require the greatest flexibility in planning and scheduling because the extent of this corrective work can vary so much. Usually, the amount of work needed can be estimated fairly accurately from visual inspection of the surface. Horizontal and vertical measurements permit computation of the "area" of replacement in square inches, feet, or yards. Alternatively, area can be determined from the dimensions of uniform tiles multiplied by the number of tiles needed. However, this is not always the case because water damage sometimes rots the studs, and these will have to be replaced as well. Sometimes fire damage has been covered with sheetrock, and there may be several studs missing. It is obvious that such a wall does not have much integrity, and new studs will have to be installed. These types of discoveries can be discussed with the contractor and a cost for this additional work established before any work is started; this might be a rate per stud or some other agreed-upon measure or a price based on material cost plus a fixed fee. (NOTE: Dimensions for construction materials are currently being converted to metric units, and new standardized measurements may not be exact equivalents with currently used inch-pound units.)

Other problems likely to be discovered relate to the electrical and plumbing systems. We have worked on a number of older buildings in which we had planned to attach new sinks and new supply lines to existing plumbing only to find out when the existing fixtures were being removed that the drain connections had broken off inside the wall. Needless to say, this required additional time to complete the work and added to the costs. Once rehabilitation had been started at another older property, the owner found out that the entire building needed to be rewired. The best way to avoid such surprises is to conduct a thorough due diligence inspection prior to acquisition. This means inspecting every unit and may necessitate involvement of skilled tradespeople or other knowledgeable experts. Many people have said that inspection of 50 percent of the units will be a large enough sample to know what to expect. That may be true, but inspecting every unit leaves nothing to conjecture. When we perform a due diligence inspection, there are usually four or five units that cannot be accessed because locks have been changed or the residents are uncooperative. If we have seen, say, 195 out of 200 units, we will establish our costs for the five unseen units based on the absolute worst of the ones we did see.

To avoid additional surprises we try to do some "tear out" in the worst of the units. Usually the current owner is agreeable to allowing some tear out because it would have to be done anyway due to the obvious extent of the problem. If permission is not granted, however, we have often agreed to restore any torn out area to a condition equal to or better than it was before it was opened if the property is *not* purchased. Given the dollar amounts involved in the rehabilitation of multifamily properties, preliminary tear out is a good idea.

Methods of Construction.   There are several ways to approach the construction work. One is to use an outside general contractor (see exhibit 3.1). In this situation, several prospective contractors might be asked to provide a single bid for all the work, including both materials and labor. Selection of a contractor for the job would depend on material quality and costs, labor costs, and how long it would take to do the work. A second method would be to use in-house staff, either personnel who are already on the payroll or individuals hired specifically for the construction. Still another method is to hire a construction manager to solicit bids from subcontractors, select the ones to do the work (with ownership approval), and supervise their work. (The construction manager often performs many of the functions of a general contractor, acting as an agent on behalf of the owner. See exhibit 3.2.) There is also the possibility of using a hybrid of two or more of the methods described. The method you choose will depend on the extent of the work to be done, the types of tasks to be performed, and the availability of skilled labor to perform them, as well as the need to meet legal requirements (e.g., preparation of drawings by a licensed architect; employment of licensed tradespeople, etc.). What must be determined is the most efficient and cost-effective way to accomplish the particulars of the rehabilitation project.

General Contractor.   There are some definite advantages to using a general contractor. When specifications are prepared and presented for bidding, the resulting cost estimates (bids) essentially provide for a turnkey operation. There is also less direct supervision of construction workers and virtually no involvement of site management personnel in the construction process itself. However, the disadvantages of using a general contractor often outweigh the advantages. Uncertainty regarding previously undiscovered conditions in areas to be rehabilitated (e.g., broken connections inside walls) and the potential for interference with residents who are living in the building are just two problems that can arise when a general contractor is used. On the other hand, if the rehabilitation requires a complete "gut" job, a general contractor may be the wisest choice. Being unfamiliar to the residents, the contractor would be able to work without interference from them. Also, a general contractor knows better what work has to be performed in what order—in a gut job, most of the existing plumbing pipes, electrical wiring, and heating components (radiators, piping, ductwork) would likely be removed. In such a situation, the construction crew would turn the property over to management one building at a time.

In-House Staff.   As long as there are problems regarding uncertainty of the work to be done and potential for interfering with existing residents, it may be more advantageous to have a construction team that is intertwined with the management of the property. That this is a key issue has been demon-

E X H I B I T   3.1

Traditional Method—General Contractor

1. One general contractor contracts with owner.
2. Design and construction are two separate efforts—no continuity.
3. Adversarial relationship between architect/engineer and general contractor.
4. Layering of bonding occurs with the general contractor furnishing bonds to the owner and subcontractors furnishing bonds to the general contractor.
5. Usually less value analysis during the design phase.
6. Usually a guaranteed lump sum bid at the beginning of the project.
7. Phased construction coordinated by general contractor.
8. General contractor has lump sum contract with owner.
9. General contractor controls schedule.
10. Owner depends on the architect and general contractor for design, costs, and schedules.

Reproduced with permission from Bentil, Kweku K.: *Fundamentals of the Construction Process* (Kingston, Mass.: R. S. Means Co., Inc., 1989).

NOTE: This exhibit and the one on the facing page delineate distinctions that are often made within the construction industry but do not apply absolutely to all rehabilitation projects.

---

strated over and over again by lenders who have taken properties back. For some reason, they consider the use of in-house staff to be the most expedient and the least expensive because it seems to be true at the beginning. There is no question that by utilizing in-house staff, management of the property and management of the construction become the responsibility of a single entity, which is basically a sound idea. However, existing maintenance personnel are usually already occupied (property maintenance), and while they may have some background related to construction, they often lack the day-to-day experience that would have developed their construction skills so that they could work efficiently. In addition, utilization of site staff usually means there are few or no cost controls.

Inefficiency and higher costs are the main disadvantages of using in-house staff. Even when the maintenance staff has been augmented by hiring additional "construction" workers, problems remain. First consider efficiency. Having maintenance personnel fulfill routine work orders for maintenance of the property and, in addition, perform rehabilitation construction work is counterproductive. If someone is required full time on a property for maintenance work, that individual will have no time for other work. Likewise, when additional people are hired to work exclusively on construction, the manager still considers them part of the maintenance department. Thus, for example, emergency rodding of a drain pipe might involve not only the existing maintenance personnel, but also some of those hired to work exclusively on construction, which is an immediate inefficiency. This inefficiency comes about because some site managers are not particularly knowledgeable about construction, but they do understand how maintenance

E X H I B I T   3.2

Construction Management Method

1. Several prime contractors contract directly with owner.
2. Design and construction are not handled by separate parties, so there is continuity.
3. Cohesive team effort between architect/engineer and construction manager.
4. Reduces layering of bonding.
5. Value analysis and cost control during design.
6. No guaranteed costs at the onset of the project (unless it is a guaranteed maximum price contract).
7. System integrated but permits phased construction.
8. Construction manager has incentive to reduce costs to owner.
9. Owner retains more control of the schedule and can plan cash flow to his or her advantage.
10. Involvement of the construction manager during the planning and design phases provides the owner with source of independent information about probable costs and schedules.

Adapted with permission from Bentil, Kweku K.: *Fundamentals of the Construction Process* (Kingston, Mass.: R. S. Means Co., Inc., 1989).

---

should be performed and how maintenance workers function. Another problem related to efficiency is the sense of urgency in trying to complete the construction work in a timely manner. Sad to say, maintenance workers are paid by the hour as your employees, and they may feel no pressure to complete the job. Besides, once the job has been completed, some of these people will be without work.

A very pointed example of such inefficiency occurred at a property we were evaluating for possible purchase. The property comprised slightly more than 200 units in several buildings. Eight maintenance workers were employed there, and during the course of inspection one day, all eight were seen walking from one building to the next. There was absolutely no control. Can you imagine the full compliment of maintenance personnel walking a property in different directions at the same time? No actual work was being done, and the top wage-earner among them was being paid more than $25 an hour.

This leads to the other concern—higher costs. Costs are high when in-house staff are used because of wasted time and because these people never really know whether they are maintenance workers or construction workers. This is not just theory. In many rehabilitations started by the lender or the current owner of the property, far more money was paid out over a longer period of time and the results were far less satisfactory when in-house staff did the work.

Construction Manager and Prime Contractors.   Hiring a construction manager who becomes part of the management staff offers several advantages,

Construction Manager—Agreement

A construction management agreement is a legal document that spells out the respective roles and responsibilities of the construction manager and the property owner. Compensation should be commensurate with the amount of responsibility—and risk—assumed by the construction manager through the agreement. Insurance coverages required of the construction manager and indemnification of the owner against third-party claims of negligence on the part of the construction manager are other key issues to be covered.

Standard forms are available from different professional organizations. The form adopted by the American Institute of Architects (AIA) takes a traditional approach to construction management—the construction manager serves as agent of the owner and does not assume risks of construction. The construction work is performed by *prime contractors* who contract directly with the owner. The form adopted by the Associated General Contractors of America (AGC) takes a hybrid approach that combines construction management with general contracting—the construction manager is given full responsibility for the performance of the various trade contractors and may be required to set a guaranteed maximum price for the construction. (The construction manager performs as a *general contractor,* contracting with various *subcontractors* to do the actual construction work.) In this situation, the construction manager has interests of its own to protect, and the manager's interests may conflict with those of the property owner.

including better coordination of the work and greater control over some costs. The individual hired as a construction manager should possess the ability—and be given the authority—to make quantity purchases of such things as appliances, carpeting, kitchen cabinets, and other items unique to residential property. Because he or she is part of the apartment management team, when the construction manager makes such purchases, the costs can be borne directly by the property—without the mark up typically added by a contractor or other middleman—thus effecting substantial savings. This also means that the costs of the construction-specific materials (e.g., sheetrock, lumber, nails, screws) and labor will be borne by the contractors hired to do the work and should be included in their bids. (Differences between the traditional method and the construction management method of contracting can be seen from exhibits 3.1 and 3.2.)

Actually, what has been most efficient for our projects is having our own construction management company. This is advantageous because the construction management company is an extension of our property management business, and its employees work in concert with the site management staff. Each rehab job is divided into two major components—the common areas and apartment interiors. If the roof has to be replaced, a roofer is hired, and that contractor provides both material and labor for the job on a finite contract basis. The same is true for exterior painting, landscaping, swimming pool repair, hall and stairway work, parking lots, and the like. For the most

---

Criteria for Evaluating Contractors
• Reputation for quality work
• Track record for timely performance
• Availability
• Local Base
• Size of business

---

part, these jobs include materials and labor in their specifications and, except for hall and stairway work and parking lot paving, this work can be done with minimal inconvenience to both contractor and existing residents. It is the apartment unit interiors that are more difficult to schedule.

The best way we have found to handle the rehabilitation of unit interiors is to hire a contractor to do the job from trash out of the unit through installation of cabinetry, plumbing, etc., to final painting. The unit is inspected when it has been "construction cleaned" by the contractor. At that point another contractor is brought in to install the carpeting, and then in-house maintenance personnel install the appliances and double-check all the mechanical installations. Finally, a cleaning contractor puts the apartment in a rent-ready condition. This procedure allows for maximum control over both the quality of the work and its coordination with the marketing effort. If the perception of the property begins to change in a positive way during the rehab, coordination with the leasing effort becomes critical to the financial success of the rehabilitation. (Note that while this approach has worked for our projects, prevailing local practices may warrant different divisions of labor or require different procedures.)

Selection of Contractors.   Ideally, the rehabber should be able to choose the best prices and schedules from among several bidders for each type of work. Who is asked to bid on different types of work will depend on the method of construction to be used.

Four characteristics of the contractor are key to success of the job and a good relationship with the rehabber. The contractor must be reputable, have a track record for timely performance, be available to do the work, and have ties to the local area. The first three would be required for any job at any time. Being reputable means the contractor will perform the work in accordance with the specifications, use the materials that are specified, and complete the job in a workmanlike manner. The only way to know this is to have used the contractor before (and been satisfied with the prior work) or to thoroughly check references. If a contractor is not reputable, there is no reason to proceed further. Timeliness of performance can be checked with references, although this is primarily a historical check. Availability can be a critical issue. A contractor might have so many jobs currently in work, that your time schedule cannot be met. (Note that this discussion ignores the

---

Advantages of Locally Based Contractors
• Availability to do work
• Availability for call back to redo unsatisfactory work or complete an installation
• Access to local sources of supply and replacement parts
• Greater efficiency

---

issue of costs and presumes there is no absolute requirement to select the lowest bidder.)

The fourth consideration—being locally based—has been mentioned previously. Engagement of local contractors is usually advantageous for several reasons. One whose work is locally based is more likely to be available to do work in the area. This is really important if a contractor has to be called back to redo unsatisfactory work or complete an installation. In addition, the contractor may have access to local sources of supply—and discounts—that are not available to the rehabber. Being locally based is directly related to efficiency—it facilitates pickup of supplies and replacement items that are part of the materials provided by the contractor. Even outstanding success with a contractor on a previous job elsewhere is no guarantee. In my experience, when contractors work outside their local area, attention to the job tends to suffer. In some cases, nonlocal contractors may have to live on the rehab property for a time, but this only seems to work for about six to eight weeks. In fact, the only reason they would do this is because there is no work in their own locality. Their hearts remain "at home," however, and that is where they want to be.

An additional point to consider is the size of the contractor's business. Hiring a large firm to do a small job is often a mistake. Large contractors generally prefer to do larger scale jobs. The only reason they would take a small job is because they need money at that time. However, if a better job comes their way, they will more than likely leave your job for the larger one. It is much the same as hiring someone who is over-qualified for a particular job. Some people accept a job because they need to work, but as soon as a better job comes along—one more to their liking or better matched to their qualifications—they will leave. In a rehabilitation project, the loss of a contractor as the construction work moves into full swing can be deleterious to your overall schedule and the critical path of performance.

We have had the greatest success using small contractors. In some instances, a one-man company has been contracted to do apartment interiors. This person had the capability of hiring additional laborers as required. Sometimes we have used several small contractors to do the same type of work, each one working independently, to increase overall productivity. In essence, they had to compete with each other to work on more units. This tactic depends on the speed at which the rehab must progress and the availability of appropriate contractors. The advantages of using a small contractor are efficiency and better control. The disadvantage is that the contractor must be proficient in several trades—namely carpentry, plumbing, and electricity. Local requirements can be another restraint—it may be necessary to have a licensed electrician approve all electrical work if not actually perform it. In some areas, all the different construction trades may have to be licensed.

In letting bids for a rehabilitation project, it is just as important for you to sell the contractors as it is for them to sell you. In this type of situation, you need the contractor as much as the contractor needs you. You expect the contractors to perform to your specifications in a timely manner and they expect to be paid for that work. Thus, it is important for the contractor to know that payment for work done will be made in a timely manner as agreed. The contractors should also be given an opportunity to check your references with other contractors you have used previously. This will provide assurance to the contractors, and they will likely pay more attention to your job.

In analyzing bids for construction work, pay particular attention to price and the basic attitude of the contractor supplying the bid. The analysis should also reveal who will run the job and be in daily contact with the construction management team. One thing I have never done is "peddle" the bids—i.e., tell one contractor the price another contractor quoted and offer an opportunity to beat it. Not only is this practice unethical, but it generally precludes any future opportunities for business with the contractor who does not get the job. The contractor will rightly believe there is no point in bidding to your specifications because the bid price does not matter. Since you never know when you will need a particular contractor again, possibly even for the same project at a later stage, peddling of bids should be avoided. However, once a bidder is selected, it is reasonable and proper to go back over the various line items and try to negotiate a better price for certain items for which the contractor's bid may have been slightly high. However, this should only be done *after* the contractor had been selected. (Note that this discussion ignores the need for contractors to provide performance or other bonds and proof of insurance; these are common requirements of construction contracts.)

Timing the Work.   The time frame of work is critical to the process as a whole. I would argue strongly that there are more pitfalls in rehabilitation than in new construction. Obviously both types of work include the cost of material and the cost of installation, and scheduling is an important consideration. Weather and other external factors affect both new construction and rehabilitation, and sometimes one trade cannot begin work until some other trade has finished. In a rehabilitation, however, one trade could take longer than budgeted if a previously undiscovered problem becomes an issue. As noted earlier, the best way to preclude this type of situation is to do some exploratory tear out as part of the due diligence. There is no question that this exploration will cost money; and if the property is not purchased, the prospective buyer will be required to restore those areas to an equivalent or better condition than before they were explored. However, this is money well spent compared to the potential downside of lost time and extra expense if it is not done. No reputable contractor will agree to do a job in which all of the pitfalls are not immediately apparent unless a sizeable contingency fee is added into the contract.

One thing that can increase the time requirement is correction of flaws in the original construction. It is really rather foolish to make a cosmetic correction if it will only be a short-lived cure because failure to correct an underlying flaw will only lead to a recurrence, probably within an even shorter time span. For example, one property we rehabbed had dormers protruding from a false mansard roof, and all of the wood had been rotted because the original construction allowed water to accumulate at the face of the dormers. Changing the design before reroofing was started solved the problem completely.

Usually exterior and common area rehabilitation work can be done quite rapidly. Of course, this also depends on the time of year. In northern states, for example, cold winter weather may preclude beginning exterior work before May, and it will have to be completed before November. Interior work can be done any time, but it is the work inside the apartments that requires the most coordination and takes the longest time. How many units can be rehabbed in a month will depend on the occupancy, the availability of contractors, and the amount of work required in each unit. We have done as many as 25 per month and as few as two or three per month.

A *construction loan* provides short-term financing for building projects, and the funds are usually released in stages related to construction progress. If a construction loan is granted for a period of eighteen months, it is very important for the time frame of work to be organized and carried out so that all of the construction work can be accomplished in much less than eighteen months because time must be allowed for remarketing the rehabilitated property. The construction loan cannot be paid off if the property has not achieved stabilization (occupancy *and* income).

The reason that the time frame is so critical is that most lenders, when providing construction loans, will establish a time limit for completing the work. In a way this is good because remarketing of a property cannot begin until the perception has been changed. The perception cannot and will not be changed until physical change is strikingly apparent.

Carrying costs are a major related concern—as soon as work is completed and contractors have been paid out of borrowed funds, the carrying costs increase because the lender has increased the amount of the outstanding loan. If the rehab is completed quickly but the market does not accept the property at a comparable pace, the higher carrying costs will be extended over an even longer payback period.

The only situation in which the time spent on physical change and the time it takes to alter market perception will be relatively equal is when a property has been taken back by the lender (e.g., foreclosure), and the lender has made a concerted effort to evict undesirables and create a stable environment. Neither marketing nor exterior construction work is required. It is during the period when there are no police calls and no infringement on the neighborhood by the property that the negative market perception slowly begins to dissipate. Because the lender has already halted the negative impacts, all the rehabber has to do is enhance the positive aspects of the property.

This distinction can be a solid argument when a rehabber is shopping for financing, and a lender insists on a very short construction time frame. If the lender will allow more time to complete the construction, the change in perception can be taking place concurrent with the physical changes inside the apartments. With an aggressive approach, it should take no longer than one year to complete a basic cosmetic rehabilitation. However, if negative perception is a major consideration, the lender must be made aware of the importance of additional time to turn that perception around. (A lender once allowed us to take four years to complete the interior rehabilitation of a property.)

Residents on the Premises.   Completing a rehabilitation with residents living at the property is a two-edged sword. On the positive side, those who remain provide income that reduces the shortfall during the recycling process. Although this is of great benefit, it is not without problems. Residents in place constitute three major impediments to the construction process. First is increased time. Unless the property undergoing recycling is to be a "gut" job, construction cannot proceed unit by unit in an orderly progression. This means construction workers will have to move around to different areas of the building. Relocating or shifting tools and equipment is inefficient and time-consuming; it reduces the amount of time spent on actual rehabilitation construction in a given day. In addition, the owner will have to wait until their leases expire for some residents to move out. Care must be taken during the rehabilitation so as not to disrupt the lives of these residents any more than is absolutely necessary. (Note that this discussion does not include the issue of rent control laws because they have not been part of our experience. Such laws can affect both rental rates and move-outs.)

The second impediment is increased cost. Time is a function of money, and if workers must skip around from one vacant unit to another, it will take longer to complete the work, and this will add to the cost. The fact that all of the units will not be done at one time is likely to diminish the rehabber's capability to purchase materials in volume, which will increase the costs of materials.

The third impediment is a greater need for management due to the increased need for services. Because there are some residents you want to retain, it is important that these people receive a higher level of service during the rehabilitation than they were receiving before you assumed management of the property. This will not be easy because there will be more dust, dirt, and noise in the common areas and emanating from individual units under construction. There will be some times when utilities will have to be turned off—another inconvenience for these residents. These considerations mean more time must be spent managing the physical asset than would be required in a stabilized management situation. In addition, management personnel will be continually evaluating the current residents—there are likely to be more evictions as well as more complaints.

The recycling of an apartment property that remains partially occupied—the vast majority of apartment rehabilitations are done this way—is not without social implications. Part of the skill requirement for professional management personnel is understanding these social implications. Although market analysis may have given a strong indication of how the resident profile should evolve once the recycling process is completed, there can never be total certainty. For this reason, all of the staff's "people skills" should be utilized to cater to each and every resident at the beginning of the process.

In a matter of one or two months, the nonpaying residents will have been identified and can be evicted. Also during this time, those who will not follow the rules and regulations you have established will also become known, but it will take perhaps another month for them to be evicted as well. (Because laws regarding eviction vary by jurisdiction, understanding of local notification requirements and procedural details is imperative.) This will still leave a nucleus of residents with whom you have an opportunity to work. The point is, even before you begin the rehab, you should set the tone for the way the property will be managed.

According to psychologists, adults are often like children—where there are no rules and regulations, they will do as they please; when there are firm rules to be followed, most people will follow them. If the rules are laid out clearly and concisely, it becomes relatively easy for the manager to identify the residents who choose not to follow them and to remove those residents from the property. This goes back again to the issue of market perception. A property cannot change in the eyes of the market until it is perceived to change. Once the drug dealing, the loud and raucous activity, and the hooliganism that may permeate the neighborhood have been purged from the property, it will be demonstrated to those people who might otherwise be leaning away from those activities that they can change with the property. Retaining these "changeable" residents will enhance the cash flow during the rehabilitation and provide the basis from which to build the new resident profile. Even those who choose not to stay because they cannot afford more rent or because they believe they do not fit in will abide by the rules until their leases are up, thus providing a period of paying residency with few problems. The key to achieving this is to treat every one of the residents as a valued customer—until or unless they prove unworthy of that treatment. (Managing the property during the rehabilitation is detailed in chapter 6.)

Preparation of Specifications

Too often properties have been rehabilitated using the bidder's specifications for the work rather than the owner's specifications. This seems to be a prevailing practice among lender-owners.

A *specification* is a written description of the construction work to be done. It describes the kind and quality of materials to be used and the mode of construction (type and extent of work), including dimensions and other particulars that define the job, as the basis for estimating costs. On acceptance by or agreement between the parties, the specification becomes part of the contract between them.

Specifications include two separate types of costs—materials and labor. In my own experience, the quality of materials was higher (and their costs lower) if they were purchased beforehand and supplied to the contractors for installation. Purchasing of materials by the rehabber not only eliminates the mark-up on these items, but also provides internal quality control. Analysis of the economics of alternatives is also facilitated. (As noted earlier, we established a construction management company to serve as "general contractor" for our rehabilitation projects. Specific installations and finishing work are contracted out—in essence, we provide the materials and the contractor provides the labor. This approach may not be acceptable in some locales.)

There are exceptions, of course. Roofing material, paint, and the like are best supplied by the contractor, but the rehabber should be able to require assurances that materials meet the required specifications for the job as well as established quality and content standards that may be needed to comply with building codes. Sometimes a contractor may be able to purchase at better prices or from sources not available to the rehabber. Also, some specific jobs require licensed contractors (e.g., installation of furnaces or boilers, work on elevators), and that may affect provision of materials.

Line-Item Specifications.   Once all of the items to be corrected are identified and the extent of the work is known, it is imperative to prepare detailed specifications of how it will be accomplished. Many tasks may seem very simple and, therefore, not worthy of documentation; nevertheless, detailed specifications should be prepared for *all* of the work to be done. If a new roof is required, specifications for that work are best prepared by a structural engineer. Most of the work on the other components of the so-called common areas of the property will be quite straightforward in that a certain amount of tear out and installation of new materials will be required. However, exceptions to this abound. For example, sections of the eaves and soffits that have been damaged because the roof leaked or from general neglect over a long period will have to be replaced. That which is obviously in need of replacement may not be the entire extent of the work—additional problems could be discovered once the work has begun. This is why the prepared specifications should allow for the job to be bid in its entirety *(standard specification)* but include a line-item specification as well that provides for a cost per lineal foot or per square foot or square yard for additional work *(nonstandard specification)*. Thus, when a change in the work specification is issued *(change order)*, any additional work has already been priced. To the extent that such an approach can be utilized, it is recommended.

Most apartments will require varying degrees of work because each one is in a different state of disrepair. A line-item specification makes it easier for a contractor to bid on the work without examining every unit. In fact, an inspection that permits the contractor to see the types and extent of work needed in a representative unit may suffice for bidding on standardized work items. Subsequently, each unit can be inspected immediately prior to performing the work. At that time, each of the line-item specifications can be analyzed for application to the particular unit and a total price for the unit can be established.

For our projects, a line-item specification is developed for the individual apartments based on an inspection of every unit. Certainly there must be an initial clean up and tear out so that the unit is prepared to accept new materials. This will be done in every unit. Any particular installation or type of work that will be generally applicable to all the apartments is identified and standardized. If we have determined that all kitchen cabinets and bathroom vanities will be torn out and replaced with new ones, these become standard line items for every unit. This work is straightforward except for the underlayment. The due diligence inspection should have revealed whether the underlayment has to be replaced and in which units this applies. Then, an additional line item can be inserted for replacement of the underlayment as a nonstandard specification—i.e., work is to be done only on an as-needed basis.

Line-item specifications are also developed for work that is likely to vary from unit to unit—for example, repair or replacement of ceramic tile in shower and bath areas. As might be expected, some units will require more repair and replacement than others, and not every unit will require work. To avoid having to bid each unit separately with a contractor, we establish norms and seek bids that quantify specific tasks. For example, in the bathroom, if no work is required for a particular line item, there will obviously be no charge. If ceramic tile has to be regrouted, that work might be charged on the basis of the area (in square feet) or the number of tiles. If the sheetrock beneath the tile has to be replaced, the work will likely be charged on a square-foot basis. This facilitates the bidding process and expedites agreement on the amount of work to be done and the rates to be charged. We would never say, "here are two hundred units, go to work." Instead, we release five to ten units at a time for a contractor to work on, and the specifications and original bid figures are discussed for each of those units—and agreed to individually—before the contractor begins to work on them.

The walls are of critical importance to the ultimate result of the rehabilitation. If drywall is to be replaced, a separate line item should establish the cost per sheet or half sheet of drywall (or per square foot), including taping and surface preparation. Preparation of walls that require no other work is also critical and should be itemized. Remember, when the entire unit is completed and ready for occupancy, it should look brand new. New cabinets in kitchens and bathrooms, new carpeting, and a fresh paint job are not enough. The walls in apartments in older buildings have been painted time and again. If a property is in poor condition as a whole, you can be sure the paint jobs have not been of the highest caliber either. Nail holes that have been poorly spackled and remnants of paint drips and chips, when painted over, still give the impression of an old wall despite the coat of fresh paint. Extra money should be budgeted for preparation so that the walls will be smooth and look new when painted again. Although a prospective resident is not likely to reject an apartment out of hand because a paint drip or an improperly spackled nail hole is visible, such flaws will affect the overall perception. With all else being new, the walls must give the impression of being new, too. Everything that can be done to enhance a prospect's first impression must be done.

Another small item that goes a long way to create a positive impression is replacement of electrical outlets and switches. Here again, repeated painting is likely to have created a buildup over existing outlets and switches as well as their respective cover plates. Specifying new outlets and switches adds to the appeal of the unit and provides that every outlet will be tested to make sure all are in operational condition. The same is true for plumbing. Any drains or supply lines that are installed by the contractor must be operational. At first glance this may seem perfunctory. However, you would be surprised how many contractors will install items but never test them to see if they work. All contracts for the construction should include a requirement for installations to be operational. Ultimately, the burden is on the rehabber—all work should be inspected before any payment is made. Anything that is passed over initially or only works for a brief period will only add to the costs of maintenance later.

Other Requirements.   Regardless of the construction method used, it is very important to establish and maintain specific requirements for the con-

Contractors' Bonds

Bid Bond—Assurance that, if the contractor's bid is accepted, the contractor will furnish performance and payment bonds and enter into a contract with the owner within a specified time period.

Payment Bond—Assurance that the contractor will pay for all labor, material, equipment, supplies, and subcontractors used on the project. Sometimes called a "labor and materials payment bond," it protects the owner against claims and liens after the project is completed and final payment has been made to the contractor.

Performance Bond—Assurance that the contractor will perform and complete the contract as per agreement.

Supply Bond—Assurance that the supplier will furnish the quantity and quality of material according to the contract. This bond protects the general contractor.

NOTE: These types of *surety bonds* constitute three-way contracts between a bonding company (surety), the contractor (principal), and the property owner (beneficiary). Performance and payment bonds are most commonly encountered. They are designed to protect the owner from construction risks related to nonpayment of suppliers by the general contractor or failure to complete the project as contracted.

tractual arrangements. Thus, the specifications for the job or jobs should also cover adjunct equipment to be provided by the contractor, who will be responsible for necessary permits, and requirements for the contractor to provide payment and performance bonds (typical) and certificates of insurance (proof of coverage).

Concrete work, asphalt paving, roofing, and other quality-graded materials will require reference standards to be matched. This may be accomplished by citing standard specifications established by the American National Standards Institute in conjunction with associations of materials manufacturers. Provisions for completing outdoor work in inclement weather may also be required.

For strictly cosmetic rehabs, mere physical replacement of cabinets, appliances, and plumbing fixtures on a per-item basis may require no architectural design or drawings. However, addition of new walls to subdivide the space inside units as well as changes that require relocation of plumbing fixtures or electrical outlets will require specific drawings as part of the rehabilitation plan. Consultation with a knowledgeable general contractor or a rehabilitation architect can save much consternation and expense in developing a solid overall construction plan. Even if new drawings are not required, it may be appropriate to reference current "as is" drawings in regard to replacement installations and correction of code violations (e.g., structural problems); these drawings should be obtained from the seller regardless.

Consideration should also be given to organization and timing of construction. While provisions for bonuses and penalties are common in construction contracts, in the recycling process these clauses are not all that advantageous. Two requirements of the contractual arrangement do make all the difference in the world, however. First of all, the timetable (work schedule) should be established in writing. If the contractor knows what is expected—and when it is to be done—ongoing communication and inspection will foster timely completion. Second, payment should always be made promptly, as agreed. For long projects, a series of partial payments is often scheduled and may be based on work completed. Payment in full before the work is completed should be avoided.

Depending on the complexity of the work and the nature of the contractual arrangements to be made, it may also be appropriate to address provisions for arbitration of disputes, time constraints on completing the work, methods of payment, and changes to the work (change orders). Properly prepared specifications will assure that all prospective contractors are bidding on the same types of work in the same manner.

Bidding the Work

Once specifications have been established, and the method of construction has been chosen, contractors should be invited to submit bids. (Usually three sources are sufficient for comparison on a specific job.) The specifications should set forth all of the requirements of the job or jobs to be bid on. If some items are negotiable, it is well to have bids based on a uniform set of specifications and negotiate on selected items later. Also, if it is known in advance that the periodic draws against the construction loan funds are fixed in time (set dates) or related to specific stages of the rehabilitation, this information should be included in the request for bids. Alternatively, it may be appropriate to request a payment schedule from the contractor as a basis for establishing draw dates and amounts. The request for bids should include a requirement for the contractor to provide references and other qualifications to do the job. (A sample list of work to be performed in apartment interiors is provided in exhibit 3.3.)

Analyzing Bids.   There are three items to analyze in examining each of the bids received. The first, obviously, is price. The second is the contractor's references. If possible you should ask to see previous work and talk to prior customers. It is important to know the quality of the contractor's work and his or her compliance with time schedules. The third important consideration is change orders. Instead of asking for a single price for the job, we ask the contractor to delineate a price for each function. This way, it is easy for us to analyze and compare bids on a "task" or "job" basis. It is also easier to negotiate a change in the specifications to avoid a drastic cost increase. The incident described below provides an example.

EXHIBIT   3.3

Example of Work Items—Apartment Interior

Kitchen
Cabinet removal
Install new cabinets
Install countertop(s)
Install vinyl flooring
Clean and oil exhaust fan(s)
Install double-basin sink
Replace faucet
Replace sprayer (with hose)
Install garbage disposal
Replace angle valves
Replace light bulbs

Bathroom
Recaulk wall tile
Replace wax ring
Replace toilet seat
Install medicine cabinet
Install fluid master
Install overflow gasket
Replace light bulbs, including heating lamp
Replace faucet, bathtub
Replace faucet, sink
Clean and oil exhaust fan(s)

Other Interior Work
Painting
Cleaning, including carpet shampoo
Cleaning, without carpet shampoo
Remove carpeting
Secure subfloor
Install miniblinds
Install threshold
Install solid-core door
Install hollow-core door
Replace door stops
Change air conditioning filter
Change thermostat
Install peep hole
Replace light switch
Install duplex receptacle
Replace pull string
Replace 9-volt battery (smoke detector)

This list is typical of work we have had done. It assumes that the items can be accomplished—e.g., drain lines in the kitchen sinks can accommodate disposals. Contractors are asked to bid on the specific work and include a list of parts and unit prices for materials they will provide (e.g., plumbing pipe, valves, and fixtures such as rebuilt faucets; electrical switches, receptacles, and light bulbs; drywall sheets, mud and tape for finishing walls, primer, and paint). Cabinets, appliances, and fixtures are supplied to the contractor for installation.

Original specifications for unit kitchens called for installation of new cabinets in an area where there had been a light fixture centered directly over the sink. At the time the specifications were prepared, no one realized that installation of the cabinets, as specified, would result in the existing light fixture being off-center. This error in the specifications became obvious only after the work had been started. However, the fact that these were line-item specifications, with each price separately delineated, meant only one issue and one cost had to be addressed. The extra cost of recentering the light fixture over the sink turned out to be $40. Although it was impossible to measure a financial return on the $40 increase in investment, the aesthetic impression that resulted from this change was considered essential to creating the overall impression that was desired for the unit.

Whenever there are any questions regarding pricing, the rehabber should not hesitate to ask someone else's opinion. Going back to one of the professionals who helped identify problems in the first place could prove invaluable. (I have also checked prices with contractors we had used in the past but who were not involved in working on the particular property because of their unavailability or because the property was located outside their market area.)

Bid prices for certain types of work are likely to vary from one contractor to another. It is important to ascertain that the bids are all estimated on the same basis and that the bid from any one contractor is consistent within itself—in other words, labor rates for the same kind of work do not vary and prices for specialized trades are within range locally (i.e., the going rate).

Contractors' bid prices estimate two types of costs—direct and indirect. *Direct costs* include labor (wages and benefits for the contractors' personnel), materials (building parts, permanently installed equipment, etc.), and heavy equipment to be used in the construction process (cranes, bulldozers). If work is to be subcontracted by the contractor, the subcontract costs are a direct cost as well. *Indirect costs* are also incurred by a contractor in the performance of the work, and these must be figured into the bid price. Workers' compensation, payroll taxes, insurance, and the contractor's business overhead and profit are other costs that must be covered. A properly prepared bid will also include a factor for *contingencies,* although this amount is usually related to the relative vagueness or specificity of the property owner's rehabilitation plans.

Time and the Budget.   Time is of the essence in the bidding process—specifications must be prepared (based on inspection and analysis of the property and the market), and bids must be received during the loan contingency period. However, in many instances, the deal will be closed and the loan in place when the final bids are received. It should be obvious that the initial analysis and preliminary budget must be reasonably accurate. Once the bids are in, they must be analyzed in relation to the rehabilitation budget. If the bids grossly exceed the budget and the available funding, some items will have to be scaled back or eliminated, and these budget cuts must be made without jeopardizing the market position projected for the property.

Once this bid-to-budget analysis is complete and construction contracts are finalized, a critical path for construction must be established. This critical path must set forth a timetable for construction that will be in concert with the market analysis done prior to acquisition. This initial timetable should allow for some flexibility—it must take into account the potential for discovering additional problems and yet keep pace with expectations for marketing and renting.

The Critical Path Method of Construction Scheduling

The critical path method of scheduling construction identifies specific tasks, the order in which they must be performed, and the time required for completion of each one. Usually there are several concurrent series of activities or sequential paths for a given project. The one that requires the most total time represents the shortest period in which the work can be completed.

The simplified diagram below assumes that tasks 1, 2, 3, and 4 and tasks 5 and 6—two separate series of tasks in the rehabilitation of apartment interiors—must be completed in sequence before task 7 can be started. Since tasks 5 and 6 require 5 total days, they represent the critical path. Combined with task 7, the critical path for these tasks would require allowance of 7 days for completion. For a rehabilitation project, there are likely to be many such series of tasks that must be considered in establishing the critical path for the job as a whole.

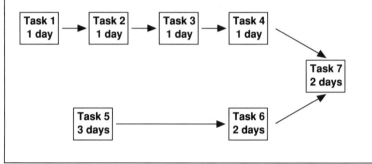

Budget Considerations

When operating a property with stabilized occupancy, the accuracy of the operating budget is very important to the analysis of net operating income (NOI) for the period. Usually operating budgets are prepared annually, and performance is analyzed monthly. All professional real estate managers utilize such budgets. This is the only way the manager can know the amounts of income and expense expected for a particular period. The key is planning. Managers should plan well and carefully because it is much easier to adjust for variances from a specified budget than to deal with a situation where nothing is expected—and therefore everything new becomes a crisis. When you approach a lender to obtain financing for a rehabilitation project, one of the most important components of your rehabilitation plan will be a budget. This budget must account for projected income and expenses related to operating the property during rehabilitation as well as specific costs of the rehabilitation work.

The recycling process has a major impact on the operating budget for a property. Without exception, occupancy will decline, and so will rental income. Some items of operating expense may be reduced because of this—for example, if heat is included in the rent, the cost of heating apartments may be lowered by controlling the amount of heat provided to vacant units—but other expenses will inevitably increase.

There is no way to predict how rapidly apartments will be vacated or exactly how many vacancies will ultimately result once the rehabilitation is started. This is disconcerting, but there are ways to budget for operations during a rehabilitation and thus provide a guideline. During the due diligence period, two very important facts can be uncovered—the caliber of the residents and the condition of the property. The first is determined from a review of current leases and analysis of the resident profile; the second is derived from a thorough inspection. The two will affect and be affected by each other. No doubt the property will have been suffering from general mismanagement and physical neglect for some time. Even if occupancy has remained reasonably high, rents are probably below market rates and actual collections will be down as well. Inevitably, the socioeconomic level of the residents will have declined because qualifying procedures will have been relaxed.

There is a definite correlation between the caliber of the residents and the physical condition of the property. There are likely to be three types of residents: slow-pay or no-pay, poor housekeepers or rule-breakers, and those with nowhere else to go. The slow-pay or no-pay variety of resident should be evicted immediately. There is no reason to retain any residents who are not paying rent. Keeping them only increases the management burden and does nothing to increase income. (Note that state and local laws prescribe procedures for dealing with nonpayment of rent and evictions, and these must be followed.)

However, those who are extremely messy housekeepers or who violate the rules and regulations prescribed in the lease need to be differentiated. Some of these people will continually resist any change and will repeatedly violate rules and regulations; they have no intention of changing their behavior, and they should be evicted for cause as soon as possible even if they are paying rent. Another group are psychological followers: If something is messy, they will adapt themselves to it, even if messiness is not their choice—they tend to do what others do. Still another type is the resident who violates the rules but, when order is restored, will capitulate and abide by the new rules and regulations. These latter two groups can likely remain because they will change as the property is changed.

The last type of resident is the saddest of all. These people are mostly senior citizens who may have moved in when the property was in good condition and a fine place to live—they have watched it change; they have lived through its decline. However, they will not necessarily be supportive of the rehabber's efforts to restore its former condition because they realize that the rent will go up, and some of them will not be able to afford the new rents that have been projected. This displacement process (sometimes called *gentrification*) is a part of apartment recycling that is painful on both sides. On the bright side, however, is the fact that many of these people can afford to stay—and they will stay and be model residents.

Operating Income.   For purposes of budgeting, it is probably safe to expect that the vast majority of the residents in place when the property is purchased and the rehabilitation is started will not be there when the recycling process has been completed. The number of residents who move out by their own choice will depend on the magnitude of the rehabilitation required. If only a minor facelift is needed, coupled with a strengthening of the level of professionalism in managing the property, 75 percent turnover in the first year (nonrenewals plus evictions) would be a reasonable expectation. Despite the high percentage, this is not likely to have a major impact on the property because the rehabber can begin marketing much *sooner*—at a much earlier stage in the process—thereby replacing those who do not renew or are evicted.

On the other hand, if the property is in need of extensive rehabilitation, 90 percent nonrenewal and evictions may be a more reasonable expectation. This will be further complicated by the fact that marketing will begin *later,* and the ever-present negative perception of the property will last longer. Until it is recognized in the market that a positive change is taking place, those who know the property will resist the physical change. To put it bluntly, the first prospective residents who seek out the property when it is ready for remarketing are likely to be people who are unfamiliar with the property and have no negative preconceptions. It will be painful to accept an application from one of these people only to have it cancelled within 24 hours. Obviously, the applicant will have talked to someone who has said that the property is not a good place to live.

For budgeting purposes, especially on the income side, it may be three months or longer before the property can be remarketed. Given that, it is prudent to be conservative in budgeting income *during* the recycling process. Conservatism is especially important in acquiring financing. If the rehabilitation can be accomplished on a fast track, it would be wise to budget for 50 percent vacancy at some point during the rehabilitation. If the process will be spread over two or two and one-half years because of financial constraints, it would be wise to budget for at least 30 percent vacancy.

Operating Expenses.   The expense side of the operating budget will be somewhat easier to evaluate. Certain pragmatic decisions should have been made about the current management staff as the due diligence was being performed. It is almost universal that most distressed properties are overstaffed, those in a lender's REO portfolio in particular. There are two reasons for this: Lenders will usually keep a large staff in place so that problems at the property are kept to a minimum. In addition, they will frequently attempt to accomplish a rehabilitation using the existing site maintenance staff, which is not a good idea.

When the rehabber assumes operational control of a property, one of the first things to be done is an assessment of its maintenance needs and the number of maintenance personnel needed to accomplish the required work. Contrary to the commonly touted notion, there is no rule of thumb regarding how many units can be handled by one maintenance worker. The ratio will depend on the age of the property, its condition, the resident profile, and the level of service that must be maintained during the rehabilitation. The same is true of the office staff. The need for leasing personnel will not be as great at the start of the rehabilitation as it will when the property begins to show signs of physical change. Initial office staff should be limited to a site manager and possibly an assistant, depending on the size of the property.

Another expense that should be reduced in the early stages of the rehabilitation is advertising—there is no reason to advertise then. Some utility costs might be reduced—e.g., heat and water consumption, which vary with occupancy. Sometimes it is possible to negotiate for a reduction in waste disposal costs based on reduced occupancy, but this benefit cannot always be expected.

Other than the items identified here, the operating expenses should be rather typical for a property of comparable size in that location. Typical, of course, has many definitions. In this context, I mean that real estate taxes, insurance, basic services, and administrative costs are likely to be about the same as in a stabilized situation.

A word of caution regarding budgeting is in order. When dealing with lenders, it is unwise to mix rehabilitation costs and operating expenses. It is far better to classify operating expenses as exactly what they are. If there is a shortfall, it should be covered by contingency funds budgeted for the rehabilitation. Also in this context, painting of rehabilitated apartments and certain maintenance items that would normally be covered in the operating budget will become part of the rehabilitation budget. Once an apartment is turned over to management for marketing, all attendant costs other than correction of contractor defects should be considered operating expenses.

Rehabilitation Costs.   The last consideration is the rehabilitation budget itself. Obviously, this budget will be developed from the bids for the rehabilitation work. (A list of typical components of a rehabilitation budget is provided in exhibit 3.4.) This does not mean that certain items will not be modified or deleted from the rehabilitation budget because of inordinately high cost. The ultimate rehabilitation budget will only be adopted after all tests have been performed to see if the investment return will merit all of the planned costs (economic analysis of alternatives).

Remember, all of the pitfalls of new construction are present in the re-

E X H I B I T   3.4

Rehabilitation Budget Components

Permits—required building permits.

Electrical—wiring repairs or replacement (upgrading) inside walls as well as repairs or replacement of ceiling light fixtures, wall switches, and outlets.

Plumbing—piping and connection repairs or replacement inside walls as well as replacement of faucets, sinks or basins, bathtubs, toilets, etc.

Elevator—repairs or replacement (upgrading) of installation.

Heating system—repairs or replacement of furnace(s), air-conditioning unit(s), and distribution equipment (radiators, ductwork, etc.).

Foundation—repairs or other adjustments.

Roof—repairs or replacement.

Painting—surface preparation as well as materials and labor.

Windows—repairs or replacement of framing and glass as needed or outright installation of new windows.

Appliances—installation of new refrigerators and/or stoves as well as new additions (dishwasher, disposal, microwave oven).

Cabinets—repairs or replacement of existing cabinetry or installation of all new cabinets.

Carpeting—replacement of existing carpeting and/or preparation of floor for first-time installation.

Draperies/blinds—replacement or new installation of window coverings.

Materials—other construction materials and installations (may be components of contract bids for specific work).

Labor—construction and other labor.

Landscaping—clean up of lawn and plantings and/or design and installation of replacement lawn and plantings.

Parking lot—repair and restriping and/or paving of parking area.

Contingency—funds to cover needed work discovered in the course of rehabilitation preparation and/or construction.

Depending on the extent of the work to be done, allowance for architectural drawings may be needed. In addition, costs of "demolition" (tear out or removal of existing fixtures, drywall, tile, etc.) should be included. This list only addresses types of work. It may be more appropriate to differentiate common area expenses (foundation, roof, parking lot, etc.) from those specific to unit interiors. Not considered here are issues of environmental compliance and its attendant costs, which may be addressed as a separate line item or included in the contingency fund amount.

---

cycling process, and to them are added the uncertainties of discovery while the work is being done. The key difference is that new construction is building from scratch while rehabilitation is making corrections to something what was previously built and has deteriorated over a period of time. As a consequence, costs for each item in a rehabilitation are likely to be higher. A new roof is not just installed; the old roof must be removed and hauled away before the installation. Superficial problems with plumbing may or may not herald similar or worse problems inside the wall or floor. This is why it is so important to establish a contingency fund for the rehabilitation. If there is any reason to suspect more problems than are immediately apparent, additional money should be allocated in the rehabilitation budget.

In addition to the costs of the rehabilitation construction and other work, consideration has to be given to the carrying costs of the loan. (Financing the recycling process is covered in chapter 4.) Regardless of any income generated by the property, real estate taxes and mortgage interest will be due and payable as scheduled. As the amount of the loan increases with each release of construction funds, debt service requirements will escalate proportionately. In developing the documentation to apply for financing, it is imperative to consider not only the time frame for the physical work to correct existing deficiencies, but also the time it may take to change the perception of the property in the market. The latter issue should not be taken lightly. As has already been indicated, it will take longer to change the market perception than to alter the property. Caution is advised regarding estimates of time; they must be realistic. The rehabber's hopes and desires will not shorten the time one bit.

Impact of Change Orders.   Initial construction work should be monitored very closely. This is especially true of the work inside individual apartments. The first four or five completed units will essentially become prototypes for the rest of the project. They provide an opportunity to fine-tune methodologies and evaluate the results of the planning. The contractors themselves may suggest more efficient or more cost-effective means of performing the work.

When the first one or two units are completed, the following questions should be asked.

- Does this unit meet the criteria that the market dictated?
- If not, what changes have to be made—can be made—to meet those criteria?
- Will the changes measurably add to the costs?
- Can changes be made to save money?
- Although this opportunity for additional change may add to the construction costs, will it also enhance the marketability of the unit and/or increase the return on invested capital?

These questions relate to the economics of alternatives. All of them are valid, and some of them are likely to occur during any rehabilitation. An example from my own experience is presented below.

Inside the apartments, there was a small wing wall (mid-height room divider) between the kitchen and the living room. This had been specified for removal in an effort to make the units appear more spacious. The work would necessitate repairs to the drywall and the floor. After construction was started, someone suggested the possibility of not removing the wall but rather installing a countertop on it to create a built-in kitchen table. The idea appeared to have merit, so two prototype units were completed utilizing the tabletop concept. Prospective residents immediately opted for this built-in kitchen feature, and as a result, the construction specifications for this particular style of unit were altered to include tabletops. In this case, the built-in tabletop feature was something that would garner more rent as well as *reduce* construction costs because the tabletop cost less than the tear out and repair expense for removing the entire wing wall.

Such paybacks are not always the case because adjustment of the economics of alternatives is an ongoing process. Conceptual ideas are important, but they must be in harmony with market dictates, which are critical to the success of the rehabilitation.

The Economics of Alternatives

Analysis of the economics of alternatives looks at the changes to be made to a property from the perspective of their impact on rent (achievable increase) and return on invested capital (acceptable rate). Decisions regarding discretionary work require a positive impact on rent pricing to warrant their inclusion in the rehabilitation plan. Many physical things must be done to a property that cannot be measured in such an analysis. Examples of this nondiscretionary work are a new roof, boiler repair or replacement, or any item that is demanded by the market to lease an apartment or that is required under municipal code to correct existing violations. As noted earlier, these types of changes will not generate additional revenue.

The goal of rehabilitation is quite simple: *Maximize income with a minimum capital expenditure.* This does not mean using inferior products and workmanship to reduce costs. It is an evaluation of proposed improvements—either alone or in combination—that will maximize rents. For example, if the market analysis indicates that the majority of the better properties you want to compete with are providing 14.3-cubic-foot refrigerators, is it prudent to provide larger ones? The question is: If a 14.3-cubic-foot refrigerator sells for approximately $400 and a 16-cubic-foot refrigerator sells for $475, will the larger refrigerator return more rent? If refrigerator capacity is the only difference between apartments, the rehabber will get no more rent for having spent $75 additional on rehabilitating the apartment. In an earlier discussion of base cabinets in the kitchen, it was pointed out that the $35 difference in price between a cabinet with one drawer and one door and a cabinet with three drawers would not achieve any additional rent. These comparisons are requisite to an analysis of the economics of alternatives.

Sometimes a group of improvements must be considered. For example, it may be determined that the market indicates new kitchen cabinets, new kitchen appliances, and a new bathroom vanity are all in order, and the rehabber opts for those changes but decides not to replace the carpeting. In this case, optimum rent cannot be achieved for the unit—based on the market, and everything else being equal. Further exploration of the example may explain this. Suppose the rent for the apartment was $365 per month initially. Suppose further that, predicated on the market, the rent would be $465 per month after completion of all necessary cosmetic corrections on the building exterior and rehabilitation of the apartment interior, including the appliances and cabinets, fresh decorating, *and new carpeting.* Keeping the old carpeting in place diminishes the appearance of newness resulting from all the other changes.

Some additional assumptions can be made about what might increase the rent and provide a reasonable return on additional invested capital. Suppose a couple of competitors' offer all that you are offering and in addition include a dishwasher in the kitchen. Market analysis has revealed that the only difference between your newly rehabbed property and its competition is the dishwasher. Furthermore, rents at these competitive properties average $10 more per month for each unit. If a dishwasher costs $300 installed, and you are able to get $10 more rent per month as a result of adding the dishwasher, this one item represents a 40-percent return on invested capital ($120 per year ÷ $300 cost). It should be apparent that a 40-percent return on this incremental increase in invested capital justifies the expenditure.

Conversely, an additional item may *not* be worthwhile. Suppose no one in the competitive market offers microwave ovens. If a microwave oven can be purchased for $100 but there is no way, the rent can be increased an additional $2 or $3 per month to cover this investment, it would not be prudent to do so.

Sometimes it is advantageous to provide an additional low-cost amenity that makes your apartment superior to the market and will help you rent up even faster. Bear in mind, however, that when the rehabilitation is complete, *everything* on your property will be *new.* For this reason alone, *it will be superior to its competition.* That being the case, it may be wise to wait until there have been two or three turnovers in an apartment before adding this type of amenity, which could be paid for out of reserves at the later date.

There is nothing magical or scientific about analyzing the economics of alternatives. It is a trial-and-error process that computes the cost of adding an amenity or a group of amenities and measures the increase in rent that these amenities will bring. If an adequate return on investment is indicated, it is wise to add them. What is an adequate return? It is impossible to answer this question with any certainty because of differences in benefits from different amenities as well as differing expectations among investors. Other considerations such as long-term maintenance and eventual replacement of an item should not be ignored in this type of analysis. It is reasonable to assume, however, that if an 8-percent return can be achieved with safety, a significantly greater return than this will be needed to accommodate risk—at least an additional 5–10 percent. Every addition to the rehabilitation costs increases the amount of venture capital needed and, hence, increases the overall risk in the recycling process. (The issue of risk is discussed in more detail in the context of investment analysis in chapter 5.)

CHAPTER
4

Financing the
Recycling Process

Exhaustive market analysis and thorough evaluation of the real estate are fundamental to planning a rehabilitation, but financing is what makes it a reality. A real estate deal is nothing without financing. When a likely candidate for recycling has been identified, the decision to proceed with acquisition and rehabilitation must not only be accepted by the investors; it must be ratified by a lender. The climate for financing has changed radically. The savings and loan debacle as well as numerous bank failures have resulted in tighter controls on lending. A performing asset as the required basis for a loan, as opposed to a pro forma statement based on projections, is what makes rehabilitation loans extremely difficult to obtain.

The Market for Apartment Financing

Historically there have been numerous sources for financing investment in apartment properties. Savings and loan associations were interested in financing new construction as well as existing properties. Insurance companies and pension funds were next in line, while commercial banks had been strong sources for construction loans but not for permanent financing.

In the past, the analysis required for underwriting loans on multifamily properties was directly proportional to the amount of money that a lender had available for permanent loans. However, growing numbers of nonperforming loans and increasing government review have led to changes in the underwriting process. Today loans are evaluated on a strictly economic basis—i.e., the property must be able to support the loan being sought. That this must be accomplished *without* a tax write-off is a consequence of the Tax Reform Act of 1986. Previously, the real estate market had been stimulated by tax advantages written into the Economic Recovery Tax Act (ERTA) of 1981, which was passed to stimulate recovery from the recession of the late 1970s. In that environment, many developers believed the combination of tax advantages and inflation was here to stay—there was less emphasis on market analysis and the economic strength of a property and more emphasis on tax advantages and the certainty that inflation would bail out even a marginal deal.

Real estate cycles dictate the types of construction and financing that are prevalent at a given time (exhibit 4.1). Problems come to the surface when inflation is very low or nonexistent. Yet it is virtually impossible to stop a project that is already under way, even if economic changes suggest otherwise. Once construction financing is in place, a development has to move forward in order to make its payroll and generate a profit for the developer. The result is overbuilding. Even on a fast track, it is rare to complete a project from land acquisition through construction to lease-up in less than three years. Once the process has been started, the deal acquires a life of its own and continues regardless. When added to the fact that real estate is one of the last bastions of pure competition, a cyclical progression is inevitable. Once a segment of the real estate market is overbuilt, development of new rental space (apartments, offices, store space) will remain static until demand catches up with supply.

The point of all this is that there will always be areas of the United States where one segment or another of the real estate market is overbuilt (i.e., supply exceeds demand) as well as areas where demand is greater than the existing supply. The key to successful apartment recycling is analysis of every deal based solely on its economic viability. Just as investors will look for quantity, quality, and durability of income, so will the lender.

There is nothing magical about apartment financing. If thorough analysis indicates that a property is economically stable and viable, there will be a lender to finance investment in it. However, lenders prefer that the borrower also has equity or capital at risk in the deal. That way both the borrower and the lender have something to lose—if the borrower has the potential for loss, the risk to the lender is reduced.

In addition, as part of the loan application, lenders require prospective borrowers to provide a substantial amount of information about their business and personal finances and about the property to be purchased. When the borrower is a business entity and more than one individual is involved (e.g., a partnership or corporation), certain information is typically required from all of the principal participants. Exhibit 4.2 lists the kinds of documents we have been asked to submit; the lender's list was very specific as to what information was required and when it was to be submitted.

EXHIBIT   4.1

Real Estate Cycles

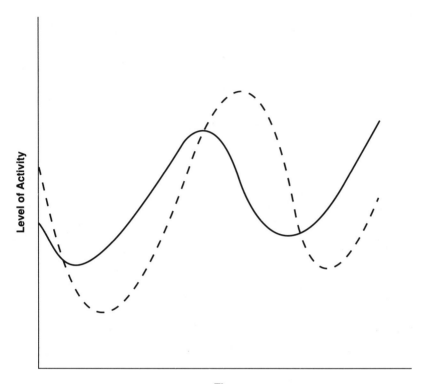

The real estate cycle (broken line) follows the business cycle (solid line). Slowing business activity (a downward slope of the solid line) is characteristic of a period of recession; in the real estate cycle, new construction declines as a result of overbuilding (a peak in the broken line) and leads to a period of adjustment during which occupancy declines and rent concessions are widespread. A deep trough indicates depression; in real estate, occupancy and rents are severely reduced. An upward slope signals beginning growth or recovery; in the real estate cycle, this reflects accelerated demand for rental space and increased new construction. The business cycle culminates in prosperity (the peak in the solid line) which leads in real estate to new levels of overbuilding.

Illustration reproduced with permission from *Principles of Real Estate Management, Thirteenth Edition* (Chicago: Institute of Real Estate Management, 1991).

E X H I B I T   4.2

Loan Application Documents

1. Loan application form (e.g., Multifamily Loan Application, FNMA form 1053).
2. Copies of executed documents related to the borrower's intended form of ownership (e.g., partnership agreement identifying general partners and/or guarantors, articles of incorporation, sole proprietorship).
3. A schedule of real estate investments, including a cash flow analysis showing current income and expenses, original loan balance(s), current loan balance(s), current lender(s), and lender's contact(s) for each investment property owned by the borrower and/or principal participants.
4. Current financial statement (last 90 days) and income tax returns (last 3 years) for the borrower and/or principal participants.
5. Verification of deposits for each bank account or other holding listed in the financial statement(s).
6. Credit references, personal and/or professional (including contact, title, company name, address, and phone number).
7. Statement of experience (owning, managing, or building income properties) for the borrower and/or principal participants.
8. Certification of previous multifamily and real estate investment experience, including a list of multifamily and commercial properties in which the borrower (and/or principal participants) participated as a Principal in the past 10 years, indicating that no defaults, foreclosures, or deed-in-lieu of foreclosures have occurred on the listed properties. (Attach explanation of each default.)
9. Credit reports (usually ordered by lender on borrower and/or principal participants).
10. Loan payment history/mortgage verification for the subject property (name and address of lien holder and loan number) as well as any other properties owned by the borrower and/or principal participants.
11. Property operating statements for the past three years and the current year-to-date plus a pro forma for the next full year for the subject property.
12. A certified current rent schedule, including unit number, unit type, resident name, current rent, street rent, and lease commencement and expiration dates—signed by both management agent and borrower (and/or principal participants).
13. Delinquency report indicating residents whose rents are 30, 60, and 90 or more days past due, including the amount of each delinquency.
14. Occupancy history of the subject property for the last 12 months.
15. A management plan for operating the subject property (marketing and maintenance programs, resident application screening policies, etc.).

Loan Terms.   Although there are exceptions, the maximum loan amount commonly available for financing an apartment property is 80 percent of its purchase price or appraised value (loan-to-value ratio), and a minimum debt coverage ratio of 1.2 is required. Such a *takeout or permanent loan* is usually contingent on a stabilized, performing operation. The loan-to-value (LTV) ratio is a measure of the lender's risk of loss. The debt coverage ratio (annual NOI divided by the annual total payment of principal plus interest) reflects

E X H I B I T   4.2 (*continued*)

16. Management resume profiling the managing agent's multifamily experi-ence—previously and at the subject location with the existing resident profile.
17. A copy of an executed management agreement that specifies the term and compensation.
18. A copy of a current, valid, executed lease.
19. Copies of vendor contracts.
20. A list of site personnel with their resumes (including duration of employment and compensation).
21. Certificates of occupancy as required by local jurisdiction—per building or per unit. (If certificates of occupancy are not issued, lender may require a signed letter from an appropriate official defining the local practice and verifying that there are no known building code violations.)
22. A copy of the entire current property insurance policy and the paid receipt. (Lender may specify additional or different insurance coverages as part of the loan agreement.)
23. A letter from the municipality stating that the subject improvements may be rebuilt to current density if they are damaged or destroyed.
24. Copies of real estate tax bills and water/sewer bills for the past three years.
25. Copies of utility bills for the past three years.
26. Tax account number and tax jurisdiction for the subject property (needed by appraiser).
27. Title insurance for the property naming the lender as mortgagee (needed by surveyor).
28. A survey showing all easements on or affecting the subject property, appropriately certified (needed by appraiser).
29. Aerial photograph of the property (2 copies).
30. A schedule of capital improvements (significant capital expenditures) for the period covered by the operating statements in item #11.
31. List of professional services utilized by the borrower—attorney(s), accountant(s), in-surance agent(s), etc.
32. A statement of intended use of the loan proceeds.

The foregoing list is not intended to be all-inclusive; it is representative of the kinds of information we have been required to provide. Note that a particular lender may have more extensive or different re-quirements based on its policies and practices, the particulars of the property, and the amount and terms of the loan. If the property is located in a jurisdiction with *rent control*, a copy of the rent control law may be required. Other documentation commonly required "as necessary or appropriate" includes a copy of any site or building plans, a copy of an executed ground lease, and a copy of the sales agreement if the property was purchased within the recent past (e.g., three years).

the amount of debt service that can be carried. This may seem overly simplis-tic, but it is not. Acquiring financing today is quite straightforward. You have to shop around to find the best terms for your financing needs. Apart from willingness to make a loan on a particular property, there are several other considerations that will affect your selection of a particular lender.

- The amortization term—the number of years during which principal and interest payments are to be made.

- The interest rate—the specific percentage *and* whether it is fixed or adjustable.
- The number of points to be paid—one point equals one percent of the loan amount.
- The amount of the application fee.
- Whether the loan is recourse or nonrecourse—if the borrower is personally liable for the loan or if the lender can only foreclose on the property that secures the loan.
- Whether there is a penalty for early repayment.

Ownership of the bank may be a consideration, too, especially if the local bank in a small community has been bought out. Often the new owner is a large institution from another state. Such out-of-town owners may require loan decisions to be reviewed and approved by their home offices, far removed from local issues and personalities. The ideal situation is one in which the borrower can talk face-to-face with a loan officer who knows the local community and the particular property—and who will want to know the borrower on a personal level.

One of the best loans available in recent years is the delegated underwriting and servicing (DUS) loan underwritten by Fannie Mae. The advantages are that this loan is nonrecourse and it provides for a long amortization period (30 years for properties more than 10 years old; 25 years for properties 10 years old or younger) at market-accepted, fixed rates and with minimum points. The disadvantage is that there is a sizeable penalty for early payment because this type of loan is sold on the bond market. (The Federal National Mortgage Association—Fannie Mae—operates secondary mortgage markets, buying FHA, VA, and conventional loans at auction and issuing mortgage-backed securities which are traded on the open market.)

Because this book deals with conventional housing, no consideration has been given to federal- or state-supported loans that may require renting a certain percentage of the units to low- or moderate-income households. However, for a property located in a neighborhood in transition, this type of loan might be considered as a way to enhance income while the negative neighborhood perceptions are being changed. Such a loan might be underwritten by a local commercial bank that has made a commitment to financing projects under the Community Reinvestment Act.

The Attitudes of Lenders.   The most logical source for a rehabilitation loan would be a commercial bank, either by itself or in conjunction with a community reinvestment organization. Such organizations and the Community Reinvestment Act have prompted commercial banks to look at rehabilitation more favorably. New construction has always seemed to be less problematic for a commercial bank to underwrite. The primary reason for this is that there are fewer contingencies and unknowns in new construction. As indicated in the preceding chapter, it is often difficult to know how much correction must be made to physically cure the defects in a property, and this uncertainty has been a great impediment to financing apartment rehabilitation.

The lender must be convinced that a loan for a rehabilitation project is less of a risk than one for new construction—i.e., because the total investment in the rehab candidate is comparatively smaller. This depends, of course, on the basis for comparison. It is very difficult to establish specific per-unit costs for new apartment construction that are *appropriate* for comparison with a rehabilitation project because differences in location (region) and target market are major factors in determining these costs. A new property being built in an upscale neighborhood with the intent of attracting upscale renters will incur higher construction costs because of larger unit sizes and inclusion of all the additional features and amenities appropriate to that market niche. However, apartment recycling is generally *not* an upscale venture. A hypothetical situation should make the point.

Suppose a new property is being designed to attract middle-income renters—its rents are in the range of $450–$600 per month. One-bedroom apartments will be between 600 and 650 square feet in area, and two-bedroom units around 750–800 square feet. Each apartment would include carpeting and a full kitchen with a stove and refrigerator—and possibly a dishwasher and disposal. Amenities might include a small clubhouse and a swimming pool, but there would be no sheltered parking. Using such a basis, construction costs, including land, might average $38,000–$45,000 per unit. In the same general locale, an existing property that is currently suffering from mismanagement and physical neglect might be reasonably assumed to have an acquisition price ranging between $10,000 and $20,000 per unit. [NOTE: The prices stated here are suggested averages and not a suitable basis for comparison of specific properties being considered for rehabilitation.]

As can be seen from this hypothetical example, a property in need of rehabilitation can probably be acquired for one-fourth to one-half of the cost of new construction. The rehabilitation must be factored into the equation, of course, but even if rehabilitation costs will run between $5,000 and $6,000 per unit (this figure presumably includes common area corrections), the differential is still great. Using the high-end figures cited here, it would cost $4.5 million for a 100-unit building constructed new, while acquisition and rehabilitation of an existing building of the same size would be only $2.6 million (less than sixty percent of the new construction cost).

What does this mean in terms of the economic analysis? It means the rents that ultimately must be charged in order to provide a reasonable return to the investor will be significantly lower. It also stands to reason that there will be greater demand for a property that offers amenities similar to those of new construction and is itself new in many ways.

This is what must be stressed to a prospective lender. The lender does not have the same risk-reward goal as the entrepreneur whose view is, the greater the risk, the greater the reward. The lender is renting money to the entrepreneur so that the property can be acquired and rehabilitated. The lender's goal is to receive a finite return on the amount of the loan over a very specific period of time; the risk to the lender is that the money will not be paid back. Therefore, the lender must be convinced that a particular property can be rehabilitated and achieve higher rents within a specific time period. The lender should be able to agree that the risk is worth taking. This is not to suggest that a rehabilitated property will compete directly with a new one. However, a rehabbed property will have a broader spectrum of potential renters because its monthly rents will be considerably lower than those in a newly constructed building. The niche for the older, rehabilitated property will ultimately be the strongest argument you can make to a lender who is hesitant about financing a rehabilitation.

Two other issues that seem to work against rehabilitation of older properties are uncertainty and the time required. The uncertainty is related to exactly what construction will be required because the rehabilitation is being done to an existing building. Once the process is under way, it is very likely that some areas will require additional remedial work that was not part of the original rehabilitation budget. This is why exploratory tear out and expenditure of a small amount of money during the due diligence process usually pays off well. Not only will the purchaser have a better understanding of the real estate and its rehabilitation needs, but the prospective lender will have greater assurance that the rehabilitation budget has been thoroughly planned and analyzed and that possible contingencies have at least been considered. (A reasonable amount should be included in the rehabilitation budget for contingencies to provide a safety net for both the rehabber and the lender.)

The time requirement is likely to be the most difficult point to sell to the lender. The rehabber has to have a firm idea of how long it will take to complete the rehabilitation and rerenting and then to attain a stabilized NOI so the property can be refinanced. To accept a *construction loan* for acquisition and rehabilitation for a period of only one year is to flirt with disaster. In apartment recycling, there is a substantial difference between physical change and perceived change. The main difference between a construction loan for new development and one for rehabilitation is the time required to achieve the goal. New construction generates excitement and anticipation; as it nears completion, there is already substantial interest in the property. A rehabilitation, on the other hand, has to effect changes, not only physically to the property but also perceptually in the market. For new construction, a lender might project six months to build, six months to rent up, and six more months to achieve a stabilized income and, on that basis, offer an eighteen-

---

Types of Financing

Construction Loan Money borrowed on an interim or temporary basis to finance construction—including rehabilitation. Because of the greater risk involved, interest rates are higher than for long-term financing. Funds are released as work is completed *(periodic construction draws),* and the loan is repaid out of the funds obtained for permanent financing.

Minipermanent Loan A short-term (3–5 years) interest-only income property mortgage, usually made in conjunction with a construction loan, used when long-term permanent financing cannot yet be supported by the property's cash flow; also called *miniperm loan.*

Permanent Loan A long-term (10 or more years) loan used to finance the acquisition of an existing property or to replace a construction loan for new development or rehabilitation; also called a *takeout loan*—a mortgage. The loan is repaid *(amortized)* in equal periodic installments by which the principal is paid down to zero at the end of a fixed period and interest is accrued on the outstanding balance.

---

month construction loan. For a rehab project, construction will likely take much longer than six months because of having to work around existing residents and, in some cases, wait until leases expire and create new vacancies. It stands to reason, then, that one year, and often longer, is more realistic for the construction period for a rehabilitation. The metamorphosis in how it is perceived will still be taking place after the rehabilitation has been completed. Once the property has successfully achieved a new image (market perception), it will take additional time to stabilize its rental income. From this rather simplified discussion, it can be argued that if new construction would be given one and one-half years before permanent financing could be sought, a rehabilitation project will require at least two and a half years to reach that same point. The time required to accomplish the perception change will depend on how negative the perception is at the start. The more negative the market perception, the more time required to overcome it.

This is the particular point that must be made to the lender. The only way a lender is likely to consider an extended period for a construction loan is if your market analysis is detailed, complete, and convincing. Once the construction has been completed, extending the repayment period tends to make lenders quite nervous. The toughest sell of all will be convincing the lender to extend the term of a rehabilitation loan long enough to provide the rehabber with a safety net because there is no definitive way to determine how long it will take to change the market perception of the property. On the other hand, great strides have been made regarding rehabilitation loans. Lenders today sometimes offer a minipermanent or *miniperm loan.* This is an interest-only income property mortgage that is used because a longer-term permanent loan is not yet supportable by the property's cash flow. It is usually made in conjunction with a construction loan and usually has a term of three to five years.

The Costs of Financing.   A construction or rehabilitation loan will cost more than a permanent loan in the same market situation for several reasons. Because the property is being altered, the short-term risk is greater, and this requires a greater yield to the lender through higher interest rates. The higher rates also provide an incentive to the rehabber to stabilize the income and refinance the property as soon as possible.

While it is important to provide adequately for construction costs in the rehabilitation budget and allow for contingencies, there is a downside to this approach. The lender will charge you points on the gross amount of the construction loan commitment—any funds not used will still require the payment of points up front. I would argue, however, that this is the most inexpensive insurance you can have. Budgeting for the downside helps to protect the upside of an investment.

Although it is not impossible to finance a rehabilitation by itself, this is not done often if at all. Assuming you already own a property, such a rehabilitation loan would create a second mortgage (the amount outstanding from the acquisition loan would be primary). Because no lender wants to be in a secondary position, it is common practice to refinance the outstanding debt along with the required rehabilitation. Thus, if a property has debt amounting to $3 million and rehabilitating it will cost $1 million, the rehabber would need to borrow $4 million. Here the loan-to-value (LTV) ratio becomes all important. The property must be appraised to determine its value both as is and after the proposed rehabilitation. In most cases, lenders will provide financing based on an 80-percent LTV ratio. Because value is being created in the process of the rehabilitation, the LTV ratio is applied to the *value as completed.* From the lender's standpoint, the most important condition during the loan period is that debt is to be serviced from the NOI, and any shortfall will be paid out of the construction loan, which increases the indebtedness. This is an important consideration because lenders will not allow the owner of the real estate to extract any cash from the property during the construction period. This, of course, puts pressure on the borrower to complete the rehabilitation and bring the property to a stabilized condition as rapidly as possible. Because there will be no return to the investors until the property has been refinanced, the sooner the property is refinanced, the sooner the positive effects of the time value of money will occur. All of these reasons encourage the rehabber to complete the recycling process as soon as possible.

The source of the property can sometimes impact the costs of financing. A lender who is holding a property as a nonperforming asset may be willing to negotiate favorable loan terms in order to return the property to a performing mode. A wide array of factors contributes to a lender's decision not to follow its *standard underwriting procedures* for determining the risks in a given loan and setting an appropriate rate and term. I recommend performing all your own financial analyses based on the assumption that, for any loan you obtain, the lender's standard underwriting practices will prevail. Any exceptions to this rule should be viewed as a bonus.

Lender Relations

Once financing has been obtained, regular communication between borrower and lender is critical. Uncertainty breeds fear—it is important for the lender to feel comfortable about the loan and the borrower. The plan you prepared as the blueprint for the rehabilitation should be followed, and your progress should be reported periodically. Communication can be in the form of a telephone call or a face-to-face meeting—the relationship established during the loan negotiations will probably set the tone for how formal (or informal) this has to be. At a minimum, the schedule for disbursement of funds by the lender will require inspection and progress reports to justify each payout. Disbursement of funds when certain amounts of work have been completed is typical of both new construction and rehabilitation. While release of funds for new construction may be tied to specific stages of the process (e.g., completion of 50 percent of the concrete work), rehabilitation funds may be disbursed on a more flexible schedule (e.g., a certain percentage of the loan may be released each month). The disbursement schedule (draw requests) will be negotiated between borrower and lender and spelled out in the loan commitment documents; the timing of releases should be coordinated with the construction schedule.

I believe the key to enhancing lender relations is to go beyond what is required and establish regular monthly communications regardless of the draw schedule. Very few lenders make loans based solely on character any longer, but there is no question that a proven track record is important for a continuing relationship with a particular lender. In my own case, it was much easier to arrange repeat business once we had established a track record with a lender.

No one likes surprises, least of all lenders, and no one wants to tell a lender anything that is negative as long as the loan is performing as agreed. However, early warning of any changed circumstances—problems or successes—should enhance a loan officer's level of comfort regarding a particular borrower and a specific property.

Good lender relations are fostered by regular communication. Rehabilitation construction is most often undertaken with residents living on the property. In such a situation, some rental income is being generated, but it may not cover all of the current operating expenses, let alone any existing debt service requirements. During the physical construction stage, all of the shortfall must be covered by the rehabilitation loan. This should have been expected and included in the rehabilitation budget. Meanwhile, it may become apparent that the perception change is not taking place as rapidly as had been planned from the market analysis. This is something that should be communicated to the lender.

Another type of difficulty arises when there are problems with the construction. Sometimes a construction problem requires a solution that was not part of the original rehabilitation agreement. In such a situation, I recommend that you determine the best solution to the problem and inform the lender—even before steps are taken to correct the problem. Some minor changes might be allowable under your loan agreement. If small problems and their solutions are presented to the lender immediately, you will be in a much better position to negotiate approval of an exception to the loan document if a large problem arises.

The success of your rerenting program is another subject for regular communication. You may discover that the negative market perception was somewhat overstated initially and, in fact, the property is renting faster than anticipated. In such a situation it is certainly wise to inform the lender of the property's success. This will increase the lender's level of comfort. Conversely, if the marketing effort is not moving as fast as was projected, it is wise to let the lender know immediately. Some people might advise against this. (Why bring up a problem if it has no effect on the loan today?) The fact is, however, that the problem could become bigger as time goes by, and informing the lender early may allow the borrower to work out a contingency plan if it becomes necessary.

These examples are not meant to imply a desire to amend the loan agreement by extending it or making other changes "as needed." The construction loan agreement is a binding contract, and the borrower is obligated to comply with it. However, exceptional situations do arise, and that is why contingencies are anticipated, at least broadly. Completion of the rehab construction does not guarantee rental income, which is the basis for permanent financing. Good lender relations can provide opportunities to work things out amicably and in everyone's best interests. For example, we were recently able to extend a construction loan for three months with no penalty and no additional interest because the takeout lender required two more months of stabilized income before making a permanent loan. This probably never would have happened—certainly it would not have happened as easily—if we had not already established a good relationship (i.e., communication link) with the rehabilitation lender.

The Role of the Title Company

Disbursement of loan proceeds can be effected in several ways. The borrower may be required to document construction costs and amounts expended as well as the percentage completion of the work—including certification of that information from the general contractor and/or architect—as part of a request for the lender to advance loan funds. (An example of a draw request format I have used is shown in exhibits 4.3a and 4.3b; a complete list of contractors and contract amounts is typically included.) In addition, the request must be consistent with the rehabilitation budget. Usually, the lender has a title company handle the disbursements, and release of the funds may be subject to the lender's right of inspection to verify construction progress.

There are advantages and disadvantages to this arrangement. In the first place, if a title company prepares the checks for the construction draws there will be a fee for this service. There is no question that some control is lost by the borrower if an outside party is preparing the draw checks. Also, assuming there is a specific day on which contractors get paid, if the person who prepares the checks at the title company is sick or on vacation, the checks could be delayed a day or two. Small contractors in particular may have problems if they have to wait for their money. On the other hand, the rehabber may pay the contractors directly and then request a draw for reimbursement. Regardless of who prepares the draw checks, an inspection by the lender or the lender's representative must be made *before* the funds will be released.

The key issue in construction draws is the collection of *lien waivers*—signed statements that the contractor has received payment for work done and therefore relinquishes any claims against the property. In recycling apartments, we have dealt with many small contractors. (When a general contractor is utilized, payment is made directly to the general contractor who is then responsible for paying the various subcontractors.) If the contractors are not paid, they are in a position to file a lien against the property for the value of their work (materials and labor). Such a *mechanic's lien* becomes an encumbrance that must be satisfied (removed) before construction funds can be released or permanent financing can be obtained. Therefore, all contractors should be required to sign a "waiver of lien" at the time they receive payment for work performed or beforehand (example forms are shown in exhibits 4.4 and 4.5). If the appropriate lien waivers are not obtained, the borrower normally must obtain a cash bond for 150 percent of the amount of the lien.

The advantage of using a title company is that it provides for continual review of the title status of the property, which is an additional protection for the lender. The title company also assumes responsibility for reviewing the lien waivers and authenticating them prior to releasing the draw checks. (Alternatively, the borrower will have to do this.) When negotiating a rehabilitation loan, you may not consider the lender's selection of the title company for preparation of the draw checks to be an important issue. However, you should make it your business to know (or try to find out) how the selected title company works. If you have any concerns about the arrangement, you can ask the lender to use a different service.

Here again, communication is key. Spending time with the title officer or

E X H I B I T   4.3a

Sample Format for Construction Draw Requests

OWNER'S SWORN STATEMENT

[Identification of State and County/Indication of Draw Number]

The Affiant, *[Insert Name(s) and Title(s) of Responsible Person(s), Name of Business Entity, and Ownership Form]*, being first duly sworn on oath deposes that they are the owners of the premises described in *[Insert Appropriate Site Identification]* and commonly known as *[Insert Property Name and Address]*.

That for the purposes of this affidavit, the following persons and no others have been contracted with, or have furnished or will furnish materials for, or have furnished, or will furnish equipment for, or have furnished or will furnish labor for said improvements. That this is a true and correct statement of all such persons, the amounts of their contracts, the amounts paid them, and the amount due them and of all hard costs and soft costs in connection with said improvements.

Name	Address	Index	Contract Amt	Previously Paid	This Request	Balance Due
ABC Construction Mgmt		Construction Mgmt				
1st National Bank		1st Mortgage Lender				
Anytown Finance		Lender Points				
Anytown Insurance		Insurance				
ABC Attorneys at Law		Atty for Borrower				
XYZ Trust Company		Trust Fees				
ABC County Assessor		Real Estate Taxes				
Operating Reserve						
TOTAL PROJECT COST:						

Signed this _____ day of _____, 19____
Subscribed and sworn before me this _____day of _____, 19____

[Insert Name of Business Entity and Ownership Form]

By: _____
[Insert Name(s) and Title(s) of Responsible Person(s)]

_____
[Signature (and Seal) of Notary Public]

Exhibits 4.3a and 4.3b are typical of statements prepared for draws on properties we have rehabbed. The first form is used to identify amounts paid for services *related to* the construction. The form in 4.3b is used to track specific construction work by type and cost; the accumulated totals are spelled out in the two-column box below the table. The lender (or title company) may specify the form to be followed for draw requests against a specific loan or for a particular project. Note that certification of completed work by a licensed architect may require use of a standard form—e.g., Application and Certification for Payment, AIA Documents G702 and G703 (2 pages), available from the American Institute of Architects.

E X H I B I T   4.3b

Sample Format for Construction Draw Requests

APPLICATION FOR PAYMENT AND SWORN STATEMENT FOR CONTRACTOR

[Insert Property Name and Location]   Payment Application #_____

Period_____

Contractor	Work/Materials	Adjusted Total Contract	%	Work Completed/ Materials	Total Retained	Previously Paid	Amount Requested	Balance to Become Due

Amount of Original Contract		Work Completed to Date	
Extras to Contract		Total Retained	
Total Contract & Extras		Net Amount Earned	
Credits to Contract		Previously Paid	
Adjusted Total Contract		Net Amount Due This Payment	

[Identification of State and County]

The undersigned, *[Insert Name of Responsible Person]*, being duly sworn, on oath deposes and says that he/she is *[Insert Title and Company Name]*, Contractor for the Renovation for the following project: *[Insert name and Address of Property]*.

That for the purpose of this work the foregoing orders have been placed and the foregoing parties subcontracted with and these have furnished materials or have provided labor or both for said project.

That the amount of such order or subcontract is as stated above and that there is due and to become due them respectively the amounts put opposite their names or materials or labor or both.

That this statement is made in compliance with the statutes relating to Mechanics' Liens and for the purpose of procuring from the Owner final/partial payment in accordance with the terms of the contract and is a full, true and complete Statement of all parties furnishing labor and/or materials, and of the amounts paid, due and to become due them.

Subscribed and sworn before me this _____day of _____, 19___

Signed _____
     [Signature (and Seal) of Notary Public]

Signed _____
     [Signature of Responsible Person]

E X H I B I T   4.4

Example Lien Waiver Form—Unconditional Waiver

The undersigned has been paid and has received a progress payment in the amount of $_____ for labor, services, equipment, or material furnished to *[Name of Property Owner or Authorized Signer]* on the job of *[Name or Description of Specific Job]* located at *[Street Address, City, State]* and does hereby release immediately any mechanic's lien, stop notice, or bond right the undersigned has on the above-referenced job to the following extent. This release covers a progress payment for labor, services, equipment, or material furnished to *[Name of Property Owner or Authorized Signer]* through *[Date: Month, Day, Year]* only and does not cover any retention of items furnished after that date.

Date: _____   *[Name of Construction Company*
                                        or Individual Contractor]

                                      By _____
                                      [Name and Title of Signer]

NOTICE: This document waives rights unconditionally and states that the construction company or individual contractor has been paid for giving up those rights. This document is enforceable against the signatory if it is signed, even if payment has not been made. A Conditional Release Form should be used if payment has not been received.

This form is provided as an example only. It should *not* be used unless payment in full has been received for all work completed to date, including final payment for the job as a whole. Note that advice of legal counsel should be sought regarding applicability of any such form in a particular state. (R. S. Means Company is a potential source for a standard form for Waiver of Lien, Material or Labor.)

Courtesy of Peacock Construction, Inc., Lafayette, California.

---

other person responsible for the draw process at the beginning can save much time and aggravation later. Also, you will be able to tell contractors exactly how and when they will be paid, and your own staff will know how to schedule this essential activity.

Refinancing following Rehabilitation

Typically, a construction (rehabilitation) loan is contingent on a commitment for permanent financing after the work is completed. However, permanent or takeout financing is itself contingent on the property being able to generate sufficient income. If the property has not reached a new level of income stabilization, takeout financing will not be available, and the rehabilitation loan could go into technical default. What puts real pressure on borrowers is that such loans are based on performing assets (ability to repay debt), not pro forma operating statements. The rules are really quite simple—lenders want to see occupancy at a stabilized 95 percent for six months. In the past, lenders would accept a trending of rents—the prospective borrower would be allowed to take the highest rent achieved thus far for a particular unit type

EXHIBIT   4.5

Example Lien Waiver Form—Conditional Waiver

Upon receipt by the undersigned of a check from *[Name of Property Owner or Authorized Signatory]* in the amount of $_____ payable to *[Name of Construction Company or Individual Contractor]*, and when the check has been properly endorsed and has been paid by the bank upon which it is drawn, this document shall become effective to release immediately any mechanic's lien, stop notice, or bond right the undersigned has on the job of *[Name or Description of Specific Job]* located at *[Street Address, City, State]* to the following extent. This release covers a progress payment for labor, services, equipment, or material furnished to *[Name of Property Owner or Authorized Signatory]* through *[Date: Month, Day, Year]* only and does not cover any retention of items furnished after said date. Before any recipient of this document relies on it, said party should verify evidence of payment to the undersigned.

Date:_____   *[Name of Construction Company*
                                 or Individual Contractor]

                              By_____
                                 [Name and Title of Signer]

This form is provided as an example only. It would be used to obtain a waiver *before* a progress payment is issued. A series of payments may create a series of such conditional waivers. Once a prior payment has cleared the issuing bank, an "unconditional" waiver may be submitted to the property owner or authorized signer. Note that advice of legal counsel should be sought regarding applicability of any such form in a particular state.

Courtesy of Peacock Construction, Inc., Lafayette, California.

---

and assign that rent to each similar unit as its lease expired. As underwriting has been tightened up, such trending is no longer acceptable. Today, lenders take the position that the rent is what it is. A lender is going to take the rent roll as it is in your best month of the stabilization period. (In our experience, this has tended to be the sixth month.) Occupancy itself only affects real dollars in terms of how many units are occupied. The question that remains is how much rent is actually being collected.

Planning for the stabilization period should begin at the start-up of the rehabilitation. When the first unit has been completed and is ready for occupancy, the rent established for that unit at that point in time will set the standard for the rents for the remainder of the rehabilitation activity and throughout the stabilization period. In other words, once you have determined that the property has been changed sufficiently, not only physically but in terms of how it is perceived by the market, the first new rental rate will be the trendsetter. Regardless of whether the unit is an efficiency or a one-, two-, or three-bedroom apartment, its rent will be the basis for all the remaining rents.

The effect of rent on subsequent lease renewals should also be considered in the planning stages. After the first year of remarketing, you will be faced with renewals. If you cannot retain the newly acquired residents, you are also putting the potential for referrals at risk. (Third-party testimonials and referrals from existing residents are what dispel negative perceptions and foster acceptance in the market.)

If a significant number of the new occupants do not renew their leases because you have increased the rent too much, the newness of the property as it is perceived by the renting public will quickly dissipate. On the other hand, if you set your initial rent too low, you will not be able to raise it to a substantially higher level during the stabilization period. This is why it is important to delay remarketing until you can charge—and receive—a higher rent. There is no question that this delay will increase the income shortfall, but that additional shortfall will be recouped through the higher rents after remarketing is begun. The best advise is, take care not to market too soon. (Timing the marketing effort is discussed in detail in chapter 6.)

Permanent financing requires scrutiny of operating expenses as well as income. In the first place, an objective of the rehabilitation should be more-efficient maintenance leading to a reduction in operating expenses. For example, one of the best methods of reducing utility costs is to have submeters installed for each unit (or provide for totally independent metering). You need to be aware of how utilities are handled locally; current practices in a particular market may or may not favor such a move. If submetering can be done, the installation would be a rehabilitation cost, and the return on the investment would be manifested as a reduction in the utility costs absorbed by the property.

On the other hand, it is very important to distinguish between operating expenses and rehabilitation costs. It may be prudent to regard certain rehabilitation work as "maintenance" when such categorization may preclude the need for construction permits. This is often acceptable for replacement of existing fixtures, as was pointed out in the preceding chapter on rehabilitation planning. However, the costs of all materials and labor for the rehabilitation should be budgeted and accounted as rehab expenses. Similarly, none of the property operating expenses should be accounted as rehabilitation costs. Even if this can be justified, it only leads to problems later; when the rehabilitation has been completed, all operating expenses will have to be paid out of operating income, and this will lead to disparities in the expense portion of the operating statement. When a lender begins to review operating records for the previous year, such variances could be most embarrassing.

Unrealistic numbers not only skew the performance record of the property, but also paint a false picture of its capacity to repay a permanent loan. In the future, real estate investments will be based solely on the economics of the deal—real income minus real expenses equalling real NOI. The rehabber should want to use real numbers because they are what will prevail after the refinancing is in place.

Once a stabilized NOI has been achieved, the loan terms that can be arranged are relatively straightforward. As was indicated at the beginning of this chapter, lenders will typically look for a loan-to-value ratio of 80 percent and a debt coverage ratio of 1.2. Apart from these factors, the amortization term, the interest rate, the points, the application fee, penalties for prepayment, and whether the loan will be recourse or nonrecourse will differ with different lenders. Granted, some of these additional issues are important. However, regardless of the specific terms, the amount of the loan will be predicated on NOI that is accurate and stabilized.

There will also be a requirement to establish and maintain a capital reserve fund. Most borrowers tend to negotiate for the highest possible mortgage loan and the smallest capital reserve deposit. I believe this is counterproductive, particularly if the investment is to be held for long-term growth and appreciation. If the term of the permanent loan is between five and ten years, it is reasonable to assume that ongoing capital improvements will have to be made to the property to maintain the viability and durability of the income stream that the rehabilitation generated. This is not to say that reserves should be set aside for every potential item. Typically a certain amount will be deposited out of the proceeds of the takeout loan, and subsequently a set amount per unit will be paid each month into a capital reserve account maintained and controlled by the lender. It is important when negotiating for the loan, however, that specific items you know will require capital expenditures (e.g., additional improvements) are written into the capital reserve agreement. If the loan is taken to the maximum and therefore the monthly principal and interest payments are at the maximum, and in addition there is a large reserve account requiring monthly payments that are high, there will be much less cash flow from the property. Taking all the money at the time of refinancing and having little money on an ongoing basis is poor business and greatly increases your risk. This is why it is desirable to strike a balance between the amount of the loan and the amount of the capital reserve requirement.

The last question that remains is how soon should a property be refinanced following rehabilitation. The answer is, almost without exception, as soon as possible. Even if the financing market is not as advantageous as would be desired, no one can have assurance that it will change for the better during the window of opportunity that you have for refinancing. I would argue further that a conservative approach is best. You should begin looking for a lender as soon as the property has reached stabilization. To look earlier is something of an exercise in futility; lenders will not be willing to discuss refinancing until they believe the property is viable.

Analyzing the Investment

Analysis of the investment is the culmination of all your investigations. Having found a property that meets all of your physical requirements and determined the availability and likely terms of financing it, you are now ready to analyze it financially. Because there may be several possible approaches to recycling a particular property, the objective of this exercise is to determine which alternative will maximize the investment return and thereby generate the most wealth for the investor over the holding period. There is also the possibility that, in the course of this analysis, the numbers may indicate that the particular property is not the best investment.

Real estate is only one among many investment alternatives with varying degrees of risk. The recycling process itself is a consideration because there are usually alternative approaches that can be proposed. In particular the element of risk must be evaluated. The impact of recycling on the cash flow generated by the property during the holding period must also be considered. The property must be able to generate income from which operating expenses will be paid. The remainder, if any—i.e., the NOI—determines how much debt service can be carried. The NOI is also the basis for estimating the value of the property, both "as is" and when the rehabilitation is completed.

This chapter will bring together these various considerations to explain the scope of investment analysis. It concludes with a discussion of several tests that are commonly used to analyze investment viability. These tests afford the opportunity to weigh the investment potential of a particular property and measure the effectiveness of various rehabilitation alternatives.

The Scope of Investment Analysis

In analyzing an investment, a series of mathematical formulas are used to calculate financial outcomes in different circumstances. Once you understand the formulas and their mathematical objectives, the testing process becomes one of simply inserting the right numbers into the formulas—entering them in a hand-held calculator or computer spreadsheet program—and performing the calculations. The challenge is to use the proper numbers or, as we will refer to them here, the right cash flows.

Historically, cash flow has been defined as NOI minus debt service. (When applicable, funds allocated for capital expenditures or reserves, or both, are also deducted from NOI.) Note that there is no consideration of federal or state income tax in this definition of cash flow. Use of this *pre-tax cash flow* removes from consideration the need to establish an investor's federal and state income tax brackets. (Because the implications for individual investors vary widely, after-tax cash flow, which includes consideration of cost recovery and the benefits of passive losses, will not be addressed. However, an individual's after-tax cash flow is a more precise measure and is definitely a consideration in his or her personal investment decision.)

Many real estate investment analysts place overwhelming emphasis on the test results themselves. I would argue, however, that the tests only have validity if the initial assumptions and resulting cash flow figures are reasonable and can be expected to be realized. It is reasonable to say that most real estate deals that fail, do so as a result of investors making unreasonable or unrealistic projections regarding the amount of money and the time needed to achieve their goals.

An important component of investment analysis is the *time value of money,* a concept which states that a dollar in hand today is worth more than a dollar that has been promised in the future. Several common cliches support this definition: "The more, the sooner, the better" and "a bird in the hand is worth two in the bush" are just two examples. If you have a dollar in hand today, one major risk is immediately taken away—that of never receiving the dollar, for whatever reason, at some future date. Fear of never receiving the dollar is probably the main concern, but there are several other factors that should be considered when deciding that sooner is better than later—specifically, inflation and opportunity cost.

Inflation—too much money chasing too few goods—is a prime consideration. Inflation in the United States has been on a roller coaster ride in recent years, and the fact that economists have difficulty agreeing on projected inflation rates merely adds to the risk inherent in waiting for a return on invested capital. In addition, money not used for one type of investment can be used instead for another investment opportunity, whether it is a real estate venture, the stock market, certificates of deposit, or passbook savings accounts. The benefits are obvious: Investment compounds and enhances wealth.

The point is, money in hand today has a readily identifiable value and the future is uncertain—the further an investment is projected into the future, the greater the risk. It is the comparison between the risk and the ultimate reward that leads to the investment decision. The cash flows that are received today are reality; the cash flows projected for tomorrow are speculative. The accuracy of all such projections is solely dependent on the assumptions made, based on the overall economic picture and including finite market trends. These projections cannot be a wish list or a dream; they must be a pragmatic assessment of overall market indications.

Investment Alternatives. The fact that an investor is considering a real estate venture is just the beginning. Within the real estate marketplace, the investor usually has several alternative choices available. No two apartment complexes will be identical. Location is the primary distinction; however, the condition of the physical assets is also different. Even properties in the same market are affected by subtle nuances within that market. As a result of all these differences, it is impossible to have a standard plan for recycling apartments that can be applied to all such properties. However, the objective should always be to maximize a property's position within its market for the duration of the holding period.

The recycling process can be as drastic as gutting the entire property and changing apartment configurations, building lines, and topographical features—in essence, re-creating the property. Conversely, recycling can be as subtle as a change in management—i.e., implementing new policies and procedures. These two examples represent the extremes. The recycling process itself will most likely be somewhere in between. However, there is a tremendous spread between these extremes, and only the most diligent and exhaustive study of the market affecting the property will give you the knowledge and confidence to begin the change.

Every day, newspaper advertisements tout apartments that are "newly remodelled," but in that context, remodelled is often only a buzz word. Closer scrutiny usually reveals that newly remodelled means new carpeting and fresh paint in the units. Statistics indicate that renters do not flock to an apartment community because an ad states that it is newly remodelled. Frankly, properties that require new paint and new carpeting throughout tend to have much more wrong with them, and prospective renters are not naive.

It should be obvious after thorough analysis of the market that if a minimum of physical and managemental changes is all that is necessary to bring a property to its optimum position in the market, very little time will be required to effect the change, and cash flows from the property will tend to be more predictable (i.e., the investment is less risky). On the other hand, if extensive physical change is required, it can be assumed that the cash flow will be reduced for some time, and ultimate yields will have to be projected further into the future to determine when the property will achieve its optimum position in the market. The degree of change and the time required are components of risk analysis.

Risk Analysis. If an investor has capital readily available, there are many alternatives for investing it. However, the alternatives will be limited by the amount of capital available and the risk of the potential investment. The amount of capital will preclude examination of investments beyond the capability of the investor's financial position. Because of this, there is little reason to examine the size of the investment here. The decision the investor must make is whether to use all of the available capital for one investment or spread the capital over several investments. Someone who has $100,000 may choose to invest $50,000 in real estate and hold the remainder in a passbook account temporarily.

Before deciding on a particular investment, the element of risk must be examined. For example, the stock market can generate high yields, but there is always some potential for loss of the original capital. In addition, brokerage fees reduce the return. On the other hand, an investor could receive a lower return on invested capital that is highly liquid and guaranteed safe (e.g., a passbook savings account).

If an investor is willing to forego some liquidity, while still having the guarantee of a return on 100 percent of the invested capital, a certificate of deposit or a treasury note (one-year term) or bond (extended maturity) might be the answer. These instruments pay back at the end of a prescribed term, but interest may be lost if the funds are liquidated prior to maturity. Because investment in real estate means a loss of instant liquidity, comparison to a fixed-term instrument may be more appropriate.

In seeking a risk-free rate of return, investment advisors consider government securities to be a benchmark—U.S. Treasury notes and bonds provide a fixed rate of return for a defined holding period. The question that remains is how many basis points above a so-called risk-free rate must an investor receive to feel comfortable with an investment. This question is a reasonable one to ask, but not an easy one to answer. When the investment involves rehabilitation, two other questions must be answered first: "How long will it take to achieve the optimum yield for the property?" and "How much change will be required?"

Also, when making drastic change, the principle of *highest and best use* must be examined. The four criteria for highest and best use are: physical possibility, legal permissibility, financial feasibility, and maximum profitability.

Change and Time.   Change must be examined first because any change to a property changes the risk. One hopes that the change will reduce the risk over the long term. However, there is a basis to project future yields based on present conditions, regardless of the condition of the property and the

---

Criteria for Determining Highest and Best Use

Physical possibility—anticipated changes (e.g., creation of additional rental units, replacement of mechanical installations) may depend on existing utilities or the condition of the structure (e.g., sufficient sewerage capacity for higher occupancy; a roof that can support an air-conditioning unit).

Legal permissibility—for a rehabilitation project, the use must be consistent with existing zoning, and planned improvements must comply with building codes and other applicable laws (e.g., environmental regulations).

Financial feasibility—whether the rehabilitation will yield an adequate return on the investment. Corrections to meet building code requirements can be extremely costly and, thus, reduce the potential return.

Maximum profitability—whether the rehabilitation will yield the highest value or price consistent with the rate of return warranted by the market—i.e., maximum productivity.

---

profile of its existing residents. Many times it is apparent that if the property is left unchanged, yields will diminish. Thus, any change that is projected should anticipate a change in the resident profile and in the property's rent structure. Whether the desired rental rates will be achieved and the resident profile will be changed are considerations related specifically to risk. No single item can stand alone—each is interwoven with many other factors and considerations.

A hypothetical example will illustrate some of the pitfalls of change.

Suppose thorough market analysis has revealed that to optimize a property's potential in its market, units must have new kitchens—including kitchen cabinets, countertops, vinyl flooring, light fixtures, and appliances (stove and refrigerator)—plus installation of new carpeting, addition of vanities in the bathroom, and complete redecoration. Assume that these changes will cost $3,500 per unit.

Consider further that this $3,500 must be invested on top of the initial purchase price paid for the property and that a particular unit may or may not be occupied. As to time, assume it would take approximately two weeks to perform the needed rehabilitation work in a given unit. So far your assumptions have been reasonably straightforward. However, a problem arises when you multiply the construction time by the number of units. If there are 100 units in the building, two facts emerge that have a potentially negative effect on your projections—the time requirement and the level of occupancy. Obviously, if you can only do one unit at a time, it could take almost four years to complete the work (two weeks multiplied by 100 units). While this is far-fetched, even if all the units are vacant and unlimited labor is available, the entire building could not be done in less than three months.

Because most apartment properties that face recycling are, in reality, "going concerns" with occupancies between 50 and 85 percent, it is fair to assume that this entire process—including consideration of occupied apartments, acceptance of the change by the market, and the logistics of performing the rehabilitation—could take up to two years. Then questions arise as to how likely the existing residents are to resist this change and whether the majority might move out when their leases expire. Consider, too, the fact that even though there has been a physical change to the property and a change in its clientele, the market may not yet perceive that the property has been improved.

This analysis is incomplete without an examination of rental rates. If the rent for one unit can be increased by $50 per month ($600 per year total), the result would be a return of 17.14 percent on the $3,500 unit rehabilitation investment in the first twelve months of a new lease, assuming no additional downtime for a unit. However, if the rent can only be increased by $25 over the previous market rent, the return on investment diminishes to 8.57 percent; the return would be even less in the first year if construction is completed and the unit remains unoccupied for a protracted period.

If the cost of funds had been 9 percent, the lower yield in the example is below that rate and demonstrates how change and time together can drastically affect a project's risk. Surely no one would invest in a property with an expected yield that is *below* the cost of funds. Obviously, the investment has to be analyzed over the projected holding period, and that analysis must include consideration of all 100 units.

The purpose of this particular example is to show that unexpected change made over a given period of time can yield disastrous results. The longer the change is ongoing and the greater the magnitude of the change, the less predictable the outcome—i.e., the greater the risk. Most of the time it is fair to say that if proper market analysis is done, the change will be positive and the ultimate result will be beneficial. Proper market analysis increases predictability and thus decreases risk. However, care must be taken in projecting the time it will take to achieve a positive result, otherwise the overall yield may not be worth the risk because the reward will be inadequate.

Desired Return.   What then is an adequate return? There is no standard measure for this. An adequate return will be determined by the investor based on the degree of risk and the ultimate reward. For example, if an investor's goals and objectives include high risk with commensurate return—e.g., drastic change in the context of apartment rehabilitation—demand for a high rate of return on the investment (e.g., 50 percent) may be appropriate and commensurate with the risk. Conversely, if little or no change is necessary to enhance the investment potential, an investor may require a much lower rate of return to warrant investment.

Due to differing risks, different rates of return are required for analyzing investments. As suggested earlier in this discussion, investment in real estate may be compared to a fixed-term instrument; the maturity of the instrument should match the expected holding period of your intended investment. This can be demonstrated with a hypothetical example—e.g., a property to be held for five years.

Let's assume that the risk-free rate on five-year U.S. Treasury bonds is 6 percent. To this, you would add a factor to compensate for the real estate being less liquid than government securities and for the fact that the real estate must be managed—in this case, one percentage point. This raises your return rate to 7 percent.

For purposes of comparison to other investments, you would factor in an additional *risk premium*. A risk premium is commonly established by comparing the risk of the investment to the risk of a standard investment portfolio such as Standard and Poor's Index of 500 Common Stocks. Investment analysts assign a variable ("beta") to describe the degree of risk in an investment; as a basis of comparison, the standard (e.g., the S&P 500) is assigned a beta of one. The beta for an intended real estate investment would be determined from an evaluation of such things as the level of occupancy, the caliber of the tenants, the overall management of the property, and its general fiscal condition. This is a somewhat subjective interpretation of available facts regarding the property and the rental market.

To develop this example, we will assume you consulted an investment advisor who has indicated that the risk premium on assets with a beta of one is 7 percent. Furthermore, your analysis thus far has indicated that your intended investment is only 75 percent as risky as investment in the stock market, in which case your risk premium would be 75 percent of the 7-percent standard or 5.25 percent. Adding the risk premium of 5.25 percent to the risk-free (but illiquid) return rate of 7 percent would set your desired rate of return at 12.25 percent.

The lower risk of your intended investment might have been based on a property with a high level of occupancy (greater than 95 percent), very few or no "problem" residents, little or no turnover, income that is steady and regularly exceeds operating expenses, and generally good management being compared to a stock market that is rather volatile. However, if a candidate for recycling has a low level of occupancy (e.g., 50 percent or less), and many or most of the occupants might be characterized as "problem" residents, your evaluation would be very different. As is often the case for such properties, the attendant rent loss and collection problems would probably be coupled with generally poor management, making this investment considerably more risky than the beta one standard. If your assessment indicates it is one and one-half times as risky as the stock market, your risk premium would be 150 percent of the 7-percent return on a standard stock portfolio or 10.5 percent. Adding this to the risk-free return rate of 7 percent would set your risk premium at 17.5 percent.

The numbers in this example merely demonstrate the potential differences in risk premiums for real estate investments. The risk premium for a particular investment must be defined for the individual investor.

Examination of Cash Flows.   As was explained in an earlier chapter, the very nature of the rehabilitation process results in uneven cash flows. The analysis of cash flows begins at the inception of the investment or, if rehabilitation is considered in the mid-life of an investment holding, at the inception of the rehabilitation. This means there are existing levels of occupancy and rent collection, and because the operating expenses of the property are already established, the NOI is known. However, as rehabilitation is started, occupancy levels will change for two reasons. First, even if there are numerous vacant apartments at the outset, eventually a time will come when occupied apartments will have to be vacated so the rehabilitation can proceed. Second, the resident profile will begin to change. Many times the new (preferred) resident profile will not begin to evolve until later in the rehabilitation process. Before that takes place, however, the existing residents will begin to be uneasy because of the changes that are taking place around them and in anticipation of the increase in rent. In my experience, most of the remaining original residents will choose not to renew their leases.

Thus, for some period of time during the rehabilitation, the cash flow will be reduced (it may even represent a loss). Eventually, the cash flow will become positive and begin to increase, and if projections were correct, the ultimate new and desired cash flow will evolve. The obvious concern, however, is how much time it will take for the cash flow to become positive and then stabilize at the new (higher) level. (*Stabilization* in this context means income projections account for rent increases the market will bear and no longer have to account for concessions or extraordinary vacancies, and there are no extraordinary operating expenses—in other words, income exceeds expenses so that NOI is positive and growing.) If you project a three-year period to attain the optimum cash flow and it actually takes five years, you will miss your time projection by 67 percent! More importantly, your financial position could seriously affect the survival of the investment.

When considering a rehabilitation, it is essential that the potential negative cash flows be considered before you begin the process. A worst-case scenario should be anticipated. For example, if the investor chooses to fund the rehabilitation from cash flow and has no additional source of revenue, the cash flow could be eroded as a consequence of the rehabilitation, and the investor might end up losing the property because the recycling process has been started but cannot be completed. Also problematic is the situation in which an investor may agree to fund part or all of the rehabilitation costs out-of-pocket. If the progress of the rehabilitation results in negative cash flows, additional out-of-pocket funds will be needed to cover the cash flow shortfall. If several investors are involved, each one must understand the extent of the personal financial obligations that can arise. Note that if the investors have formed a *limited partnership,* only the general (managing) partner or partners are obligated to provide additional funds; the limited partners generally assume no financial liability beyond their initial investment.

It is critically important that the possibility of change—especially reduction—in cash flow during the rehabilitation process is considered when financing is being sought. Frankly, many rehabilitations have been projected far too optimistically by the rehabber, and whatever reserves had been set aside to cover cash flow shortfalls turned out to be woefully inadequate. My recommendation is, if you think it will take two years to complete the rehabilitation and bring the property to a point where a permanent loan can be sought, you should try to have the term of the construction loan extended by at least 50 percent—i.e., to three years. This will provide a slightly larger margin of safety for the investors. It may also be prudent to analyze a worst-case scenario to have a clearer picture of your downside risk.

Valuing the Property

Investors and real estate professionals frequently look at a property and determine very quickly that some change is needed in order to enhance its position in the market. Too often, however, in making projections to enhance the real estate or to optimize cash flow, the analyst fails to consider the property in its "as is" condition. I would argue that nothing should be planned, and certainly no action should be taken, until the property's as-is condition has been determined. In fact, you have to know the current financial condition of the property before you can begin to make reasonable predictions about its economic future.

Evaluation "As Is."   Planning a rehabilitation can be likened to a first-time visit to a large shopping mall. In that situation, you will look at the directory of stores, determine where you want to shop, and then find the store on the map. However, before you can begin to walk toward that store, you must find out where you are—the "you are here" spot on the directory. Before you begin to plan a rehabilitation project, you must know where you are now— i.e., the as-is value of the property.

This is not as simple as it may seem. The current NOI will be reasonably easy to ascertain. After all, no projections are needed to find out current NOI. The income is what it is. (Regardless of what the present owner or manager would say, the rent and occupancy levels are as high as they can be with the current management and the policies and procedures that are in place, given the property's location and current condition.) The current operating expenses should be analyzed carefully, however. The dollar amounts should be checked to be sure they are commensurate with the size and condition of the property. The amounts for specific expenditures should be a reasonably accurate reflection of the property's operations.

The difficulty in ascertaining the as-is value of a property arises when you try to determine the durability of the current income stream. You may anticipate no additional capital outlays other than those that would be essential to maintain the property in its present condition, but other factors must be considered, too. As noted earlier, when a property begins to deteriorate physically, its perception in the marketplace also begins to diminish. The analysis of the investment must project the speed at which these degenerations will occur.

Capitalization Rates.   For purposes of computing value *(V)*, net operating income *(I)*—regardless whether "as is" or "as projected"—is divided by a capitalization ("cap") rate *(R)*. A *capitalization rate* is any rate used to convert income to value; typically it is a percent expressed as a decimal fraction. In addition, an adjective (equity, yield, recapture, overall) is usually applied to the rate indicating the relationship involved.

The capitalization rate is extracted from the market and is a reflection of the typical buyer's analysis of the risk inherent in a particular investment considering the anticipated future benefits from it. The best way to determine a valid capitalization rate is by examining recent market sales (net income divided by sale price provides a yield rate). Local brokers and appraisers can also provide capitalization rates for comparison.

Dividing NOI by the capitalization rate will yield an estimated *market value* for a property. Market value is the price at which a seller would willingly sell something and a buyer would willingly buy it if neither were acting under unusual pressure. It is based on the implication that both buyer and seller are acting as typical participants in the transaction. This must be differentiated from *investment value,* which is the price an investor bound by special circumstances will agree to pay. Investment value relates to equity ownership; it is an individualized or personal value as compared to market value, which is impersonal and detached.

Obviously, the higher the capitalization rate, the lower the value and, conversely, the lower the capitalization rate, the higher the value. It is indeed

---

Definitions of Value

Market value—the most probable price, as of a specified date, in cash or in terms equivalent to cash, or in other precisely revealed terms, for which the specified property should sell after reasonable exposure in a competitive market under all conditions requisite to a fair sale, with the buyer and seller each acting prudently, knowledgeably, and for self-interest, and assuming that neither is under undue duress.

Investment value—the value of an investment to a particular investor based on his or her investment requirements.

---

possible (and highly probable) that the market-derived capitalization rate might be viewed by a specific investor as either too conservative or too optimistic depending on his or her requirements for yield and assessment of risk. As a capitalization rate moves up or down, it is the market's reflection of risk for the neighborhood, the property, or both.

Use of Appraisal Techniques.   Derivation of a capitalization rate and applying it to NOI to estimate value gives a valid indication of the as-is value of a property. The as-is analysis should not end there, however. It is important to verify the accuracy of the first estimate of value.

Appraisers utilize three approaches in determining value. I have just described the *income capitalization approach.* The other two—the sales comparison approach and the cost approach—provide a check on the income capitalization method.

In the *sales comparison approach,* the analyst examines bona fide sales of similar properties and adjusts them for location, amenities, condition, and time of sale. A more detailed analysis is accomplished by reducing the sale price to dollars per unit, per room, and per square foot. Dividing the value of the property (obtained using the income capitalization approach) by the number of units provides a per-unit value that will indicate whether or not the subject property correlates with the comparable sales. Note that some adjustment may be necessary—positive or negative—for differences between the property under analysis and the market sales. (In evaluating sales data for other multifamily properties, I have found it expedient to use a per-unit basis for comparing their selling prices and average rents with those of the subject property.)

The *cost approach* to value utilizes an estimate of the construction cost for the property under analysis. This would be the current cost of replacing the existing improvements, *minus* the loss in value from depreciation (from all causes), *plus* the value of the land (as if vacant). This approach has little validity in ascertaining as-is value—it is quite laborious and requires estimates of depreciation (something that is very hard to measure). Its usefulness is in examining the *principle of substitution,* which states that when several similar or commensurate commodities, goods, or services are available, the one with the lowest price attracts the greatest demand and widest distribution. If the purchase price of a property is $45,000 per unit, but new construction would only cost $40,000 per unit, the principle of substitution would indicate that this is not a wise investment.

When you are considering properties for potential rehabilitation, it is highly doubtful that the acquisition price on a per-unit basis would approach what it would cost to build the property new. If the expense of rehabilitation combined with the acquisition price would push the cost of the property over the cost to build it new, a reevaluation would certainly be necessary. Even then, it is imperative to analyze the benefits that accrue to the property because of its existing location. If there are no other opportunities to build apartment buildings—because of absorption of land in the market area, zoning restrictions, or other reasons—it may be prudent to pursue the investment in an existing property even if the combined costs of acquisition and rehabilitation exceed the cost of new construction.

Evaluation "As Projected."   Once the as-is value of the property has been ascertained, it is essential to determine its value "as projected." This is where the *time value of money* theory comes into play. You are no longer dealing with the present, but rather projecting the income stream into the future. In addition, the income is going to be uneven in the early years of the investment due to the recycling process. The following example examines the NOIs for a hypothetical property from acquisition to income stabilization.

In the year of purchase, the NOI will be the same as that used in estimating the as-is value. It is probable, however, that during the succeeding two or three years, the NOI will be reduced substantially due to a changing resident profile, a loss of residents due to evictions and nonrenewals, a need to keep some units vacant so that they can be rehabilitated, and increases in operating expenses as you provide continuing service to existing residents.

Assume the following amounts of NOI will be generated during the next few years (the entirety of the recycling process, including the five-year holding period):

NOI at the Time of Purchase	$70,000
During the Recycling Process—Year 1	$65,000
Year 2	$55,000
Year 3	$75,000
Year 4	$100,000
Year 5	$125,000
Year 6	$135,000

Using a 10-percent cap rate, the as-is value of the property would be $700,000 ($70,000 ÷ .10). Applying the same cap rate to the NOI as

Assumptions for the Valuation Example

A rigorous valuation calculation will examine realistic projections of NOI (projected gross income *minus* operating expenses) for the intended holding period. It will utilize appropriate capitalization rates extracted from the market and applicable to the particular property; in all likelihood, the rates will be slightly different. In addition, consideration will be given to debt service (mortgage principle *plus* interest) based on scheduled draws against the construction loan and the terms that apply to the respective loan amounts. The anticipated cost of recycling the property and the time it will take to complete the process will affect the calculations as well.

For purposes of demonstrating analysis of the investment, a single example is used for all the various calculations. It is based on the amounts of NOI already shown in the text for the expected five-year holding period. Financing is presumed to be based on a loan-to-value (LTV) ratio of 75% of the total amount needed—i.e., acquisition price *plus* recycling cost—to be repaid at a fixed rate of 9.5% for a 30-year term. Although it is more typical to have multiple draws against the construction funds and repayment of them on an interest-only basis, it will be assumed that the entire amount is available at the beginning of the project and being amortized during the holding period. This permits use of a single amount for annual debt service and simplifies the example calculations. Tests requiring application of discounting will utilize a discount rate based on the terminal cap rate (9.5%) *plus* an allowance for inflation (3%). The following specifics should be noted.

Acquisition price (value "as is")	$700,000
Recycling cost (rehabilitation loan)	175,000
Loan amount ($875,000 x 75%)	656,250
Investor's equity (total cost − loan)	218,750
Annual debt service payment	66,217
NOI in the year of purchase	70,000
NOI in years 1 through 6—Year 1	65,000
Year 2	55,000
Year 3	75,000
Year 4	100,000
Year 5	125,000
Year 6	135,000

Initial cap rate = 10%
Terminal cap rate = 9.5%
Discount rate = 12.5%

affected by the recycling process, the value would be $650,000 in year 1. This is $50,000 less than the as-is value of the property. However, if the projected year 6 NOI ($135,000) is capitalized at the same 10-percent rate, the projected value would be $1,350,000 *(the terminal value)*. This is $650,000 more than the as-is value of the property, and it will require five years to achieve it as well as a considerable amount of work and substantial risk.

Keep in mind that the $1,350,000 terminal value you have projected is for five years into the future. In order to compare the potential advantage of acquisition and rehabilitation, it is necessary to discount the future indications of value to the present time. This is where the *time value of money* enters the picture. These calculations account for *value enhancement* over the holding period. Such a measurable increase in value becomes a selling point to persuade potential investors of the merits of a particular proposal.

The ability to discount future cash flows to an acceptable present value depends not only on the accuracy of the forecasted cash flows, but also on using the correct discount rate. The main difference between capitalization rates and discount rates is inflation. Capitalization rates found from market data (discussed earlier in this chapter) are applied only to a single year's income—there would be no inflation to affect capitalization rates directly. On the other hand, discounting techniques use forecasts of future cash flows; and because these future figures can be affected by inflation, discount rates must take projected inflation into account. It is fair to assume from this that discount rates will generally be higher than capitalization rates. An easy formula to remember is: Discount rate approximately equals capitalization rate plus inflation rate. This applies when you are calculating market value. (Note that in testing investment alternatives, you are measuring investment value—i.e., the potential return on the investor's capital.)

Tests of Investment Viability

Analysis of the economics of the investment will provide sound evidence for (or against) undertaking the recycling of a property. Five tests that can be performed to conduct this analysis will be examined here—net incremental increase in value, internal rate of return, net present value, return on investment, and payback period.

Application of Specific Tests.   *Net incremental increase in value* is particularly valuable because it begins with the cost of the investment today and takes into account the cost of the rehabilitation. It measures *value enhancement* over the holding period, and a measurable increase in value becomes a selling point to persuade potential investors of the merits of a particular proposal.

Using the example from the preceding section and applying a 10-percent capitalization rate to the cash flows, the value of the investment will be increased from $700,000 at the time of purchase to $1,350,000 at the end of the holding period (terminal value based on projected year 6 NOI). This $650,000 enhancement represents an increase in value of 92.86 percent over the initial investment. However, this does not take into account the cost of achieving the increase. Deduction of the rehabilitation cost of $175,000 from the

---

Tests of Investment Viability
* Net incremental increase in value
* Internal rate of return (IRR)
* Net present value (NPV)
* Return on investment (ROi)
* Payback period

$650,000 total yields an incremental value enhancement of $475,000. This represents a net incremental increase in value of 67.86 percent.

For this property, the investor will get back not only the entire initial investment, but also a $475,000 increase in wealth.

Other analyses apply the discounting principle. The discount rate represents the opportunity cost of investing in the particular property rather than in other financial assets. Thus, the discount rate is based on the rate of return on financial assets whose risk is equivalent to the risk of investing in the property under consideration.

Internal rate of return (IRR) finds the rate of return at which the discounted value of all benefits received during ownership is equal to the value of your equity in the investment. The IRR is the discount rate applied to the cash flows—i.e., the yield rate.

To demonstrate IRR, several specific assumptions will be made about the ongoing example. First, the entire rehabilitation loan amount ($175,000) will be taken up front. Second, the lender will make a loan based on the total amount needed for thirty years at 9.5 percent interest. The acquisition price plus the rehabilitation cost comes to $875,000 ($700,000 + $175,000). Using a 75-percent LTV ratio, the total loan would be $656,250. Annual principal and interest payments on this would amount to $66,217, which will have the following impact on the annual cash flows projected during the five-year holding period.

	Annual NOI	– Debt Service	= Cash Flow
Year 1	$65,000	$66,217	(1,217)
Year 2	$55,000	$66,217	(11,217)
Year 3	$75,000	$66,217	8,783
Year 4	$100,000	$66,217	33,783
Year 5	$125,000	$66,217	58,783
Year 6	$135,000		

Note that with the rehabilitation completed, the quantity, quality, and durability of the income stream is measurably improved. You assume that this signals a reduction in risk such that a somewhat lower capitalization rate can be used in calculating value, and you opt for a 9.5-percent rate.

Applying this lower capitalization rate to the year 6 NOI yields a terminal value of $1,421,053 ($135,000 ÷ .095), which will be the assumed sale price. Furthermore, the mortgage at that point will have been paid down to $631,581, and that must be taken into account. Assuming a 4-percent cost of sale, the net proceeds at the end of year 5 will be as follows.

Sale price	$1,421,053
Cost of sale (4%)	− 56,842
Mortgage balance	− 631,581
Net proceeds	$ 732,630

The net proceeds are added to the cash flow for year 5 to yield a total cash return of $791,413 ($732,630 + $58,783)—before consideration of federal income tax.

All of the cash flows, including the net proceeds from sale in year 5, have been discounted to a point where they equal the $218,750 initial investment in this property (the owner's equity), representing an IRR of 30.312 percent.

On the other hand, *net present value (NPV)* discounts all expected future cash flows to the present using a predetermined desired rate of return. It is calculated by subtracting the present value of the capital outlay from the present value of the expected returns. In this way, NPV tests whether more or less money may be earned from an investment compared to other investments of similar risk.

Earlier in this chapter, the discount rate was defined as a capitalization rate plus an inflation rate. For purposes of calculating NPV, a 3-percent inflation rate will be added to the 9.5-percent terminal capitalization rate from the IRR calculation to yield a discount rate of 12.5 percent. Applying this discount rate to the series of cash flows yields a net present value of $237,742.54. This means that the investment will make more than you were willing to accept. Had the number been negative, the investment would not have been attractive.

NPV is the sum of the projected values as discounted to the present time. Thus, all the values are measured in today's dollars.

NPV is based solely on projected cash flows and the opportunity cost of capital, and it recognizes the time value of money. Note that in testing NPV, the cash flows are measured against a predetermined discount rate or a minimum acceptable rate of return, while the calculation of IRR actually establishes a discount rate. If NPV is positive, the minimum acceptable return has been achieved; if negative, it has not.

IRR expands on present value calculations and is a measure of profitability. In general, an investment will be acceptable if the IRR is *greater than* the opportunity cost of capital. Although IRR is a precise measure, it has several weaknesses:

- Assumptions about reinvestment rates—IRR measures return on capital *within* an investment; return rates on capital withdrawn from the particular investment are not included.
- Potential for multiple IRRs—when there are both negative and positive cash flows for a single investment, it is possible to have more than one IRR (or no IRR). Generation of different IRRs suggests that the use of some other performance measure or adjustment of the cash flows or time frame would be more appropriate.
- Choosing between mutually exclusive projects—because IRR does not account for differences in capital outlay requirements, it is unreliable in ranking projects of different scale or which offer different patterns of cash flow over time.
- Differences in opportunity costs—IRR does not account for differences between short-term and long-term interest rates; it is less useful when differences in the term structure of interest rates require computation of a complex weighted average rate to obtain IRR.

Many investors prefer to use NPV rather than IRR because it avoids these potential problems.

Return on investment (ROI) is still another test. It measures cash flow against investment. However, it does not consider the time value of money.

In the example, the initial investment was $218,750. Dividing the cash flow for years 1–5 (NOI *minus* debt service) by the initial investment yields the following annual returns (percentages as decimal fractions). Here we have considered the proceeds from the sale along with year 5 cash flow.

	Cash Flow	÷	Equity	=	Annual ROI
Year 1	(1,217)		$218,750		(.0056)
Year 2	(11,217)		$218,750		(.0513)
Year 3	8,783		$218,750		.0402
Year 4	33,783		$218,750		.1544
Year 5	58,783		$218,750		3.6179

These calculations indicate that there is a negative return on the initial investment in the first two years. Then, beginning in year 3, the return is slightly over 4 percent; and in year 5 (the year of sale), the cash flow and sale proceeds yield an ROI of 362 percent. These figures can also be averaged. The total return over the five-year holding period is 376 percent. Dividing this by 5 yields an average annual ROI of slightly more than 75 percent.

ROI is a rather simplistic tool. It is comparable to IRR only when all future cash flows are equal. Because it does not consider the time value of money, the results will be less precise.

Payback period measures how long it will take before projected cash flows equal the investor's initial capital investment. However, it does not take the time value of money into account, nor does it consider investment risk or the effect of any gain or loss beyond the breakeven point (when the cumulative income from the investment equals the cumulative loss). It is best used in conjunction with other performance measures or to compare investments with similar characteristics.

In our ongoing example, it is obvious that the initial investment of $218,750 will not be paid back in full until the property is sold at the end of year 5—examination of the cash flows reveals that only $30,132 will be paid back at the end of year 4.

Calculation of the payback period will give a different answer than NPV because all cash flows before the payback date are equally weighted while all cash flows after that date are given no weight. Therefore, it is important to establish an appropriate payback period that will maximize the NPV.

[NOTE: The serial example used throughout the preceding sections has been presented in a straightforward manner to show the types of results an investor is likely to obtain when using hand-held real estate calculators or computer spreadsheet programs, which automatically calculate NPV, IRR, etc. (They come with instructions for entering dollar amounts, percentage rates, time periods, and other variable factors.) The specific formulas and calculations are not easily demonstrated here and, in fact, are beyond the scope of this book. However, the benefits of a spreadsheet approach warrant additional comment.]

Use of a Spreadsheet. In analyzing a particular property, it is wise to apply several tests to the cash flows and present the information in a spreadsheet format. (This can be done very easily with spreadsheet software in a personal computer.) Having projections for successive years displayed in columns on a page gives a very clear indication of the impacts of different factors. Obviously, the first considerations would be the conditions of sale and operation and the terms of any financing obtained. For purposes of analysis, you might assume the same loan terms for both the acquisition loan and the construction loan (rates should be based on your shopping for financing). Or, debt service may have to account for interest-only with a later balloon payment and an amortization period based on a long-term fixed rate (e.g., 30 years at 9.5 percent). Special care must be taken to adjust for loan-to-value ratio (LTV); the loan amounts will be substantially lower than the purchase price or the anticipated rehabilitation costs.

Minimally, the spreadsheet would consider dollar amounts for the following items:

- NOI in successive years—amounts will vary until stabilization.
- The price at purchase.
- The investment in rehabilitation—accounting for separate amounts for the years of active construction.
- Debt service—loan amounts and terms (financing obtained) for the purchase and the rehabilitation, with draws against the latter based on expenditure amounts or a predetermined schedule.
- Cash flows—NOI minus debt service and capital expenditures.

Calculations of NOI should be realistic. It may be prudent to include in the spreadsheet the anticipated revenues (rental income) and operating expenses that yield the NOI; this could expand the potential for adjustments to projections. If the property will be sold at the end of the holding period, the sale price (in the year of sale) would be compared to the purchase price. The cost of sale should be considered, too. The spreadsheet program would require entry of specific amounts to permit calculation of the various line entries for successive years. Pre-tax NPVs and IRRs would be calculated automatically unless the specific tax situation of the investor is known.

Best application of the testing would include development of comparison figures based not only on assumptions regarding rehabilitation and future resale (after the income has been stabilized) but also on different scenarios that could occur. You should examine the impact of holding the property "as is" for an indefinite period (perhaps stipulating that NOI would remain level over the holding period—i.e., equivalent to the amount being generated at purchase).

It is also appropriate to consider a worst-case scenario. This might reflect what could happen if the market analysis is not done carefully and realistically or if an unexpected change occurs in the market. Examples of the latter would be inability to attract prospects to your rehabilitated property, perhaps because the market perception has not changed as you projected or possibly because of a general reduction in demand (e.g., bankruptcy of a major local employer has led to a massive population exodus) or, conversely, a sharp increase in the supply of apartments at rental rates comparable to yours (new construction or other, more-appealing, rehabilitation projects). Regardless of the reason, the impact would be fewer new leases or inability to adjust rents upward and generate sufficient income to repay the loans; perhaps the income would not even cover operating expenses. Such a reduction in annual NOI and subsequent cash flow projections could force the investor to default on the loans.

An important part of this exercise is setting a desired rate of return. Due to differences in the risks of rehabilitation versus holding the property as is or considering a worst-case scenario, different rates of return would be required for each of the suggested alternatives. An example earlier in this chapter used a hypothetical five-year treasury bond to establish a risk-free rate of return, adding to it a consideration for real estate being less liquid than government securities. (Normally, you might add another percentage point or so to compensate for your management of the property. However, if you are managing the property for a group of investors, a predetermined fee would be deducted as an operating expense in your calculation of NOI; addition of a management premium to your required rate of return would amount to double-counting and could skew the calculations.)

Your confidence in your cash flow projections for the various alternatives should lead you to estimate how each of them compares to a standard investment portfolio (e.g., the S&P 500). Suppose the five-year bond rate is 6 percent and you add a 1-percent illiquidity factor. Suppose further that the risk premium standard is 7 percent. If you estimate that holding your investment "as is" is only 75 percent as risky as a standard investment, your required return would be calculated: $.06 + .01 + (.07 \times .75) = .1225 = 12.25\%$. If you assume level cash flows and NOIs for this holding option, you would calculate net equity value and ROI rather than NPV and IRR.

In projecting flat or level NOI over an extended holding period, you would need to look at only one year's figures to determine whether simply purchasing and holding a property would be a wise move. Often this calculation indicates that the capital would be better invested elsewhere to obtain a return at or above the required yield. Note, however, that level NOI yields a projected growth rate for the cash flows of zero; if steady growth could be anticipated, the required rate of return would be adjusted accordingly.

On the other hand, you are likely to be less certain about cash flows projected for a rehabilitation and resale, so you might estimate this investment to be about four times as risky as merely holding the property as is. This is the same as saying that it is three times as risky as the S&P 500 ($4 \times .75 = 3$). Thus your required return would be: $.06 + .01 + (.07 \times 3) = .280 = 28.0\%$. This required rate of return being somewhat subjective, you would calculate both IRR and NPV for a rehabilitation and resale. The same return rate would be applied to a worst-case scenario involving rehabilitation as anticipated but with diminished cash flow. In the latter case, calculation of IRR and NPV is likely to demonstrate whether there is any merit in attempting the project under adverse circumstances or if you are likely to end up defaulting on the loans.

Making the Decision to Proceed

In testing alternatives, the biggest factors have already been considered. The element of risk has been reflected in both the capitalization rate and the discount rate. In the context of apartment recycling, the determination of risk has to consider the perception of the property as it exists today, as well as how long it will take to change that perception and, thereby, achieve the projected financial results.

One final thought on the testing process. As I pointed out at the beginning of this chapter, no single analysis should be considered all-inclusive. It is only an approximation of the overall investment. The results of these tests may force the analyst to return to market data and reanalyze certain other factors that may be cause for concern. Once the tests have been completed and any needed reanalysis has been done, you should be able to be reasonably comfortable in deciding whether a particular property is a viable candidate for the recycling process.

Because each property will present different possibilities and different economic considerations, it is very important to be realistic in making projections. You must consider the long-term consequences of decisions made at the beginning of the rehabilitation process, including the extent of the physical changes to the property, the time required to accomplish them, the costs of rehabilitation and concurrent operations, and the cost of money to finance the undertaking. Also to be considered are the economic losses—the fact that rental income may not even cover operating expenses initially, let alone contribute to debt service—and the time required to change the market's perception of the property.

In analyzing a particular real estate investment, the selection of tests will depend on what the investor needs to know. The more appropriate the tests you apply, the more likely you are to have a sound economic basis for deciding whether or not to proceed. Two basic factors affect the financial analysis process—the models used and the inputs to the models. At a minimum, the appropriate models must be used and used correctly. At best, you will use more-sophisticated models and consider factors that other market participants do not take into account. As the source of the model inputs, your market analysis (demographics, rent levels, etc.) must be as thorough and as realistic as possible to provide the best possible basis for your projections. Improvements in either the models or the inputs—refining the data to reflect what is realistically achievable—will increase the reliability of the analysis and, thus, decrease risk. The riskiest investment is one that is done blindly because you do not know what outcome to expect.

Also inherent in the decision to proceed is your own sense that the investment will be successful. You have to set the parameters for the tests so that you can measure the potential for success. The question may not be how long do you *want* to hold the property but rather how long do you *have* to hold it; perhaps not *when* will there be a return on the investment, *or how much,* but *will* there be a return at all. The risks in recycling apartments are great; you have to decide at what point, for you, the benefits outweigh the risks.

6

Managing during Rehabilitation

The task of professional management is to strive for the optimum return on an investment. While property management is the key to success in operating any type of real property, it is even more critical during the recycling of an apartment property. Management becomes far more intensive because the property is going through many rapid changes. It is the responsibility of management to bring this ever-changing and generally unsettled situation as close as possible to stabilization. Essentially, this is crisis management.

In addition to managing the property, the site manager—and sometimes other members of the management team because of their presence on site—may have a role in managing the construction process. The management staff, policies and procedures, and the marketing effort must all be coordinated with the rehabilitation construction to bring an apartment recycling project to a successful conclusion.

Managing the Property

Property management is a very detail-oriented business. Managers have to adapt to any changes that take place on the property. A site manager must possess leadership qualities in order to direct the staff and yet foster cooperation (create a team spirit). In addition, this person must balance two seemingly different roles. As an employee of the owner, the manager must be forthright in enforcing the policies and procedures established for the property. As someone with direct responsibility for responding to and retaining residents, the manager must also provide good service, exhibit a positive attitude, and maintain an upbeat marketing effort.

There is really no difference between the requirements for a manager working at a stabilized property and those for one working at a property that is undergoing rehabilitation. The duties and responsibilities are essentially the same. However, it is important to understand that managing a stable property is vastly different from managing one that is in constant turmoil because of the recycling process. During the recycling process, changes will be frequent and distressing for both residents and staff. The site manager must be able to maintain a steady course despite the changes and their effects. In the context of a rehabilitation, the individual's experience and adaptability can make a difference in the outcome.

One of the first things to be done when you assume management of a property you intend to rehabilitate is to review the current situation. During the due diligence process, you should have gained some insights regarding actual and potential problems with the way the property was being managed. Once you own it, you will have to do a more careful assessment as a springboard for your proposed changes to the property.

Assessing the Current Situation.   Regardless of the level of occupancy and the overall caliber of the existing residents, the property is in trouble—a factor that was considered in your search for a property to recycle. This negative situation has been sending a very strong message to those living at the property who have probably been behaving pretty much as they pleased—e.g., paying rent late or not at all, having wild parties, working on their cars in the parking lot, intimidating other residents, and numerous other unacceptable activities. Your immediate task is to establish order. This is best done by establishing policies and procedures that will give management personnel firm direction and let the residents know what is—and is not—acceptable behavior. (Specific policies and procedures are discussed later in this chapter.) Another important task is to interview the staff members currently employed at the property (management personnel and maintenance workers) and find out what their specific duties and responsibilities are.

Dealing with Existing Site Staff.   There are two schools of thought on the treatment of existing staff at the time of management take-over. One is to purge the entire staff because they have been working essentially with no rules and are likely to have developed poor working habits and even poorer attitudes. Termination at take-over can be a wise policy in general. Once you hire people, their subsequent terminations will require unemployment compensation drawn against your account (rather than the prior owner's) and possibly severance pay. In addition, lawsuits for "wrongful discharge" are possible, and a claim of discrimination or retaliation against the employee can be difficult to fight.

The other approach is to evaluate individual staff members and keep those who can work under the new system. Bear in mind that there is one thing those staff members have that a new owner does not have at the time of acquisition—i.e., an intimate knowledge of the property and its subtle nuances. For example, sewer backups and other related problems seem to be a part of every property that is a candidate for recycling.

This is not to suggest that existing staff should be retained simply because they may have knowledge of problems that are not readily apparent on the surface. Nor should you retain them solely to acquaint you with such problems and then terminate the entire staff. Rather, I recommend interviewing the site manager and other staff members individually, just like any other candidates for employment. The same questions should be asked, and their references should be checked in the same manner. If it is possible to retain some or all of these staff members initially, the management transition may be less traumatic to the residents.

The important thing to understand is that, at the time of acquisition, the entire staff is likely to be demoralized. It is difficult to come to work every day at a property that is obviously declining toward ruination. You can rest assured that, when you begin to interview the staff as you are completing the due diligence process, your plans for the rehabilitation are going to be viewed somewhat cynically by them—no matter how glorious your ideas may seem to you. Remember, too, any property that is a candidate for recycling has probably been looked at by many other people, from prospective buyers to mortgage lenders. In addition to the fact that there has been no plan to correct the deficiencies of the property, and probably very little money available to do so, the site personnel are afraid for their jobs. They realize that new ownership—and management—could mean the end of their jobs. It is important for you to be sensitive to these feelings. Much more information can be obtained if the person being interviewed does not feel that he or she is being interrogated, and you will have an opportunity, one-on-one, to assess each staff member's ability. A good question to ask in these formal interviews is, "What would you do if you were setting the policies for the operation of this property?"

Human beings work best when rules are clearly set forth as specific policies and there are procedures for implementation and enforcement. Frankly, most people prefer to comply with established rules rather than be seen as renegades. In my own experience, there were usually some prior staff members who were willing and able to do what was acceptable; but they were stymied because there were no rules, and they had neither the experience nor the drive to find better ways of doing things.

Developing the Site Management Team

In determining how large a management staff is required, the prime consideration will be the site manager. The overall demoralization of the residents, as well as the existing staff, requires that the manager take command of the property and the staff immediately. I would argue that the chain of command is extremely important—the site manager must have authority and be able to pick his or her staff. Your guidance should remain an important factor in the staff selection, however, and you should interview the entire staff yourself initially. Even though there will be no need for leasing agents as such at the outset of the rehabilitation, you may determine that the current site manager is not adequate for the job, and one of the leasing agents might be able to assume the site management responsibilities. Actual creation of the management team should be left to the site manager you choose.

Choosing a Site Manager.   This person should have a strong personality and the ability to be a leader. At the beginning, these criteria supersede all others. New policies and procedures will be established and these must be implemented and enforced.

Another important criterion is organizational ability. One thing we have found repeatedly is that site managers who have operated with little or no outside supervision tend to develop their own, sometimes atypical, ways of doing things. For example, during the lease audit performed as part of the due diligence process, you may find that the leases are not in order and that they do not match the current rent roll. This is an indicator that the current manager lacks organizational skills, and such skills are an important requirement during the rehabilitation. Answers to the questions you ask and the facts you uncover during your examination of the management office will speak volumes.

When there has been little supervision of the site manager, asking what has been expected will probably reveal that the minimal requirements were being reasonably met. It has been said jokingly within the industry that, if there are no problems, supervisory personnel do not visit the property. There is a lot of truth to this. If accomplishment of certain items will reasonably satisfy the owner, doing these thing will mean fewer visits to the property by the owner. In such situations, the site manager can do pretty much what he or she pleases once the owner's needs are fulfilled. Most of the time this means little or nothing extra is done. Unfortunately, this situation is all too typical of an owner of a property in trouble or when a lender has taken such a property back. There is no burning desire on the part of ownership to visit a property that is declining, where the people on it are demoralized. Because there is nothing uplifting there, an owner will look for reasons not to go to the property. That is why, during the interview, it is valid to ask the existing site manager to tell you exactly what has been expected of him or her by prior ownership or management.

Communication and interpersonal skills are next in importance. Local government officials, financial institutions, investors, and others will be visiting the property from time to time, and they have to be dealt with in a straightforward but friendly manner in order to enhance your credibility with them. The site manager will be your intermediary with these people, and you should want someone who will represent you well.

On the other hand, marketing skills are not very important at this early point. The property is still a long way from the rerenting phase of the reha-bilitation. Of course, having a manager who possesses the marketing skills required for that rent-up will be a bonus. In managing a residential property that is being recycled, an individual who lacks both marketing and people skills is not likely to be successful as a team leader.

Other Management Personnel.   The number of management person-nel is an important consideration. Regardless of the size of the property, two people will be needed in the management office at the beginning of the rehab—a manager and an assistant—to provide the necessary coverage dur-ing a work week that will span six days. At this point, the management office will not be a leasing office, but the establishment and communication of poli-cies and procedures will necessitate far greater resident contact and more frequent and thorough property inspections than under ordinary circum-stances. This means all site personnel will have to be people-oriented and organized. Keeping residents happy is an important part of site management.

The major initial efforts will be directed to collecting rent from existing residents, enforcing policies and procedures, and following through on evic-tion proceedings. None of these tasks is easy; if a property has more than 500 or 600 units, you may want to consider adding a second assistant. There is no hard and fast rule as to when a second assistant is necessary; it depends on the work load faced by the management team. Sometimes a part-time person is all that is needed. While it is obvious that payroll should be minimized during a rehabilitation, it is also imperative that your new policies and pro-cedures are enacted quickly and enforced diligently.

Maintenance Personnel.   Good maintenance people are hard to find. As with the management staff, interviewing all of the existing maintenance staff is advisable. It may be said that, once a maintenance worker acquires bad habits, there is no way that person will change. Yet there are instances in which the establishment of specific procedures and work rules has led to very high levels of performance. The formal employment interviews should expand on your earlier conversations with the maintenance personnel during the due diligence process.

In considering the skills needed to perform the job, the so-called people skills should not be overlooked. Maintenance personnel will interact directly with the residents, and residents opinions of the property will be based in some measure on the services they receive and the manner in which it is delivered—i.e., the workers' attitudes.

There is no ironclad method for making a hiring decision, nor is famil-iarity with the property a particular advantage, as the following example indicates.

A maintenance man had worked at the property for twelve years. During the due diligence, the man had shown that he was extremely knowledgeable about the property and its problems. In fact, he had proposed solutions for some of them and made numerous other suggestions for changes. In the formal interview, he expressed enthusiasm about working under the guidelines that we planned to establish. However, the man had to be terminated shortly after we took over management; although he talked a good program, he never produced any results.

This error in judgment was not particularly costly. It just necessitated interviewing more people and hiring a replacement, and we had learned some things from him about the property. The truth is, it often takes several changes before you assemble a team that can work together and be in harmony.

When choosing maintenance personnel for a property undergoing rehabilitation, several criteria must be established. The first thing to realize is that maintenance personnel will not be directly involved in the rehabilitation construction work. However, they will do some work on the rehabilitated apartment units. That role will be discussed first.

Rehabilitation Responsibilities.   Our experience indicates that it works out best if the maintenance staff have exclusive access to the areas used for storage of cabinets, countertops, appliances, and certain building materials purchased in volume directly by the owner. Because of this, the maintenance staff are required to assist in the unloading and later delivery to the units of these materials as they are scheduled for use in the rehab. For the same reason, they should be responsible for the final unit preparation—since appliances are stored by the maintenance staff, it is best to have them installed by those same personnel. This way the appliances will not be removed from the secure location until they are needed. Similarly, any window coverings or other items not included in a contract for turnkey construction of the unit rehab should be installed or completed by the maintenance staff. This affords an excellent opportunity for maintenance personnel to test all plumbing and electrical installations, just as they would in the turnover of any vacant unit.

Common sense also plays a part in this final checking, since small oversights on the part of the contractor—e.g., tightening loose screws—can often be fixed by the maintenance worker in a few minutes, and the contractor does not have to return to the unit (even though the contractor is responsible for the work). This does not mean the contractor gets a pass. The contractor should be told about such oversights, and if they are a recurring problem, you should indicate that a deduction will be made from the contractor's payment. On the other hand, a large oversight or an improper installation in a rehabbed unit should be brought to the contractor's attention for immediate correction.

In the past at our projects, initial demolition or "trash out" of the unit to be rehabbed used to be included as part of the maintenance staff obligations, but that is no longer done. Now, removal of carpeting, cabinets, floor coverings, tub enclosures, and the like is part of the contractor's specification. The reason for this is quite simple. We received numerous complaints from contractors that the maintenance crew had created more work for them by doing a messy tear out. We subsequently found that having the contractor's crew do their own tear out meant no overlap of responsibility and no room for argument.

Maintenance Responsibilities.   Although the maintenance personnel may be involved in the rehabilitation to some extent, their primary responsibility is to provide service to the property and the residents in place by responding to work orders. When choosing maintenance personnel, it is important to select people who have the skills needed to solve particular problems inherent within that property. For example, if a property has hot-water baseboard heat and uses a low-pressure boiler system, it would certainly be advisable to have at least one maintenance worker with the ability to deal with the routine maintenance of this heating system.

As you can see, by having a clear delineation of responsibilities, the maintenance staff can be kept to a minimum, and they can fulfill their primary responsibility of responding to work orders for existing residents and the common areas of the property as well as performing very specific tasks in the rehabbed units because scheduling this work is relatively easy.

Size of the Maintenance Staff.   How many maintenance people are required for a particular property is more difficult to answer than the same question regarding the management staff. In fact, the answer depends on several variables. First and foremost is the skill of each maintenance worker. Quality of work and speed must also be considered. You have to evaluate whether the work was done correctly the first time (no callbacks), and how quickly it was completed. Some people work faster than others, and this must be taken into account. Similarly, the number of callbacks can easily be assessed so that an experienced manager can determine the speed at which a task should be performed to do it correctly.

Also consider the types of work being performed in occupied apartments and the common areas. In a rehabilitation project, it is important to include maintenance requirements when considering where to make changes. If certain areas generate repeated expenditures for maintenance—in terms of work orders, time, and money—it may be worthwhile to evaluate these problem areas as part of the rehabilitation. A good example of this is sewer rodding. If a property has had recurring sewer problems, rather than purchase a high-powered rodding machine, consider installing new sewer lines as part of the rehabilitation. This is a sizeable cost, but when weighed against the repeated costs of rodding and maintenance plus the inconvenience to residents, the expenditure may result in a savings of both money and grief.

The only way to categorize and delineate the responsibilities of maintenance personnel during the recycling process is to prepare detailed job descriptions for them. Because every property is unique, its requirements for maintenance will differ. Particular consideration should be given to ongoing maintenance. Providing service to the existing residents will foster resident retention and help to maximize income during a period when occupancy naturally tends to decline. Careful analysis of the operating expenses incurred under previous management will be of great assistance in determining what is needed.

In establishing manpower requirements, consider the number of vacant units that will be part of the rehabilitation at its start-up and the number of units that will be occupied, possibly throughout much of the construction period. An excellent program to follow is to provide the best possible service to the existing residents without replacing costly items that will ultimately be disposed when a particular unit is rehabilitated.

Another consideration is the part these personnel play in the rehabilitation. As noted earlier, there are several critical areas of the rehabilitation process in which maintenance personnel participate. These are unloading, storage, and installation of appliances, and making a final check of the unit's mechanical installations prior to occupancy. This will be easy to schedule because the rehabilitation contractors' turnover schedule can be interfaced with the routine maintenance schedule. There is an additional obvious benefit to having maintenance personnel do final mechanical checks. Even though construction management personnel will have inspected each unit carefully prior to acceptance of the work done by the contractor, maintenance personnel having an opportunity to double-check the work means that, if problems occur later, a maintenance worker cannot say that the contractor was in error. This also further delineates responsibility and accountability.

Obviously, a recommendation to have one maintenance worker for 50 units—or for 80 units or 100 units—would be erroneous. Clearly, the number of workers will depend on the type of work or specific tasks required, the speed with which jobs can or must be performed, and the competence of the people performing each task. The situation is optimum when maintenance as such, combined with their rehabilitation duties, provides full-time work for each member of the maintenance team, and little or no overtime is required. When establishing a maintenance team during a rehabilitation, this should be the manager's goal.

One final thought about maintenance staff: Do anticipate some changes when the rehabilitation is completed. First of all, the staff size will not have to be increased as occupancy increases following rehabilitation. This is because the additional tasks staff performed during the rehabilitation are no longer required, and there should be fewer service requests for the newly occupied units. (The construction contractors' work having been checked by both construction management and maintenance personnel assures this.) What will change is the scheduling of maintenance work. To best serve the property—and the owner—the manager should, from the outset, hire maintenance personnel who want long-term employment and have a good attitude about work.

Policies and Procedures

Your policies and procedures for the property will be established as a result of your due diligence efforts, which should have included analysis of the policies that have been in place at the property as well as those extant within the local marketplace. For a property undergoing recycling, the implementation of rigorously enforced policies and procedures will have much the same effect as turning on a light in a dark room. The change from a complete absence of policies and procedures—or nonenforcement of those that were in place—to firm but fair policies and procedures will be a shock for the existing residents. However, change in general (the recycling process) can only begin when change in the particular (management policies) is enforced.

Policies critical to changing the image of the property and establishing property management operations are needed first. In an effort to reduce the shock to the existing residents, it is best to plan for implementation in phases. Collection policies are needed immediately so they can be enforced within the first thirty days. Criminal activity should be forbidden, and local police should deal with lawbreakers. Lease renewals, relocation of residents to rehabbed units, and other resident relations policies must be established so that they can be explained to those who may query the management staff.

New policies and procedures—community rules, if you wish—should be presented to the existing residents within one week of the beginning of new management. (It is assumed that new management will become effective on the first of a month, since that is a fairly common practice.) The residents will need to know several things—

- What specific policies are being implemented.
- Whether they replace, modify, or augment something already in place.
- When they become effective.
- How they will be enforced.

All of the policies and procedures that you establish should be implemented only after careful research and evaluation of the current market, the current position of your property within that market, and its projected position when the rehabilitation has been completed. Policy changes should never be considered frivolously; this is especially true of those policies that have a lasting impact (e.g., allowing pets on the property).

Exhibit 6.1 is a list of management functions and resident activities that should be addressed in standard operating policies and procedures. This list should not be considered all-encompassing because each property will have some unique requirements that must be addressed. However, it can serve as a general guideline for the types of policies needed at any residential property.

The policies and procedures you establish will be the basis for the property's operations after the rehabilitation is completed and when stabilization has been achieved. You will also need to establish policies and procedures for hiring, training, and otherwise dealing with the site staff. Some specific policies and their ramifications are discussed in the following sections.

Collections.   More than likely collections will have been a problem. The new collection policy—or enforcement of the existing one—should become effective in the month following take-over. This will allow the residents to make appropriate financial adjustments. People who have made a habit of paying their rent on the fifteenth or twentieth of the month because there was no penalty before are likely to accept a first of the month due date when told what the new policy is and how it will be enforced. Obviously, such a thirty-day phase-in of the new collection policy is likely to further increase any existing delinquencies; however, immediate enforcement could create irreparable damage for that majority of the residents who would otherwise comply with the policy. Besides, landlord-tenant law or applicable municipal codes may require a specific period of notice.

Criminal Activity.   One policy that should be enforced immediately is the removal of residents who are committing unlawful acts. This is the first step in demonstrating to the outside world that change is taking place. During the due diligence process, local government officials—especially the police department—should be contacted to find out what type of unlawful activities, if any, are known to be taking place on the property. Once new management is in place, the police should be invited to begin the clean-up process immediately. The all-important change in the property's image begins with the establishment of a good working relationship with local government officials, and having the police arrest lawbreakers is one of the best ways to launch this process. Purging a property of lawbreakers not only creates a more wholesome atmosphere for the residents, but also begins the long process of changing the market perception of the property. When it becomes apparent that you are sincere in your desire and efforts to change the property, remarks about it will change from negative to positive.

Lease Renewals.   As indicated in an earlier chapter, many residents who have paid their rent and generally abided by whatever community rules and regulations are in force will choose not to renew their leases when they

E X H I B I T   6.1

Types of Policies and Procedures

Rental Policies
- Requirement for applications and leases to be in writing
- Use of a standard form for rental applications (compliance with fair housing requirements)
- Whether a credit bureau or other means will be used to verify applicant information and what information will be checked
- Uniform qualification standards for acceptance of residents (minimum age—need for guarantor, ratio of rent to household income, minimum period of employment, references from prior landlord, credit references, etc.)
- Lease term (standard period—e.g., 1 year; acceptability and handling of longer or shorter lease terms)
- Security deposits (other deposits—e.g., pets; return of deposits; use of move-in/move-out inspection checklist; damage exceeding ordinary wear and tear)
- All adult occupants required to sign the lease
- Renewal of leases (terms, notice, etc.)
- Subleasing (written permission of landlord required; landlord approval of sublessee)

Collection Policies
- Rents due on first of month (grace period, late fees)
- Method of payment (check or money order preferred; handling of NSF checks)
- Nonpayment of rent (eviction notice, legal proceedings, legal fees)
- Withholding rent for nonprovision of services

Maintenance Policies and Procedures
- How to request services
- Requirement for written work order
- Time frame for response
- Emergency maintenance (access to units, notice to occupants)
- Record keeping (distribution of work order copies; who completes forms)
- Parts and supplies stocked (items, quantities, inventory system)

---

expire. One policy we have used successfully to counter this involves offering them renewal leases for another term at the same rental rate or only a slight increase. This has been done when there were a sufficient number of vacant apartments available for rehabilitation and when it was known that the rehab construction would take longer than one year. The reason is obvious. A good resident who pays rent on time is a valued customer, and retaining that resident helps maintain the income stream. It must be understood, however, that many residents who have been satisfied with conditions as they were will be uncomfortable with the changes being made at the property. What this means is that policies designed to purge some of the residents will only add to the general exodus from the property. Certainly, the faster the resident profile is changed, the more rapidly the market perception of the property will change.

Accounting and Record Keeping Policies
• Handling of security deposits (escrow and/or interest-bearing account)
• Deposit of collected rents
• Handling of cash receipts
• Chart of accounts (relating income and expense items to budget categories)
• Income and expense records
• Budget variance
• Requirement for written purchase orders (authorizations, dollar limitations)

Emergency Procedures
• Types of emergencies (procedures for handling specific emergencies)
• Chain of responsibility (who can notify emergency services; who contacts property owner, insurance agent, etc.)
• Access to the property (whom to contact; specific arrangements)
• Media contact (who contacts media; types of information to be given out)
• Resident in-unit emergencies (illness, death; notice to family; notice to authorities)

Rental policies must take into consideration applicable laws. Security deposits may be subject to payment of interest, and residents may have to be informed about where those funds are being held (financial institution, account number). Occupancy guidelines (minimum and maximum number of occupants for each unit type or size) may be established in local fair housing laws, or they may be prohibited altogether. Leasing practices and apartment marketing strategies must be nondiscriminatory as required by fair housing laws.

Specific policies and procedures are also needed regarding employees and employment beyond those covered in the text. Particulars to be addressed include qualification of job applicants; checking of references; salary and performance review; work day, work week, days off and holidays; and employment benefits such as insurance, vacation, and sick time. These may be set by the management company or the property owner, and they must comply with wage and hour laws and equal employment opportunity laws.

In the context of apartment recycling, policies and procedures should also be established regarding construction activities (purchase and storage of materials; access to rehab areas; role of maintenance staff; supervision of the work, etc.). These may be set by the construction manager.

Rules and regulations that residents are required to comply with are often incorporated into the lease document (as an appendix or rider). These spell out such things as use of on-site coin laundry equipment, disposal of garbage and household trash (including requirements for recycling paper, glass, etc., as appropriate), replacement of batteries in smoke alarms, limitations on noise or other disturbances, recommendations for personal security (keep unit doors locked; locks on windows; access for visitors), recommendation or requirement for renter's insurance, requirement for automobile insurance, definitions of visitors and guests, and parking assignments. They should also reiterate rental, collection, and maintenance policies and may include specifics regarding pets and return of security deposits. In particular, they should spell out the kinds of behaviors for which the landlord can terminate the lease (nonpayment of rent, illegal activities).

Relocations within the Property.   Another policy that must be considered relates to the transfer of existing residents to newly rehabilitated units. This should not be a problem, but a firm policy must be established. Bear in mind that most of the residents probably live at the property because of their income level—they cannot afford to live in a more-desirable and, possibly, more-expensive apartment community. When rehabilitated units are ready for occupancy, it is likely that few of the existing residents will be able to afford the increased rent. Relocation of these residents will probably not be a large part of the rerenting process, although there will be some who will avail themselves of this opportunity. A good policy to follow is to offer residents a nominal incentive to relocate in the building (e.g., pay for the telephone hook-up in their new apartments). At no time, however, should a rent discount be offered as an incentive to move into a newly rehabbed unit. The unit is in the best condition that it will ever be. No matter the quality of the resident, once an apartment is occupied, it will never look as good as it does on the day its rehabilitation was completed.

Employee Policies.   This discussion of policies is incomplete without some mention of policies regarding staff appearance and dress requirements. It is difficult to demand a certain type of dress for employees unless uniforms are provided. However, I strongly urge that some uniformity of appearance be required among maintenance workers at the property. Ideally, all maintenance personnel will at least wear shirts that are the same color. These shirts should be purchased as a property expense, and the workers should be required to keep them clean. This way you can include sewn-on name tags that include the property name. (Remember, the name of the property will likely be changed, and additional or different colors may be used in the new design theme. Coordination of company colors and "uniform" shirts is a good idea.) A mode of dress can also be strongly urged for the management staff. This may be handled best as a dress code indicating some things that are not acceptable as business attire (e.g., blue jeans and tee shirts). Regardless of where site personnel work, cleanliness should be mandatory. The important thing to emphasize is that employees represent the property to the residents and to the community at large. Appearance is an important part of their professional image and reflects on the property's image.

Certainly it is better if people can be salaried and not have to be paid overtime. However, the law is very clear about this—an employee must have management (executive, administrative, or professional) responsibilities and meet certain other tests to be exempt from the overtime requirement. The majority of the workers at the property will be paid an hourly rate, and they will be entitled to one and one-half times that rate for hours worked in excess of 40 hours per week.

Personnel policies should be explained to employees at the time of employment. For site staff who are held over from prior management, your policies should be explained at the time of management take-over. Policies should cover the work day and work week, including hours to be worked (start and end times) and breaks (lunch or other meals). Specific policies should address pay periods, overtime pay versus compensatory time, and benefits that will be provided to them (e.g., paid holidays, vacation time, and sick days or personal holidays). If medical or other insurance is made available, they need to know whether it is prepaid by the employer or the employee contributes toward it. If there is to be a probationary period, it should apply to all new employees—I strongly recommend this and urge that it be applied prior to benefits accruing. A check of equal employment opportunity laws is in order to assure that your policies are nondiscriminatory.

None of the foregoing policies is any different than those needed for a stabilized property. However, in my experience, there is usually some turnover of employees before a solid team is established. To facilitate administration and be sure they are uniformly applied, all employment policies should be in writing, and every employee should have a copy of them. (The employee should be required to acknowledge that this information has been received and is understood—also in writing.) If everyone understands the policies, there will be few questions and less opportunity for conflict to arise when an employee is terminated. Fair policies and practices foster good morale.

Resident Relations

Most rehabs are not "gut jobs" requiring existing residents to move out. Just as surgery is a shock to the human system, rehabilitation is a shock to a property and its existing residents. There are three property management activities that should be focused on during a rehabilitation.

1. Maintaining a continuity of services provided to established residents in order to maximize the amount of rental income.
2. Evicting residents who do not pay rent or who cause problems for management and other residents.
3. Keeping those residents who do pay their rent and behave properly.

Bear in mind that the third group occupy units that must be rehabilitated at some point. It will take a great deal of skill to convince them to stay in the first place and then to coordinate their relocation to newly rehabbed apartments. (The relocation process is addressed elsewhere in this chapter.) During the transformation of the property, the management team will have to acquire, polish, and make use of so-called people skills. Having established management policies and procedures, they will need toughness to enforce the rules and then to evict those residents who do not abide by them. On the other hand, they must be sensitive to the problems facing the residents they want to retain. Rehabilitation is disruptive, and these residents will have to be provided more (and better) service to compensate for the previous lack of it.

In this situation, effective communication is the key to resident retention. Residents should be informed of the plans for the rehabilitation initially and the progress of the construction periodically, as well as how they will benefit from the various changes. Because you need their cooperation, it is imperative to invite it beforehand and express appreciation for it afterward.

Resident Rules and Regulations.   The best way to deal with the inherent conflicts that are likely to take place during a rehabilitation is to establish specific rules and regulations for the residents to follow. These should be clearly presented, simple but enforceable statements based on your management policies. These rules and regulations may not be strictly enforced at the very outset. The important thing is to get them down in writing and then make sure copies are provided to all the residents.

Before you create new rules, however, be sure you know and understand those that are already in place, even if they were not being enforced before you took over. It may be more important to advise residents of the change in management and, accompanying it, the change in policy—i.e., that *existing rules will now be enforced.* A good example relates to policy regarding how to deal with residents who pay their rent late. If you take over the property on the first of the month, it is a good idea to send the residents a letter reiterating what is already in their leases. More than likely, the lease will state that the rent is due on the first of the month and delinquent after the fifth of the month. A late charge may also be in order after the fifth. If this has not been enforced for some time, it is imprudent to take over the property one day and enforce such a major policy the next. A fairer approach is to write to the residents explaining what the policy is and stating that, effective *next* month, the policy will be rigorously enforced. This gives you twenty to twenty-five days to alert existing residents about the policy. Many will comply simply because the rule has been made known to them, but many will not. However, when the subsequent evictions proceed, swiftly and in an orderly manner, collections will begin to increase. As mean-spirited as it may seem, one eviction will be the greatest instruction for the remainder of the residents. The important step is to make sure everyone on the staff understands *how* the eviction proceedings are to be handled.

Dealing with existing residents while a property is in transition is difficult at best. How the rules and regulations are developed and presented, and the way they are enforced, will determine the type of response you will get from your residents. Tough, but fair; stern, but compassionate—these are the guidelines, and they will require the fullest application of your people skills.

Managing the Construction

In an earlier chapter, I recommended *against* using site staff to perform the rehabilitation construction. However, the importance of having the management team involved in the rehabilitation process cannot be overemphasized. There is no better way to create and maintain a strong bond between rehabilitation construction and property management than to have the site management staff routinely assist in the inspection process.

Members of the management staff, especially the leasing agents, are responsible for rerenting the units. They talk to prospective residents. They hear others' comments, questions, and criticisms of the rehabilitation. Too often, however, leasing agents are left out of the rehabilitation process when, because of their direct contact with prospective renters, they have gained insights that should make their input a most important factor. Members of the management staff also need to know about the progress of the rehabilitation and its quality so they can respond appropriately to prospects and residents. Recycling an apartment property is a team effort, and no member of the team should be overlooked.

Managing construction requires inspection of the work while it is in progress as well as after it has been completed. The problem is that most such inspections will be done primarily to satisfy the lender's requirements in preparation for a construction draw. These inspections are important because the job cannot progress further if the lender is not satisfied. However, it is probable that every item of work performed will not be inspected at that time regardless of who makes the inspection on the lender's behalf. On the other hand, if inspections are performed for the purpose of knowing that all work has been done in compliance with the contracts—and that everything works properly—there can be no question that the draw inspection will be satisfactory.

When the construction activity is at its peak, daily inspections (by the site manager or the construction manager) are essential. This is not because of any distrust of the contractor, but rather because you should want to know what is going on at the property every day. It demonstrates that you are interested in the contractor's performance as well as the general progress of the rehabilitation. You should also be looking out for potential problems that might change the critical path of the construction process—i.e., the performance timetable. It is not the contractor's responsibility to advise you of a problem that, if solved now, could save money later and result in a better rehabilitation. While this happens occasionally, it should not be expected. It is your job as the owner (or manager) of the property to look for such problems and to find alternative solutions that will improve the overall outcome of the job.

Inspections are laborious and highly repetitive. After a period of time, they become tedious. Because you are looking at the same items again and again, it is only natural to become lazy. The only way to avoid falling into the trap of casually looking at an item—rather than meticulously inspecting it—is to use a checklist. Property management is a very detail-oriented and repetitive business. Because of this, forms and checklists have been developed to help management personnel focus on the task at hand. Some might argue that too many forms and checklists force a person to focus on the paperwork rather than on the job. However, only those forms and checklists that are essential should be used. In a rehabilitation project, a construction inspection checklist is imperative. (An example is presented in exhibit 6.2.)

At best, a checklist can only identify types of items that should be in-

E X H I B I T   6.2

Example Construction Inspection Checklist—Unit Interior

Property _____ Date _____

Unit No. _____ Type 1BR 2BR Corner Rehab/Nonrehab	**Living Room** Flooring _____ Window _____
Hallway Entry Door _____ Flooring _____ Subfloor _____ Closet _____ Electrical _____ Other _____	A/C _____ Electrical _____ Other _____
	Dining Room Flooring _____ Electrical _____ Other _____
Bathroom Doors _____ Flooring _____ Tub/Enclosure _____ Sink/Faucet _____ Medicine Cabinet _____ Electrical _____ Other _____	**Kitchen** Appliances _____ Cabinets _____ Countertop _____ Flooring _____ Electrical _____ Sink/Faucet _____ Other _____
Bedroom 1 Doors _____ Flooring _____ Closet _____ Window _____ Electrical _____	**Bedroom 2** Doors _____ Flooring _____ Closet _____ Window _____ Electrical _____
Other	

It may be necessary or appropriate to include particulars to be checked for each item. Otherwise, those conducting the inspection must be trained to identify specifics of correct versus incorrect installations and what kinds of things to test (e.g., electrical outlets and switches, working faucets and drains).

---

spected. The critical factor is training of the management team. They must know *how* to conduct the inspection—what to look for and how to check it. This means, too, that the management staff must become familiar with the spectrum of construction tasks that should be performed for the rehabilitation. An example is the testing of new electrical outlets. An additional two or three minutes in an apartment unit with a tester to be sure that all outlets are "live" can save having to call the contractor back or avert a service request right after a resident has moved in. Having the work performed by the maintenance staff at a later time will add to the operating costs of the property as well as inconvenience the new resident, from whom you want to receive referrals. As you can see from this simple example, if routine inspections are made with great care, the draw inspection for the lender will take care of itself (all the lender wants to see is that the money requested has, in fact, been spent at the property).

Just as goals were essential in establishing the timetable for the rehabilitation, a defined chain of command is needed to assure its completion. In the rehabilitation of an apartment community with ongoing occupancy, the chain of command cannot always be clearly defined. It is important to continually reinforce an attitude of partnership in the process. Because the contractors will be paid by the construction manager, the construction manager should have direct authority over them. However, the site manager will also interact with the various contractors, and it is important to establish at the outset when and how much authority the site manager will exercise over the contractors. Because the site manager is on the property everyday, it is usually more expedient for the site manager and the management office to be a point of contact for the contractors. There will be times when contractors working in individual units will need certain supplies that are to be furnished to them and are stored on the premises (e.g., kitchen cabinets). Access to the secured storage area and coordination of the transfer of supplies is best arranged by the site manager. However, only the construction manager (or project director) should be authorized to approve completion of the work.

There should also be a clear delineation of who will communicate with the lender. The construction manager should work directly with the lender's representative for construction draw inspections; the draw itself is best handled directly with the loan officer. (Matters of policy and financing should be handled directly by the person responsible for the loan—the new owner.) Routine updates can be handled and minor problems solved between the construction manager and the loan officer. As has already been pointed out, there should be frequent communication advising the lender of what is happening at the property—good things as well as bad. Anything that could require an alteration (or exception) to the loan documents should be communicated in a face-to-face meeting between the lender and the owner. The relationship with the lender should be viewed as a long-term proposition. Even if the term of this loan is short, there is always the next deal.

Monitoring the Critical Path.   The critical path method of construction scheduling is based on a series of specific tasks, the order in which they must be performed, and the time required to complete each one. (This concept was introduced in chapter 3.) Management of the construction process requires monitoring of the critical path, which requires focusing on three distinct categories of problems.

First are unforeseen structural or physical problems that may be uncovered as the rehabilitation progresses. These must be dealt with immediately so that work can be resumed as quickly as possible. From a financial standpoint, they are why a contingency fund is established. The lender must be made aware that, in a rehabilitation, there should be a substantial contingency fund to cover unforeseen circumstances in construction.

Second are changes in market conditions. When analyzing a market, the hardest things to identify specifically are the position or status of the ever-evolving neighborhood and how negative the perception of the subject property is as rehabilitation begins. As the recycling process gets into full swing, it may become apparent that the market for this property, as rehabilitated, is stronger than you initially thought it was. This might encourage you to alter the timetable and complete the rehab faster than you had originally planned. Items you had not considered necessary might prove to be of critical importance for continuing or improving the rerenting and achieving the market position you desire—remember the example of the tabletop on the wing wall. If this happens, the rehabilitation budget must be analyzed immediately to see if any funds can be made available so that these items can be included in the rehab. Conversely, some of the items that once seemed necessary to attract a reasonable market share may have proven *not* to be that effective—a microwave oven, for example. These items should be eliminated from the rehabilitation of future units.

Third are special situations—natural disasters such as fire, a tornado, an earthquake, or the like; strikes and other forms of work stoppage—any of which could be devastating to your rehabilitation timetable. The inability to maintain a supply of cabinets and other materials could not only lead to a work stoppage, but also create other problems for a rehabilitation project. If contractors cannot continue working, they will tend to look for other work, and then they may not be available when work on your project can begin again.

The goal of the recycling process is to change the image of the property as it is perceived by renters in the market, and the objective of the critical path or timetable for the construction is to anticipate completion of the last unit rehab at the exact time when the last new resident would move into the property. This is perfection; and, while it is doubtful that things will ever happen exactly as planned, this must be the goal. Achieving it would prove that the timetable established for the rehabilitation dovetailed with the initial interpretation of the market and its perception of the property. However, the recycling process is inherently inexact, and many mid-course corrections to the critical path are likely to be needed.

Marketing

The entire recycling process is a marketing process. You are making physical changes to a property and adopting policies and procedures that will provide a particular lifestyle based on the resident profile you prepared from your original market analysis. However, it is the rerenting of the rehabilitated apartments that is the final manifestation of all the things that have been accomplished up to that point—your decisions at the outset regarding the scope of the rehabilitation, the selection of new plantings, the ultimate name change (if necessary), the personnel you have hired or retained, and the overall image that you want to project.

The normal impulse is to market the property as soon as possible. In recycling apartments, the timing of this activity is crucial. First of all, the new owner has two goals that are fundamentally antagonistic to each other. One is to attain the highest possible stabilized NOI in the shortest amount of time; the other is to minimize negative cash flow (i.e., actual losses). Marketing too soon defeats both of these goals.

On the other hand, you may acquire or have to manage a property where renting will be an ongoing process throughout the rehabilitation. Often this approach is taken when a property is located in a neighborhood that is perceived to be just as undesirable as the property itself. In a situation such as this, only the nonpayers, the slow-payers, and the lawbreakers will be purged from the property. Residents who are considered "marginal" will be encouraged to remain, and marketing will continue. A decision has been made that the character of the property, rather than the profile of the residents, will be changed in an evolutionary (rather than revolutionary) way. Rentals will be slow, and so will the rehabilitation of apartments, although changes to the exterior and the common areas should be made quickly. Such rehabilitation by evolution will require three to four years to accomplish, and during this period, the property must wait for the "economic obsolescence" of the neighborhood to disappear.

Timing the Marketing Effort. During the course of the recycling process, it is important to generate excitement about and enthusiasm for the property. There is a natural excitement created by the evolution of an old, well-worn, bleak-looking property into a new-looking attractive one. This is related solely to the physical changes that those who are directly involved with the property see each day as the property's outward appearance improves. Their first thought may be that everyone should share in this enthusiasm. However, that is an unrealistic hope because the market's perception of the property is still negative, and people are still reluctant to choose it as their home.

Something else must be understood as well. As the physical changes are being made, the property may not even appear to be undergoing any changes. If the initial rehab effort is focused on vacant units, the newness will certainly not be obvious. The exterior of the building and the grounds surrounding it may not be improved right away because some work may have to be completed before other work can be started. Another important consideration to keep in mind is that most prospective residents do not begin looking for an apartment until their leases are about to expire and a move would be imminent.

Besides, people tend to have difficulty imagining what a property will look like when it is completely renovated. If only one apartment unit is ready and the rest of the property is not, the prospect's impression of the whole property is likely to be negative. Here again, the problem is one of perception. In a stabilized property, it would be counterproductive to show a prospective resident a dirty apartment and say, "If you rent today, it will be beautiful when you move in. We will fix everything," because a prospect would not buy that. Such an approach is even less viable in a property undergoing recycling. If at all possible, the rehabilitation should begin with fanfare. Exterior cleaning or refinishing, new landscaping, and repairs to the driveway and parking lot are some of the elements that should be addressed first.

Furthermore, in order to generate the highest possible stabilized NOI in the shortest time, you must begin charging rents that are commensurate with your ultimate goal. When you begin to rerent, there will be marketing costs and additional payroll costs for leasing personnel. If you rerent too early, you may not be able to achieve the rents you projected, and the added costs may not be offset right away. Premature marketing not only adds to the operating costs of the property but tends to dampen the excitement that has been building in the site personnel. The opposite situation is also problematic. If marketing is delayed too long, staff morale will suffer because their anticipation of converting the initial excitement into rentals will have dissipated, and they will begin to question whether the property will ever really be rented. It is obvious from this that the rerenting process must be timed carefully.

The goal of the recycling process should be to complete most of the common area rehabilitation as rapidly as possible. Completion of this work will signal to the market that substantial physical change is taking place because the property will be projecting a new image to the outside world. By this time, much of the physical work will have been accomplished in areas that are easily seen by outsiders, and the only residents will be the rent-paying variety—those who remained after removal of the troublemakers and others who would be an embarrassment to any marketing effort. This is the point at which community organizations such as the Chamber of Commerce, local real estate professionals, and businesses can be invited to tour the property and see what is being done.

This is also the time to begin "selling" to residents who have stayed in their former apartments by mutual agreement. Talking to them before this time has no real advantages; trying to sell them at the outset of the rehabilitation is foolhardy. The residents will only know what they actually see, and over the first few months that the rehabilitation work is being done, they will be able to see firsthand what changes are being made. Having seen the changes you are making to the property, those who can afford the new rents will probably want to stay. What you can do to assist this process further is give them a little nudge—perhaps offering a special consideration if they will relocate to a newly rehabbed apartment (as noted earlier in this chapter). After all, being able to move into a really new home should be incentive enough.

Although some may disagree with the philosophy that the one best marketing tool is a property that looks outstanding, it should be obvious that money has been spent to present the property to the renting public. This is the time to hire leasing personnel. Initially you may need only one leasing agent to work directly with the manager and his or her assistant. An advertising campaign should be started as well. The only marketing piece needed is a new property brochure. Site signage should not be overlooked because it is an important addition to the property's curb appeal. On the other hand, promotional gimmicks and giveaways—including incentives (i.e., rent discounts)—seldom produce the results desired.

Advertisements.   While it is easy for an appliance retailer to have a special sale and advertise it heavily in an effort to lure the public into the store, in renting apartments, you are selling more than bricks and mortar—you are selling a way of life. The people you are trying to attract are seeking a nice place to live, a place they can be proud to call home. In the early stages of the marketing process, advertisements in the local newspaper will bring the very best results, but avoid such phrases as "grand opening," "all new," and "newly rehabbed." These are all shop worn and have limited (or no) appeal to renters.

Incentives are another problem area. An advertisement that says, "one month free rent," is usually an indication that the marketing of the property is in trouble. (I once saw an advertisement that read, "due to popular demand, we are extending our 'one month free rent' for another week." My question was, "by whose popular demand?" It had to be that the owner was demanding more rentals.) Frankly, my experience has shown that incentives rarely overcome whatever negative perceptions remain in the marketplace, and I recommend against them.

What you can promote in an advertisement is the items you have added to the units, such as appliances or fixtures you decided to include because your competitors provide them (e.g., a dishwasher). Also consider listing features of your units that are not common in the market but add value to your rentals because they are something the residents would ordinarily have to provide for themselves (e.g., blinds or drapes you installed to present a uniform appearance at the windows). Remember the tabletop installed on the wing wall? Any built-in item like that is promotable. Of course, these things would be in addition to the basic information that should always be included in any "for rent" advertisement—the apartment size (numbers of bedrooms and bathrooms; whether there is a separate dining room), when it is available for showing and occupancy, the location of the property (address or major intersection), the rent, and whom to contact.

Brochures. This is where you can describe your units as newly rehabbed. You may want to list new kitchen appliances, new windows, and other features and fixtures that have been replaced. It may be appropriate to distinguish replacement items from things that have been added to units so they would be more competitive (e.g., an in-sink disposal, any built-ins). If all new electrical wiring or plumbing was installed, this can be noted, too. Ideally, the brochure would be illustrated, preferably in color. The key is to show the finished product. A model apartment can be photographed as an example of how unit interiors will look. The exterior of the property should also be shown as it will look when it is completely landscaped; for this, colored drawings may have to be used if photographs cannot be taken. What is available may depend on the timing of the brochure preparation in relation to the rehabilitation construction. Architectural drawings or renderings may serve the purpose if such were prepared as part of the rehabilitation plan. Floor plans are another nice addition, especially if there are different sizes of apartments or variant room arrangements.

The brochure should include the same basic information as the newspaper advertisement. However, this is where you have an opportunity to expand on that information to characterize the property and the lifestyle it will offer. This means availability of parking, access to public transportation, and recreational facilities (e.g., swimming pools or playgrounds on the property or nearby), as well as information about shopping and schools. However, this is one area where rental rates should not be specific. Because a brochure may be used beyond the initial lease-up, stating an overall range or a representative minimum rent (e.g., rents beginning at $500) will prevent the brochure from becoming outdated too quickly.

Marketing Personnel. An important part of the marketing effort is the personnel responsible for it. You cannot expect staff you hire to have the same level of excitement and enthusiasm for the property and its potential as you do. It is true that the staff will pick up on the overall excitement because of the rehab and the fact that you are doing what you said you would do from the outset. However, they expect to be compensated for their efforts, and monetary incentives in the form of leasing commissions are a good way to encourage staff members' general excitement about the project. Two types of incentives are suggested, those paid to the individual and those earned by the group. Whether you use either or both will depend on the size of the leasing staff, which is a function of the size or needs of the property.

Individual commissions are not always easy to track because a prospect may visit the property several times, talking to one person one time and leaving a deposit with someone else. In fact, a team approach to leasing (and, thus, a sharing of commissions) can sometimes foster the type of togetherness in which everybody works together to accomplish the mutual goal of renting apartments. Bear in mind that incentives for a team must be sufficiently large to merit dividing among several individuals. This is an area that needs a lot of thought before a program is set up. Some of the things to be considered are:

> How much commission—what percentage—will be paid on unit rentals?
> What will be the basis for earning commissions?
> How many units must be rented within a specific time period?

The size of the property is also an important factor. Strategies for 100 units may not work for 500 units, and vice versa.

Specific incentives can be tied to meeting particular goals. The measure can be rate-based, or the goal might be a certain level of occupancy within a prescribed period or by a target date (e.g., one rental a day for a one-month period, or 60 percent occupancy within the first three months). Any incentive that is tied to performance helps the leasing staff "buy in" to the overall success of the program. For this to work, however, the goals must be achievable.

Dealing with Prospective Residents.   When people are making a decision about where they are going to live—a decision that means changing their driving license and voter registration records among other things—they will tend to pay the most they can afford for the best possible service and physical facilities. That is what apartment marketers must bank on. We must make available the best service and the best apartment for the price.

Remember, not every prospective resident will have a negative perception of the property, and there is no reason to alert all prospects that there has been a problem with this property in the past. Why shoot yourself in the foot? Many people who are new to the area will look at your apartments just as objectively as they would look at other apartment complexes. Half the battle in rerenting is inducing prospects to come to your property in the first place. If the rehabilitation is well done, what they see will be impressive.

There is nothing more demoralizing than someone new to the area who enthusiastically puts down a deposit on an apartment and then calls back a few hours later to say, "I've changed my mind," because he or she has been told that the property is not a good place to live. To some extent, this is to be expected. Your leasing staff must understand that this will probably happen again and again during the early phases of the remarketing and that they cannot let it overwhelm them.

There is one distinct advantage that a completely recycled apartment property will have over its competition. Right now—today—it is the newest property in the market. Everyone who rents there is going to have new carpeting, a new kitchen with all new appliances, or whatever new items you have installed in every one of your rehabbed apartments. Now the groundwork you have laid within the community—e.g., your ongoing relations with officials of the local government—will go a long way toward providing some positive feedback in the form of favorable comments to prospective residents who ask them whether your property is "okay."

In fact, the things that will do the most for the rerenting effort are a good-looking property, a nice model to show, rehabbed units that are well-finished, and leasing personnel who are friendly and helpful.

7

Evaluating the Results

Start-up of the rehabilitation sets the clock ticking in a countdown toward stabilization and refinancing. This is a most frightening thought. Regardless of the exhaustive market analysis and the due diligence efforts to assess all problems and anticipate all contingencies, the analyses are inexact. The rehabilitation process is replete with pitfalls and uncertainties, and constant monitoring is required so that corrections can be made when and as necessary. The minimum goal is to be able to refinance the property in a timely manner—hopefully for more than was borrowed for the acquisition and rehabilitation—and avoid defaulting on the existing loan. The ultimate goal is to sell the property for the highest price possible.

Ongoing analysis is necessary to determine where the property is in relation to the initial projections of where it should be. The main criterion for refinancing is a stabilized NOI, which is a measure of the success of the rehabilitation. The higher the NOI, the more successful the recycling process. Throughout the months of construction and during the lease-up period, you should be updating the various due diligence analyses and projections on a regular basis. It is imperative to monitor and measure changes in the marketplace and the financial picture as the recycling process changes the property and its perceived image. To use a rather trite phrase, you need to make frequent "reality checks."

To put the goals of refinancing and ultimate sale into perspective, this chapter reiterates the importance of ongoing market analysis and operations review. The longer-term picture requires consideration of the holding period and the need to optimize both the physical condition and the income stream of the property in preparation for the final sale.

Market Analysis

The success of the rehabilitation will be measured on the basis of the market's acceptance of the newly changed property. At each succeeding evaluation, the market position of the property must be compared with the initial projections for that future time. Obviously, if the initial income projections are met within the prescribed timeframes, the rehabilitation can be considered successful. The results will have validated the original analysis of the investment. However, if the change in the market's perception of the property does not keep pace with the initial estimate of market acceptance, the return on the investment as well as the ultimate yield on the property will suffer; and that could jeopardize the success of the rehabilitation in the long run.

Real estate transactions have been characterized as having a life of their own. This is quite true. The negotiations, the nuances of contract changes, etc., seem ultimately to function independent of the humans participating in the transaction. Sometimes the negotiations in an ordinary acquisition become so intense that market factors are overlooked and "doing the deal" overshadows all else. The same can be true of apartment recycling. Typically, once initial projections have been made and tested, the rehabilitation proceeds on its way with little or no thought being given to changes in the market and its perception of the property. Just as a driver traveling along highways and backroads must look for markers and signs to confirm that the road being taken is indeed the right one as indicated on the map, so must the progress of the rehabilitation be checked against the initial projections to be sure that it, too, is proceeding in the right direction. Apartment recycling is not done in a vacuum—the timetable or rehabilitation plan must be reviewed and occasionally altered as the market dictates.

Continuing evaluation of the competition is imperative. For a stabilized property, competitive rents and features should be checked on a regular basis—preferably each quarter. These comparisons are even more important during the recycling process because the subject property is undergoing physical changes all the time, and it is imperative to measure the market's reaction to or perception of those changes. The problem faced by most properties undergoing rehabilitation is that changes in the market's perception of the property often lag behind the original projections.

To know for sure how the market and its perception of the property are changing, competitive properties should be shopped on a monthly basis as the marketing program begins. Obviously, site employees can only visit the competition once or twice before they will be recognized as shoppers. In order to conduct the monthly market checks needed, money should be allocated in the annual operating budget to pay outside shoppers.

Once a property begins to be accepted in the market, you may find that leasing personnel at competing properties are making comments to their prospects about your property—such as, "They are trying to make changes at that property, but it has really been a terrible place for a long time." This is precisely the kind of thing you thought you were trying to overcome. Note, however, that the effort is indeed being recognized. Such a "sour grapes" commentary is a clear indication that *your property is having an impact in the market*. By trying to perpetuate the old negative perception of your property, your competition is seeking to maintain the status quo—the improvements to your property are obviously making inroads among your competitors' prospects.

In monitoring changes in the market, the key items to look for are changes in the market's perception of your property. It may be necessary or appropriate to modify rental rates or rental policies to facilitate the change in perception. In addition, the site staff should be part of the team from the very beginning. Their inputs can be helpful in preparing for the recycling and in monitoring the success of the rehabilitation and subsequent marketing effort.

Rental Rates.   The ability to raise rents at your property is another measure of recycling success. The goal, of course, is to raise rents as rapidly as possible. However, it may not be possible to maintain the rate of rent escalation as originally projected. On the contrary, you may find that your rents cannot be raised or, in fact, must be lowered. This is a situation from which it will be quite difficult to recover in the short run—and the reason for a strong recommendation *against* marketing too soon. Then again, if things are going well and prospective renters abound, you may be able to consider escalating rents more rapidly than originally projected.

There are two reasons for not achieving projected rental rates. One is the lack of prospects, which is a strong indication that the market's perception of the property has not changed; the other is some lack in the product itself. The lack of prospects can be addressed in several ways, but a word of caution is in order. Special offers, rent discounts, and similar promotions will not overcome a long-standing negative perception. When Orson Welles said in a TV commercial, "We will sell no wine before its time," he was talking about the product being at its best. The same is true of a property undergoing recycling, as indicated in the following example.

We have run specials that exceeded the specials already in place in the competitive market, with no additional success. For one particular property, the special offer provided for a lower rent initially with an automatic rent increase every quarter during a one-year lease—to recoup the discount in stages. The bottom line was an overall discount of approximately three-fourths of one month's rent at the market rate. The special ran for four months with no apparent increase in traffic or rentals until the middle of the fourth month. The special was discontinued the next month. Traffic in that next month was greater than in the preceeding month and continued to increase in subsequent months. This was a clear indication to us that the special did not bring prospects to the property; rather, the improving image of the property—i.e., how the market perceived it—is what created the increased traffic.

Rental Policies.   Sometimes rent is not the only attraction for prospects. If the rerenting is lagging behind projections, a reevaluation of rental policies may be in order. Changing policies to be less restrictive can broaden market acceptance. However, this can be very risky. For example, a property may be made more appealing by changing from a "no pets" policy to one that permits certain pets. Such a policy change can have long-term consequences and should not be considered lightly. When rentals have increased, management may want to return to a "no pets" policy, and this will surely lead to problems with the pet owners. Once pets have been accepted, it is very difficult to reverse the situation. If there are 100 units in a property and pets are permitted, it is extremely likely that at least two-thirds of the occupants will have a pet, and a change in policy does not mean that pets already on the property will automatically disappear overnight.

Another example is a lowering of resident selection standards. While lowering qualification standards may broaden the base of available prospects, it also leads to changes in the profile of the property's occupants. Lower standards can only mean a change for the worse, and that will surely undo all the preceding efforts to improve the resident profile. It could also discourage existing residents from renewing their leases. Having met the higher standards, they will have expectations of living among people who are similarly qualified.

Although policies are subject to change as ownership and management see fit, beware of frequent radical shifts in policy. The best approach to changes in rental policies is to not panic. If a good market analysis was done initially, and repeat analyses are performed monthly, any changes that are needed will probably be smaller and less drastic.

Leasing Agents' Insights.   Another consideration is input from leasing personnel. Usually they are not consulted enough during the marketing process. Some owners and managers believe that asking for the opinions of leasing staff will only yield negative feedback and excuses for failure to rent fast enough. However, if leasing agents believe they are part of the team, they can be an outstanding source of information for monitoring your decisions regarding amenities within a unit, changes to the common areas, and even your advertising campaign. Furthermore, the resident profile at the property will be changing continually during the rehabilitation. Constant feedback from leasing personnel will help you fine-tune your advertising as well as suggest items that can be added to the units to make them more desirable from the standpoint of the evolving resident profile. For example, ceiling fans had not been part of the initial rehabilitation budget for a project, but continual monitoring of the market—shopping the competition and questioning prospects—indicated that ceiling fans in the bedrooms would be a major selling point for leasing apartments with only one sleeve or through-the-wall air conditioner located in the living room. The cost of installing a ceiling fan in the bedroom of each unit was very small, but this addition had a dramatic impact—it markedly increased the closing ratio.

I would argue further that, if a team concept is established at the outset and all team members are asked for input initially, continual solicitation of their input will be a natural outgrowth of that process. A specific example should make the point.

> For one property we rehabbed, the lender had provided minimal rehabilitation funds. The property had been built in 1968 and included avocado kitchen appliances (an example of functional obsolescence). When the rehabilitation was being done in 1984, many of these appliances were still operational. New appliances were available in the avocado color, but at a stiff premium compared to the cost of standard white appliances. We were concerned that white appliances alongside avocado appliances might be a turnoff for prospective renters, so we decided to run a test. A single white refrigerator was placed in the model alongside an avocado range with an avocado range hood, and the leasing agents were asked to record the reactions of prospective renters.
>
> The results were amazing: Not one prospect hesitated about renting an apartment because of the disparity in appliance colors. In fact, the leasing agents successfully sold the fact that the white appliances were brand new. This test made the decision easy. All white appliances were purchased as replacements—at considerable savings.

White appliances remain the standard for rehabilitations as well as initial installations because they can always be matched. Other colors come and go, and often it is difficult or impossible to find exact color-matched replacements. With white, it is even easy to color-match touch-ups to cover scratches.

Operating Statement Analysis

When the rehabilitation is started, the income inevitably begins to diminish. The reasons for this have already been discussed elsewhere, but some of the points bear repeating. Once you begin remarketing, rentals will probably pick up speed initially, but income will increase only slowly. It seems that for every two new residents who move in, three others whose leases have expired will move out. Occupancy may be only slightly increased or possibly decreased. However, the important thing to measure is the income. When new residents begin to move into the property, the income begins to increase even though the occupancy rate seems to languish. This is one of the positive signs that a rehabilitation is successful. In truth, it is more desirable to have a 100-unit property that is 70-percent occupied and has many new residents who are paying higher rents than to be 80-percent occupied by previously established residents who are paying the same rates they were being charged prior to the rehabilitation. During this period, collections must be monitored very carefully; bills are paid from income not from occupancy levels.

The key items to be compared with budget projections are each month's income, collections, and occupancy. If these are lagging behind projections, the property's market position must be reassessed. Income and occupancy levels work hand in hand with continual market analysis. The income portion of the operating statement is most closely allied with the success of the rehabilitation. The rapidity of re-leasing at new or higher rents is the measure of market reacceptance of the property.

The expense component of the operating statement should not be ignored, however. If the goal is to maximize NOI, this can only be achieved by increasing income, decreasing expenses, or a combination of the two. Operating expenses must be reviewed continually. As each month's operating statement is being prepared, all budget variances should be analyzed in detail. While every area is important, some line items need to be monitored very carefully. Advertising is probably the most important such line item. Maintenance is another major consideration.

Measuring Advertising Results.   The rehabilitation will be based on certain specific assumptions and projections. As new prospects come to the property, each of them will have been attracted by certain things. The leasing staff are in the best position to find out what has been the most successful in attracting prospects to the property. Newspapers are the most commonly used and cost-effective advertising medium. However, money invested in the appearance of the property as a feature that attracts prospects—i.e., its curb appeal—will overshadow every dollar spent for advertising.

The best approach is to have leasing personnel engage prospects in casual conversation as they walk the property and view the model, asking them what precipitated their visit to the property. As with a stabilized property, regular traffic report forms for recording numbers of prospects, what they are seeking, and how they found out about the property are an efficient means of collecting specific information for analysis. Cumulative notes on days of the week and times of day when traffic is heaviest as well as specific weather conditions make it easier to adjust office hours and leasing agents' work schedules.

Budget-Related Issues. The initial operating budget will be prepared using information acquired during the due diligence process. There may be some historical data, but if the property has been poorly operated and managed, such data will be suspect. More often than not, the available historical information is very sketchy, and preparation of the budget will be based on your experience with other properties. In that case, the initial operating budget will probably be zero-based. As actual operations begin, it is essential to monitor each line item very carefully to see how your projections compare to actual costs. I recommend budgeting for operating expenses on the high side initially (for purposes of investment analysis). In that way, actual costs are more likely to be reasonably comparable with the original projections, and subsequent adjustments to the budget will be less drastic.

Note that none of the previous discussions of budgeting have included tools and equipment (a possible capital expenditure) or parts and supplies (an operating expense). It may be necessary to budget for purchase or leasing of some equipment for both the rehabilitation and the general operation of the property. In a rehabilitation project, the contractors are typically expected to provide construction equipment as needed. Provision of equipment would be a component of the bid submitted for the job. However, this expectation may or may not be met by the various small contractors hired to do specific work. In that case, leasing of needed equipment by the rehabber would be an appropriate budget item. In addition, a property that has been managed poorly in the past will probably not have on hand an adequate supply (if any) of the parts and supplies typically used for maintenance and repairs, let alone appropriate equipment for these tasks. The absence of something as simple as a handtruck can make it extremely difficult to move around appliances, cabinets, etc., if these items are purchased by the owner. An inventory will indicate what is available, and anticipated work (both rehabilitation construction and ordinary maintenance and repairs) will suggest what tools and supplies must be purchased and whether equipment should be purchased or leased.

The earlier recommendation against charging certain rehabilitation costs as operating expenses bears reiteration. Every time a draw is made against the rehabilitation loan, the size of the overall debt is increased, and this increases the amount of debt service because interest is charged on the amount borrowed; if funds are taken from the operating account, no interest is being charged. While this certainly helps lower the cost of the rehabilitation, it also distorts the operating costs upward. In truth, the few dollars in interest that will be saved by transferring items from the rehabilitation account to the operating account are a minor consideration; the problem is the impact on NOI. The increase in operating expenses decreases the amount of NOI, which is not only the basis for obtaining permanent financing but also the basis for calculating the value of the property.

The important thing to remember is that you initially budgeted income and expenses for *operating the property during the recycling process.* During the rehabilitation and rerenting, continual review of all line items in the operating budget is required. This not only tests the accuracy of your projections but, more importantly, allows you to see monthly variances and make adjustments for them. In this way, you will be able to stabilize the NOI more quickly after the rehabilitation is completed—rather than just starting to work toward stabilization at that point. This monitoring of the budget has other ramifications. If the NOI shown in the operating statement at completion of the rehabilitation is substantially different from the initial projections—and no mid-course corrections have been made to adjust for budget variances—the entire project could fail.

Preparation for Refinancing

Preparation for refinancing should begin the moment the rehabilitation is started. *No lender will consider refinancing your property until the rehabilitation has been completed and the NOI has been stabilized for six months.* In addition, lenders want to see 95-percent occupancy for a six-month period following the rehabilitation. The lender will insist on seeing all operating statements from the beginning of the rehabilitation.

The permanent loan will be based on the stabilized NOI. This is why rehabilitation expenses should not be loaded into the operating statement. The higher the NOI, the higher the value of the property and the greater its ability to service debt. Typically, lenders will use a maximum loan-to-value (LTV) ratio of 80 percent and a debt coverage ratio of 1.2:1. The success of the rehabilitation will be measured by the size of the loan that a lender is willing to make on the property. This is where all of the work from preparation through construction and lease-up comes together.

The same caution about marketing applies to refinancing. You should not begin shopping for permanent financing too soon. Until the property is actually performing, lenders will not be interested in talking with you. Once the property has achieved 95-percent occupancy and its operating statement and resulting NOI have been stabilized for a period of two months, you can begin to shop. If you can comfortably demonstrate at least two months of performance, such an asset will begin to whet their appetite.

Reassessment of the Holding Period

Most rehabilitation programs take at least two years to complete. To achieve a truly changed perception in the market usually requires a longer period. The refinancing preparations offer an excellent opportunity to reassess the potential of the changed property as well as the owner's goals and objectives.

The owner's goals and objectives are paramount in the preliminary planning process. As noted earlier in chapter 3, the intended holding period should dictate the selection of construction materials so that their longevity is commensurate with the owner's goal. When the physical rehabilitation is complete, the property will be in its absolutely best possible condition. It stands to reason, then, that at the first turnover of a newly rehabbed apartment, the carpeting will no longer be brand new. There will undoubtedly be some surface nicks or scratches on the kitchen countertop or cabinets. No matter how thorough your painting, maintenance, and janitorial people are, they cannot restore a vacated apartment to brand-new condition.

Market Considerations.   Because resident turnover signals a change in the property, it is important to undertake a new market analysis at that point. This should be done in the same exhaustive manner as the initial feasibility study was performed. The difference at this later point is that the property has already established a niche in its market. Drastic change to the property and its perception will no longer be a consideration. However, if the property did not attain the market position that had been projected for it, there remains a strong possibility that the property could backslide unless it continues to be managed intensively.

Loss of market position is not necessarily a failure of the management team. New external factors could be bringing additional negative pressures to bear against the property. For example, competing properties that had been superior to your property before the rehabilitation was started could have been allowed to run down over the two or three years your recycling process was under way. The changes at competing properties create a difference in the socioeconomic profile of the prospects entering your property's marketing area. Conversely, properties that may have been average but still somewhat superior to your property before its rehabilitation might have undergone rehabilitation of some sort themselves during this same period. This kind of change could lead to an enhancement of the entire rental market affecting your property. Another possible factor is new construction in the immediate market area, which in most cases has a positive impact on an older rehabilitated property—higher rents necessitated by the cost of new construction make your newly rehabbed property more competitive.

The preceding examples illustrate the fluid nature of the real estate market, and it stands to reason that continual evaluation of one's position in the market is imperative—not only to know what that position is, but also to determine the best time to sell the investment. Reanalysis of the market on a continuing basis provides data for reanalysis of the investment, which should also be done on a continuing basis. Investment analysis using various holding periods can provide solid information for determining the best time to sell. The investor should bear in mind, too, that other investment opportunities may present themselves at any time, and they could necessitate a change in the holding period for the rehabbed property. The goal in analyzing the holding period is to find the optimum time to divest.

Additional Improvements. The continuing market analysis measures both the property's position and its potential for improvement in the market. This will be combined with the actual knowledge that is gathered on a daily basis by the management staff as they interact with current and prospective residents. With the rehabilitation completed and the first rehabbed units being turned over, the property will have reached a plateau in terms of its physical condition. Now there are probably other opportunities to make additional changes that can be explored. Installation of ceiling fans as part of the rehabilitation was used as an example earlier in this chapter. Suppose instead that this improvement was *not* added during the rehabilitation, but that ongoing market analysis following completion of the rehabilitation has indicated that a bedroom fan is a desirable amenity and being demanded by the market. In fact, fans are being installed at competing properties. If ceiling fans will enhance the leasing program as well as increase the amount of rent that can be charged, it may be wise to consider adding such an improvement.

The objective of rehabilitation is to create as much positive change as possible and to overcome negative market perceptions. However, financial constraints may limit the changes that can be made, and consequently, the rehabilitation budget—the basis for the rehabilitation loan—will reflect choices that will yield the greatest return. When such is the case, in all probability there remain some additional changes the rehabber chose not to make. Some items may just have been overlooked during the due diligence process and therefore omitted from the original rehabilitation budget; other possible changes or enhancements may have been discovered during or after rehabilitation.

Once the rehabilitation is completed and the property has reached stabilization, the holding period should be reexamined. If the holding period is going to be several years, it is wise to consider some additional changes that will preserve and enhance the physical structure. The best example is an improvement that will conserve energy. Typically, properties that have undergone recycling demonstrate measurable loss of energy simply because the existing windows are inadequate to the task of heat retention. For such a rehabbed property, a program of window replacement will enhance the property physically and increase its value; in addition, it will reduce heating (utility) costs, which goes directly to the bottom line—it increases NOI.

You may wonder where the money for additional improvements will come from if it was not available for the rehabilitation. There are two possible ways to pay for additional improvements: One is simply to accumulate funds by setting aside a portion of the cash flow each month; the other is to establish a reserve fund from the proceeds of the refinancing and then add to it from the cash flow on an ongoing basis. The latter approach is superior because there is already a lump sum in reserve. In fact, lenders require establishment of a reserve fund as a condition of refinancing (see chapter 4). They know that once a rehabilitation is completed and most of the risk has been removed, few investors are willing to put more of their own cash into such a property on a regular basis. This is why establishment of a reserve account at the time of refinancing is so important—money that has never been received will not be missed. What is really at issue during the negotiations is the amount to be set aside initially—the lender would like the reserve account to be as large as possible, and the borrower would like it to be as small as possible so that more of a cash return on the investment in the property can be realized at that time. I strongly recommend that owners prepare a new capital improvement budget prior to negotiating for refinancing so that a continuing capital improvement program can be maintained. The selling point for the investor is that the cash flow—i.e., the periodic return on the investment—will actually increase over the holding period.

One last thought about post-rehabilitation improvements. The real estate investor should always be on the lookout for functional changes that are appropriate in the market. What was acceptable to the market two years ago may not be acceptable today; when change is in order, you should opt to modernize. Betterment of the property should always be the goal—as the property becomes more desirable in the market, the yield to the investor will improve.

Ongoing Property Management.   Although rehabbers may be reluctant to admit it, recycling a property is a hectic time. As stabilization is reached, the hectic pace continues in anticipation of the refinancing, with emphasis on preparing the property for inspection by a new lender for a permanent loan. Once the property has been refinanced, it is time for a thorough review of the policies and procedures you implemented at the beginning of the rehabilitation. The importance of those initial policies should already be quite clear—they set the standard for how the property has responded.

Earlier in this chapter, changing rental policies to enhance the leasing effort was discussed. As noted then, some policy changes are very difficult to reverse. Now that the property has reached 95–96-percent occupancy, you may wish to revisit these earlier decisions. To change policies again just because the property is fully occupied could lead to an increase in vacancies and destroy the cash flow you have worked so hard to build. This is why it was strongly suggested that initial policies should be evaluated for the longer term and any adjustments to them should not be considered solely for short-term gain.

If the policies established at the beginning of the rehabilitation had a solid basis, they will stand the test of time. After the rehabilitation is completed, it is time to fine-tune them. For example, collections should be enforced even more rigorously than they were during the rehabilitation. It is important to recognize that when you are attempting to retain existing residents, you are more likely to make deals with them. You may have permitted some residents to pay their rent in two installments rather than initiate eviction proceedings immediately because you knew that a particular resident paid the rent in full although a bit later than required by the lease. This is a practice that must be eliminated after the rehabilitation. Also, as the property approaches 100-percent occupancy, there will inevitably be fewer vacant units available for rent, and you will have to time move-ins more carefully. It is important to *not* take a lease that will start 30 days or more into the future if you only have one or two units available.

Personnel requirements must also be reevaluated. An additional leasing agent may have been hired to fulfill rental goals during lease-up. Now is the time to consider efficiency as well as things that can make a difference in a prospect's first impression of the property and continue to make a favorable impression on the existing residents. Remember, this is the time when you begin to optimize the NOI, and controlling payroll and other expenses is part of that exercise.

The Ultimate Selling Price.   To achieve the highest ultimate selling price, the quantity, quality and durability of the income stream (NOI) of the property must be maximized. From the very beginning of the acquisition process, the goal has been to bring the property to a point where it will sell for the highest price possible. Now that the recycling process has been completed, the market will have reacted to what you accomplished—that is, how well and how thoroughly you handled the rehabilitation. Because you will never know the absolutely "right" moment to sell at the maximum price, you must always strive to maintain the property at its optimum, in physical condition and market position. The final goal—sale of the property at the highest price possible—must be woven into every decision and throughout the entire recycling process.

8

The Recycling Process

In the preceding chapters, the various activities related to apartment recycling have been discussed in detail. Many of the analyses will be repeated as more current information suggests reconsideration. Given the nature of rehabilitation, the difficulty in anticipating specific problems, and the dynamics of the market during the time frame, plans and budgets are likely to be revised or adjusted more often than they would for a new construction project.

This chapter suggests a sequence for proceeding with a particular project; it also acknowledges that some activities are likely to be going on concurrently. It assumes familiarity with the local area, market trends, and the rehabilitation process. In other words, the investor has to do some "homework" in preparation for even beginning to explore possibilities. Those who have owned multifamily properties have the advantage of experience regarding the purchase—and operation—of presumabily stabilized properties as a basis for comparison. The differences between that situation and a rehabilitation (addressed throughout the earlier chapters of this book) are what make the recycling of apartments exciting as well as challenging.

Finding the Right Property

In apartment recycling, the candidate property has to be examined more carefully than one that is being purchased only for operation as an investment. Critical questions to be answered are:

- How much will it cost per unit to buy the property?
- What is the extent of its problems—i.e., can it be fixed?

- How much will it cost per unit to rehabilitate it?
- Will rehabilitation make it marketable and permit sufficient increase in rent to provide an adequate return on the investment (as defined by the investor)?
- If so, how long will it take?

Underlying these questions is the larger issue of market perception: Is the perception of the property negative? Can it be changed? Most importantly, how long will that take?

An initial inspection coupled with information about local prices for materials and labor, market rents, and how the property is perceived in its market should provide sufficient information to draft a purchase offer and negotiate an initial deal. In addition to the dollar price, the contract should provide for sufficient time to conduct an appropriate due diligence evaluation to determine the feasibility of rehabilitation and obtain financing for the purchase. Because the results of the due diligence analysis could lead to a decision *not* to proceed, it is wise to consider both best-case and worst-case scenarios in as realistic terms as possible.

Due Diligence Analysis.   This is a comprehensive evaluation of the property to determine the specifics of what *must* be done to correct physical problems and change its image, what *should* be done additionally to make it more competitive, and what *could* be done to enhance its marketability overall.

Physical Condition.   A thorough inspection of the entire property, using a checklist and making extensive notes, is imperative. Every unit should be carefully inspected (if possible) to determine exactly what work has to be done in it. This information is critical to estimating rehabilitation costs. (The example inspection checklist in exhibit 2.4 works well for preliminary inspections; from such a preliminary review, a property-specific checklist can be developed for a detailed inspection.) Structural or civil engineers, construction contractors, or other competent professionals should be consulted to help identify and characterize problems that are suspected but difficult to evaluate if you do not have such expertise.

Physical changes to be made can be categorized as structural, environmental, and cosmetic. Structural problems are particularly important because they relate to habitability. They may not be obvious during a preliminary inspection, and they may not be correctable at an acceptable cost, but they have to be corrected. (State landlord-tenant laws and local building codes will indicate specific requirements.) Environmental problems must be evaluated carefully because of the cost of correcting them and the potential liability that can arise if they are not addressed. (Some sources of environmental problems are listed in exhibit 2.7.) Often the correction of structural and environmental problems will not bring a measurable return in the form of increased rent, which increases the income of the property and, therefore, increases its value. On the other hand, correction of cosmetic problems as well as functional obsolescence will not only enhance the marketability of the property, but also have a direct impact on the rent levels that can be achieved.

Fiscal Condition. Minimally, the property's operating statements for the preceding twelve months should be reviewed. If at all possible, statements for the past two or three years should be examined as well. An expense-to-income ratio of 50 percent or less (operating expenses divided by receipts) would indicate that the property's expenses are "typical"; if greater than 50 percent, the reason for the disparity should be sought. Rental income, vacancies, maintenance expenses, and payroll are particular items to scrutinize in these reports. The rent roll, delinquency reports, and individual resident ledgers should also be reviewed for the current year and prior years (if possible) as a source of collections information.

Property Management. The site manager and other personnel who are responsible for operating the property should be interviewed to determine their role, if any, in its management under new ownership. Individuals' attitudes and qualifications should be considered. (A checklist for reviewing current management staff was provided in exhibit 2.1.) Changes in management policies, procedures, and personnel are critical to the recycling of an apartment property.

Existing leases should be matched to current occupants, and payment histories, rent amounts, and expiration dates should be compiled. Existing policies and procedures must be reviewed to ascertain what they are and how they are being implemented or enforced. Rent collection policies, personnel practices, and general administrative procedures should be examined to identify needed changes. Maintenance procedures and records will indicate the quality of service provided to residents and recurring problems that should be addressed in the context of a rehabilitation. The absence of a maintenance log is a good indication that management is part of the problem. (An example maintenance log checklist was provided in exhibit 2.2.)

The current resident profile must be characterized so that desired changes to it can be identified. (An example checklist for this was provided in exhibit 2.3.) Resident files and applications will provide much of this information as well as indicate which residents are slow in paying their rents or whose behavior in general requires scrutiny. Talking with residents will provide additional perspective on them as well as on the property and its management.

The Market. Analyses of the region and the neighborhood should be conducted. Demographic data should be collected to frame the larger picture of the population. Its size, age distribution, and income levels—plus information about renter household formation—are important for determining the desired resident profile. Information about employment levels and types of employers is also valuable (see the list provided in exhibit 2.5). The supply of apartments, demand for them, and the absorption rate should be determined. A comparative analysis of competing properties is critical to determining market rents as well as what features and amenities are available—and desired by renters. (Exhibit 2.6 presented an example form for comparison grid analysis.) The perception of the property and the neighborhood is a major consideration. If the neighborhood is perceived as good, but the property itself is not, this is an extremely positive position for the recycling candidate.

Current Financing.   This is an important consideration as it relates to the price and the value of the property. Outstanding debt can inhibit the transfer of title to the property. If debt service payments exceed NOI, this may partially explain current maintenance practices and the extent of deferred maintenance that must be addressed in the rehabilitation. It may also inhibit flexibility when negotiating the purchase price.

Other Considerations.   The due diligence period should be utilized to check with local governing bodies regarding zoning of the property, records of inspections and violations of local building codes (life safety requirements), etc. At issue are whether existing permits are current, whether there are code violations that have to be corrected, and the general status of compliance. In addition, it is important to determine the requirements of current codes. Items that may not have been considered violations (due to grandfathering) may have to be addressed in a rehabilitation. Requirements for permits for construction should be reviewed so that the fees are included in the rehabilitation cost projections and applications for specific permits can be submitted in a timely manner.

Other records to seek out include the title of the property and any liens against it. You also need to know about real estate taxes and their status—in particular, whether a new increased assessment is pending. Local, state, and federal (regional) environmental agencies may have to be contacted to determine the status of environmental compliance. (Components of the due diligence analysis were outlined in chapter 2.)

Developing a Rehabilitation Plan

The problems identified during the due diligence evaluation will have indicated what you "must do," "should do," and "could do" to the property. The planning process should take all of these into consideration—i.e., the economics of alternatives. (Rehabilitation planning was the subject of chapter 3.)

Making the decision to proceed includes choosing exactly what work will be done, how it will be performed, and in what sequence. These considerations will affect how much the rehabilitation will cost. Estimated costs are used to develop a preliminary budget. It is these early projections of rehabilitation exenditures and their potential impact on future rental rates that become the basis for analyzing the investment. If the project is worth doing, a budget for the rehabilitation as well as one for operating the property during construction (if appropriate) will have to be presented to the lender as part of the loan application.

The Planning Process.   This encompasses a variety of different activities, beginning with the due diligence analysis. Because the prospects for a particular rehabilitation can range from minor cosmetic "repairs" to complete gutting of each unit and wholesale replacement of features and fixtures, it is particularly important to explore alternative approaches and evaluate comparative costs. Examples of such differences as they relate to kitchen cabinets make the point. The choice might be replacement of doors only versus removal and installation of completely new cabinets or installation of cabinets with only one drawer and a door versus cabinets with three or more drawers. Whether an upgrade will be sufficient will depend on market expectations and the condition of existing items as well as financial constraints, and the cost differential may be the deciding factor.

Analysis of the economics of alternatives should provide additional basis for deciding what changes will be most cost-effective. (The cost of a particular change multiplied by the number of units in which that change will be made provides an approximate total for that expense.) Once a particular direction is chosen, the estimated cost figures should be used to develop a preliminary budget, looking at both rehabilitation costs and operating income and expenses.

The approach to construction—use of a general contractor, a construction manager, or in-house staff—may depend on the extent of the physical changes required. If the needed changes are minor and within the capabilities of the site maintenance staff, that may be the approach you would take. Extensive changes or work that requires specific expertise may necessitate use of contract labor. In that situation, your personal experience and the availability of appropriate professionals may favor use of a general contractor or a construction manager. Note that in some parts of the country, specific installations must by law be performed by licensed individuals in skilled trades (e.g., electricity, plumbing), and this requirement may decide how the construction will be approached. (These issues were discussed in chapter 3.) Regardless of the specific approach, who does the work will affect both costs and timing. An itemized list of specific changes to be made inside units provides a starting point for development of work specifications, which will be submitted to contractors for bids. Some items (e.g., roofing) may have to meet specific standards for material and construction; others (e.g., plumbing) may have to be installed in compliance with local building codes.

Assuming at least some of the construction work will be done by contractors, it is important to call upon their expertise to facilitate development of cost and scheduling information. Early in the process, any required architectural drawings or designs should have been commissioned. (In some areas of the United States, preparation of drawings by a professional architect may be required.) Requirements for permits must also be met.

In planning a rehabilitation, careful consideration should be given to the progression of tasks. Weather permitting, early completion of exterior work (e.g., structural repairs to roof or walls, surface refinishing, window replacement, landscaping, parking lot repairs) is desirable. Work on the exterior and so-called common areas of the property is a declaration to the market as well as current residents that change is taking place. Interior work, especially within units, requires a particular task sequence—wiring and piping inside walls must precede attachment of fixtures to them as well as painting or other finishing, and these usually must be completed before carpeting or other floor coverings can be installed. Also to be taken into account is a progression from one unit to another. When a large number of vacancies presents unoccupied units side-by-side, work can be done in adjacent units, perhaps concurrently, depending on the size and skills of the work crew and the similarity of tasks among other considerations. When there are fewer, more scattered vacancies, consideration must be given to relocation of work areas, tools, and materials, as well as the greater potential for disturbance of residents who occupy units near or adjacent to those under construction.

Planning for remarketing the property requires careful and repeated analysis of the market and the competition. Apart from hard numbers—rents, vacancies, new construction, etc.—the key consideration is change in the way the property is perceived. This may never be measurable in any objective way because it is an evolutionary process. Yet it should be readily apparent whether the perception has changed enough to permit active promotion of the property to the market niche that represents the desired resident profile. Demographic characteristics will be important defining characteristics—age, income, household size, and other considerations contribute to people's lifestyles and choices of where to live. While fair housing laws preclude advertising that appears to be directed to one group rather than another, it is appropriate to advertise the features and amenities that are present at the property. Inclusion of rental rates, or at least a lower limit (e.g., one-bedroom apartments starting at $450 per month) will permit those in the market for apartments to decide for themselves whether a particular rent is "affordable."

Having market-ready apartments presumes that policies have been established regarding marketing and leasing practices and administrative procedures related to rental applications (use of a standard form); requirements for security and other deposits; verification of applicants' employment, credit, and other information; and preparation of lease forms. This means careful consideration will have been given to resident selection standards (e.g., sufficient income to pay the rent) as well as compliance with fair housing laws and applicable state and local laws regarding rental housing.

Components of a Management Plan. The outcome of the planning process is a written management plan for the recycling of a property. At the very least such a plan will consist of a budget and a general work schedule. However, most apartment rehabs, being major undertakings, require a comprehensive plan that spells out in detail what work will be done and when it will be accomplished (sequence of tasks and time frame).

Detailed *specifications* make it easier for contractors to prepare accurate bids for the work. The specifications should address the extent of tear outs (when required); the type, quality, and amount of materials to be used and whether they will be provided by the property owner (e.g., new appliances) or by the contractor (e.g., roofing materials); and the specific labor required. Bid requests should indicate requirements for the contractor to provide bonds (performance and payment) and certificates verifying insurance coverage. (Note that in some situations signed contracts may be a requirement to obtain financing.)

The *budget* component should anticipate payments for items purchased for installation (e.g., fixtures, appliances) as well as for contracts covering materials and labor, relating them to specific draws against the construction loan if possible. It should also project the flow of operating income and expenses for the duration of the rehab. This means the likelihood of increased vacancies should be considered so that contingency funds can be budgeted (as part of the loan amount) to cover rental income shortfalls. For purposes of budgeting, it is important to distinguish between operating expenses and capital expenditures and to evaluate each of them carefully.

The *work schedule* should anticipate problems and plan for alternatives. Inclement weather may delay or stop exterior work temporarily. A previously undiscovered break in plumbing lines or electrical wiring can delay completion of one or several unit interiors. Late delivery of materials—or shipment of the wrong items—is another possible disruption. It is prudent to make allowances for such contingencies by building flexibility into the plan—project both early and late completion dates (best-case and worst-case scenarios) and establish a sequence of tasks such that some trades can be moved to other units when work in a particular unit cannot be done as scheduled.

Management changes, when extensive, should be scheduled for stepwise implementation so that everything can be accomplished efficiently and effectively. Assuming the presence of residents in some units, management of the property will take on an additional dimension. Residents must be informed about the planned rehabilitation and the potential for disruption or at least inconvenience in their daily lives (e.g., noise, dust, and obstacles). Safety of residents, site personnel, and construction workers should be evaluated beforehand.

In our projects, we try to retain as many of the existing staff members as possible. Individual interviews allow us to make hiring decisions on a case-by-case basis. If a change in personnel is in order, however, terminations and hiring will become major activities. The process can be facilitated by hiring a site manager and delegating responsibility for assembling the site management team to him or her. (Some rehabbers advocate starting management with a completely new site staff because such a policy allows you to start with a "clean slate" and precludes some financial consequences. Once someone is your employee, termination allows him or her to collect unemployment compensation—to which you contribute on your employees' behalf—and possibly severance pay; a later termination could also lead to a lawsuit. However, legal advice should be sought before such a termination policy is adopted.)

While the property owner (or the management company) should set policies and procedures, this is another area where implementation would be the responsibility of the site manager. New or stricter policies regarding handling of collections, delinquencies, and evictions are among the first ones to be enforced. The take-over schedule should provide for notification of residents about new management and new policies, including *when* and *how* the new policies will be enforced. Other steps of the progression should be included in the plan along with an expected time frame for accomplishment. This might even include anticipation of lease expirations—e.g., lease renewals and relocation of residents to rehabbed units. (Management during the recycling process was detailed in chapter 6.)

A specific *marketing plan* should be prepared to expedite reintroduction of the property to the rental market. It should include a rent schedule and address specific advertising as well as adjunct materials (brochures, application forms, leases). Close monitoring of the market during the early period of construction—especially with regard to how the property is perceived and whether the negative perceptions are being overcome—will be critical to the timing of a new marketing effort. Marketing may have to be delayed if the market perception of the property is not changing rapidly enough to keep pace with the rehabilitation. Flexibility and realistic expectations are the keys here.

Obtaining Financing

At the time an offer is made and a contract to purchase the property is negotiated, an investor should already know what loan terms are prevalent in the market. (Financing issues were detailed in chapter 4.) Once the contract is signed, it is important to expedite development of a plan for the rehabilitation because it will be the basis for financing the project—purchase and rehabilitation.

At minimum a lender will require inclusion of a pro forma budget as part of the loan application package. (Loan application documents were outlined in exhibit 4.2.) A more comprehensive plan that includes a tentative work schedule and anticipates disbursement of rehabilitation funds (the construction loan) in addition to a budget may facilitate approval of financing as well as expedite start-up of construction and monitoring of the work.

Specific loan terms and requirements will vary by location, by lender, and by project. The investor can expect the requirement of specific loan-to-value and debt-coverage ratios. (Inclusion of operating income and expense data in the budget addresses these issues in part.) Points will probably also be charged, and there may be an application fee as well as legal fees and closing costs. These are in addition to a specific downpayment. Regardless of the interest rate, the amount of the periodic debt service payments will depend on several factors, among them—

- Whether the rate is fixed or variable (and the terms of variability).
- Whether debt-service payments amortize the loan—construction financing is typically repaid on an interest-only basis (with a large balloon payment or refinancing required).
- The amount and timing of disbursements of the construction loan.

It is important to calculate cash inflows and outflows, projecting figures for several years into the future—minimally, for the estimated holding period or the time it is expected to take to complete the rehabilitation and stabilize the income. The loan terms and anticipation of specific draws against the construction loan are important components of this analysis. Use of a spreadsheet program will facilitate comparison of different potential outcomes. The projected NOIs should be evaluated to determine the viability of the investment. Calculations of net incremental increase in value, internal rate of return (IRR), net present value (NPV), return on investment (ROI), and payback period should give clear indications that the rehabilitation (as proposed) has the potential to be financially successful. This analysis of the investment is critical to the decision to proceed (see chapter 5).

Rehabilitating the Property

Closing of the sale depends on the terms of the purchase contract. Once financing is in place and the purchase has been completed, the planned changes can begin.

Apartment recycling has two components—rehabilitation (construction) and management—and often the decisions related to one will have an impact on the conduct of the other.

Construction.   Any details relating to work tasks, materials choices, and scheduling of the rehab should be finalized. This presumes that specifications have already been sent to contractors, bids have been received from them, and the new property owner has decided who will do the work.

Some additional considerations should be reviewed. Before work can begin, it will be necessary to obtain any required building permits. While this is generally the responsibility of the owner, it is often handled by the general contractor. (Note that in some locales the owner may not be allowed to obtain certain permits.) When the rehabilitation is supervised by a construction manager, the individual subcontractors may obtain the building permits.

Arrangements must be made for accumulation and removal of construction debris. Receptacles should be placed so they are convenient for the construction crew, but issues of appearance (trash does not enhance curb appeal), safety (signage and fencing may be required to prevent children from playing nearby), and residents' inconvenience (limited access to parking) must also be addressed.

If the owner expects to purchase items for installation (e.g., appliances, windows, air conditioners), consideration must be given to quantities, deliveries, and secure storage as well as responsibility and accountability for access to them. When rehabilitation of a large property requires massive replacements of fixtures and appliances, coordination of deliveries with work schedules is imperative for efficiency, cost-effectiveness, and security.

Periodic inspections of the work-in-progress (by a representative of the lender) should be anticipated. Lenders require proof of satisfactory completion of work for which payment has been made and loan draws have been requested. Documentation of purchases and deliveries of materials and proof of payment for them and for contracted services will be a requirement for release of loan draws. There may also be periodic inspections by the local building department. Their concerns are habitability and compliance with local codes.

Management.   While management may be taken over at closing on the purchase, that does not necessarily mean that rehabilitation construction can begin the next day. Notices to residents about the planned rehabilitation may have to wait until operations under new management have been set up. Because properties that are candidates for recycling typically need management changes in addition to any physical changes, construction may have to wait until new policies and, perhaps, new site management personnel are in place. It may also have to wait until some of the expected changes in the resident profile initiated by management have been completed.

The point of ownership and management take-over begins a number of activities that will go on concurrently throughout the recycling process and afterward. Operating the property means collecting rents, providing maintenance services, analyzing budget variances, and compiling reports. Some site personnel may be involved from time to time in the rehabilitation itself (final inspections of unit interiors and operational status of fixtures and appliances, for example). Once rehabilitated units are ready for occupancy, marketing and leasing will become major activities. If the rehabilitation process extends over several years, renewal of existing leases and, perhaps, relocation of residents to new units may be required.

Throughout the rehabilitation process, the presence of residents will provide numerous challenges. Maintenance services will have to be provided, and the deteriorated condition of the property may mean that these exceed the ordinary. In planning the rehabilitation, consideration should be given to facilitating ordinary maintenance by eliminating the causes (or sources) of recurring problems. Services provided to residents during the rehabilitation should emphasize repair over replacement, especially if units will soon be gutted for construction.

An important consideration to keep in mind is the desired resident profile. Removal of undesirable residents, whether by eviction or attrition, will increase vacancies and thus affect rental income. Careful development of resident qualification standards and adherence to them when the rehabbed units are marketed will assure that the desired change in the resident profile will take place. The resident profile should be monitored throughout the recycling process.

Ultimate Disposition

As noted in chapter 7, analysis of the market and the investment should be repeated periodically to assure that the project is "on track" or, at least, that potential problems are identified early. A major consideration will be the ability to obtain permanent financing. Depending on the owner's goals, resale on completion may be preferable to long-term operation of the completed rehab. If market conditions change radically, the reverse may be true. Continuing analyses will guide these decisions as well as determine the optimum time to seek permanent financing. They also provide an increasingly focused measure of the success of the project.

Some Closing Thoughts

Once the recycling process has been completed, the property will have attained a certain position in the marketplace. Regardless of the preliminary projections, the property's present position is what it is because that *is* the market's perception of it. If mistakes were made, or if items were overlooked during construction, turning back is not the answer. You must examine the property as it is today and look only toward the future.

It is important to reevaluate the original rehabilitation plan and all the other efforts that were put forth during the due diligence period. This step

The Recycling Process

- Find a property that can be recycled.
- Examine the property in light of the asking price, availability of financing, and other considerations.
- Negotiate a contract for the purchase, being sure to address specific contingencies—time to perform the due diligence analysis and determine the feasibility of rehabilitation; the need to obtain financing for both the purchase and the rehabilitation; conditions that permit cancellation.
- Conduct due diligence analysis to determine the amount and extent of the changes to be made (consult with qualified professionals as necessary and appropriate)—potential problems and contingencies should also be considered.
- Prepare specifications for the rehabilitation—including architectural drawings as necessary and appropriate—and submit them to appropriate contractors for bids.
- Estimate the costs of changes (contractors' bids can provide a solid basis for these).
- Consider options—e.g., repair versus replacement; partial versus complete replacement—analyze the economics of alternatives.
- Develop a management plan—what will be done, how it will be accomplished, who will do the work, how much it will cost, and how much time it will take. Consideration should also be given to the impact of loan terms, working with residents in place, and time to change how the property is perceived in the market. The plan must anticipate construction, ongoing management and marketing, and ultimate disposition of the property—the entire recycling process.
- Prepare a budget for the project—this should address both the costs of the rehabilitation and operating income and expenses for the duration, include allowance for contingencies, and anticipate draws against the loan.
- Analyze the investment—given anticipated costs and financing prospects, decide whether the project is an appropriate investment.
- Adjust the plan and the budget if necessary.

provides an opportunity to check the accuracy of the feasibility analyses that were the basis of your initial projections. Items that had been thought to be extremely important may have had little impact overall, while still other factors that had been overlooked initially may turn out to have played a very important part in how rapidly the market perception was changed. Time spent to review all of these factors and the roles they played in the recycling process will be of invaluable assistance when the opportunity to recycle another apartment property presents itself in the future.

The recycling of apartments is exciting, challenging, and rewarding. Throughout this book, I have tried to present the challenges of apartment recycling in a realistic manner. My hope has been to give real estate professionals and private individuals an understanding of the range of factors that affect the decisions regarding which property to purchase and whether and how much to change it (extent of rehabilitation). Planning, management, and analysis are critical processes throughout a rehabilitation. However, the key objective in apartment recycling is to change the perception of the property

The Recycling Process (*continued*)

- Apply for financing—the payback period for the construction loan should provide sufficient time to complete the work, change the market perception of the property, and achieve a stabilized occupancy.
- When the loan is approved, close on the purchase.
- Assume management and operation of the property—begin to make changes in policies and procedures, the resident profile, and the staff.
- Obtain necessary construction permits.
- Begin the rehabilitation—finalize the rehabilitation plan and any additional drawings and specifications needed and hire contractors to do the work.
- Monitor the progress of the rehabilitation construction—inspections should exceed lender requirements for release of construction loan funds.
- Prepare draw documents as scheduled—account for payments to contractors and others (obtain lien releases from contractors when payment is tendered).
- Manage the property throughout all phases of the rehabilitation.
- Monitor line items of operating income and expense and variances from budget, making adjustments as necessary and appropriate—due to income shortfalls (as residents are evicted or move out when their leases expire) this can be an especially troublesome area.
- Review market analysis data periodically, monitoring changes in market rents and the perception of the property—timing of the remarketing of the property is critical to the success of a recycling project.
- Market the property aggressively—develop an advertising campaign; budget for advertising and leasing personnel; monitor traffic and leasing results.
- Review and re-analyze the investment as the rehabilitation progresses—in particular, consideration should be given to the intended holding period and expectations for refinancing when the income has been stabilized.
- Re-evaluate ownership goals—changing market conditions may favor a longer or shorter holding period than originally intended; there may be a need for additional improvements, either for continued operation of the investment or to sell it.

in the marketplace, creating new positive images that will arouse in prospective renters a desire to live there.

From personal experience, I can say that the rewards of recycling are great. While there is opportunity for outstanding monetary profit, there is also a real sense of accomplishment for having transformed an apartment property from a place where no one would live by choice into a truly desirable—as well as affordable—place to live.

Appendix

The following is a compilation of some suggested sources for specific types of information relevant to apartment management, rehabilitation, and the recycling process. In addition to resources addressing specific subjects, there is a list of general references that provides a starting point for collecting property management-specific information. Other useful books and periodicals can be identified in *Books in Print* and *Periodicals in Print* published annually by R. R. Bowker Company and commonly accessible in public libraries as well as major bookstores.

MARKET RESEARCH

The U.S. Department of Commerce, Bureau of the Census, generates consumer demographic information on an ongoing basis (decennial census). The federal government also generates data on varied aspects of U.S. commerce and industry. *The Census Catalog and Guide* is published every 10 years. The *American Housing Survey* includes income, housing quality and costs, neighborhood quality, and related data. Selected census data are also updated and published annually in the *Statistical Abstract of the United States*. All these publications are available from the Government Printing Office in Washington, D.C.

Sources for specific local information include state data centers, regional or local planning commissions, utility companies, business bureaus, and chambers of commerce. Local newspapers often collect demographic data (including consumer buying habits) on their subscribers. The local Board of Realtors may have library copies of statistical and real estate publications.

Publications

American Demographics magazine published monthly by American Demographics Press in Ithaca, New York.
The Insider's Guide to Demographic Know-How: Everything You Need to Find, Analyze, and Use Information About Your Customers, Second Edition, written by Diane Crispell and published (1990) by American Demographics Press, Ithaca. New York.
Metro Insights published annually by DRI/McGraw-Hill in Lexington, Massachusetts.

181

Commercial Services

CACI in Fairfax, Virginia
CDP Marketing Information Corporation in Hauppauge, New York
Claritas in Alexandria, Virginia
Donnelly Marketing Information Services, in Stamford, Connecticut
Intelligent Charting, Inc., in Perth Amboy, New Jersey
Urban Decision Systems, Inc., of Los Angeles, California

Professional Associations

Institute of Real Estate Management in Chicago, Illinois (professional association of property managers with local chapters throughout the United States and Canada)
National Apartment Association in Washington, D.C. (organization of state and local apartment associations)
ULI—the Urban Land Institute in Washington, D.C. (professional association of developers, architects, and others interested in land use)

ENVIRONMENTAL RESOURCES

The U.S. Environmental Protection Agency (EPA) is divided into ten regions, each made up of several states, as indicated in the following list.

Region 1, Boston, Massachusetts (Connecticut, Maine, Massachusetts, New Hampshire, Rhode Island, Vermont)
Region 2, New York, New York (New Jersey, New York, Puerto Rico, U.S. Virgin Islands)
Region 3, Philadelphia, Pennsylvania (Delaware, Maryland, Pennsylvania, Virginia, West Virginia, Washington, D.C.)
Region 4, Atlanta, Georgia (Alabama, Florida, Georgia, Kentucky, Mississippi, North Carolina, South Carolina, Tennessee)
Region 5, Chicago, Illinois (Illinois, Indiana, Michigan, Minnesota, Ohio, Wisconsin)
Region 6, Dallas, Texas (Arkansas, Louisiana, New Mexico, Oklahoma, Texas)
Region 7, Kansas City, Kansas (Iowa, Kansas, Missouri, Nebraska)
Region 8, Denver, Colorado (Colorado, Montana, North Dakota, South Dakota, Utah, Wyoming)
Region 9, San Francisco, California (Arizona, California, Hawaii, Nevada, American Samoa, Guam)
Region 10, Seattle, Washington (Alaska, Idaho, Oregon, Washington)

Publications

Environmental Law Handbook, Eleventh Edition, published (1991) by Government Institutes, Rockville, Maryland.
Environmental Management for Real Estate Professionals written by David C. Parks, CPM®, and published (1992) by the Institute of Real Estate Management, Chicago, Illinois.
Environmental Liability and Real Property Transactions written by Joel S. Moskowitz and published (1989) by John Wiley & Sons, Inc., New York, New York.

CONSTRUCTION AND REHABILITATION

The U.S. government has mandated conversion from the English system (inch-pound) to metric measurements, and this change will eventually impact property management measurements, lease documents, cooling and heating (temperature measurements), floor load factors, unit costs, operating costs, taxes, and insurance. Construction materials (lumber, piping, etc.) are also being restandardized to metric measurements. These changes can affect construction costs as well as the availability of particular materials. Information on metric conversions and new standards is available from the Construction Metrication Council of the National Institute of Building Sciences in Washington, D.C.

The Associated General Contractors of America (AGC) in Washington, D.C., includes general construction contractors, subcontractors, industry suppliers, and service firms among its members and is a resource for construction contract documents. Another source for construction contract documents is the American Institute of Architects (AIA), a professional society of architects also located in Washington, D.C. They also provide standard forms for certification of construction work for payment.

The American National Standards Institute (New York City) in conjunction with various construction trades and related associations publishes standards for materials, construction, safety equipment, etc. Insulation, roofing materials, and plumbing pipes as well as electrical codes are among the wide array of construction-related items covered by specific ANSI standards.

Publications

Construction Renovation Formbook edited by Robert F. Cushman and John W. Dinicola and published (1991) by John Wiley & Sons, Inc., New York, New York.
Fundamentals of the Construction Process by Kweku K. Bentil, published (1989) by R. S. Means Company, Inc., Kingston, Massachusetts.
Means Repair and Remodeling Estimating written by Edward B. Wetherill and published (1989) by R. S. Means Company, Inc., Kingston, Massachusetts.
Means Repair and Remodeling Cost Data published annually by R. S. Means Company, Inc., Kingston, Massachusetts.

OTHER RELATED PUBLICATIONS

The Appraisal of Apartment Buildings written by Daniel J. O'Connell and published (1989) by John Wiley & Sons, Inc., New York, New York.
The Appraisal of Real Estate, Ninth Edition, published (1987) by the American Institute of Real Estate Appraisers, Chicago, Illinois.
How to Comply with Federal Employee Laws written by Sheldon I. London and published (1991) by London Publishing in Washington, D.C.

Income/Expense Analysis: Conventional Apartments published annually by the Institute of Real Estate Management, Chicago, Illinois.

Means Facilities Maintenance Standards written by Roger W. Liska and published (1988) by R. S. Means Company, Inc., Kingston, Massachusetts.

Negotiating Real Estate Transactions edited by Mark A. Senn and published (1988) by John Wiley & Sons, Inc., New York, New York.

Practical Apartment Management, Third Edition, written by Edward N. Kelley, CPM, and published (1990) by the Institute of Real Estate Management, Chicago, Illinois.

Real Estate Investment Deskbook, Revised Edition, written by Alvin L. Arnold, was published (1987; cumulative supplements issued annually) by Warren, Gorham & Lamont, Inc., Boston, Massachusetts.

Transition: Taking Over a Management Account published (1992) by the Institute of Real Estate Management, Chicago, Illinois.

Index

About the Institute of Real Estate Management

The Institute of Real Estate Management (IREM) was founded in 1933 with the goals of establishing a Code of Ethics and standards of practice in real estate management as well as fostering knowledge, integrity, and efficiency among its practitioners. The Institute confers the CERTIFIED PROPERTY MANAGER® (CPM®) designation on individuals who meet specified criteria of education and experience in real estate management and subscribe to an established Code of Ethics. Real estate management firms that meet specific organizational and professional criteria are granted the status of ACCRED-ITED MANAGEMENT ORGANIZATION® (AMO®). Individuals who meet speci-fied educational and professional requirements in residential site manage-ment and subscribe to a Code of Ethics are granted the status of ACCREDITED RESIDENTIAL MANAGER (ARM®).

The Institute's membership includes nearly 9,500 CPM® members, more than 3,300 ARM® participants, and nearly 640 AMO® firms. CPM members manage nearly 25% of U.S. multifamily rental housing properties and ap-proximately 36% of condominium and cooperative ownership properties; CPM members also manage 63% of U.S. subsidized housing. In addition, they manage nearly 44% of the office space and roughly 10% of the shopping center and retail space in the United States.

For sixty years, IREM has been enhancing the prestige of property man-agement through its activities and publications. The Institute offers a wide selection of courses, seminars, periodicals, books, and other materials about real estate management and related topics. To obtain a current catalog, write to the Institute of Real Estate Management, 430 North Michigan Avenue, P.O. Box 109025, Chicago, Illinois 60610-9025, or telephone (312) 661-1953.